SOUTH CAROLINA TRAILS

"Comprehensive, excellent format, clear, concise . . . a great asset to hikers."
  —Donald W. Eng, United States Forestry Services, Columbia, S.C.

"A wealth of trails awaits the experienced hiker or stroller. Maps and details on plants and wildlife enhance the guide."
  —*The Star,* Chicago, IL

"Folksy information serves to pique hikers' interest . . . a book for every hiker."
  —*South Carolina Wildlife*

"This is a guide that the conscientious upstate hiker cannot do without."
  —*Anderson Independent-Mail,* Anderson, S.C.

SOUTH CAROLINA TRAILS

Second Edition

by

Allen de Hart

An East Woods Book

The
Globe
Pequot
Press

CHESTER, CONNECTICUT

Copyright © 1984, 1989 by The Globe Pequot Press

Library of Congress Cataloging-in-Publication Data
De Hart, Allen.
    South Carolina trails / Allen de Hart. — 2nd ed.

p. cm.

    Rev. ed. of: South Carolina hiking trails. © 1984.
    "An East Woods book."
    Includes indexes.
    ISBN 0-87106-647-5
    1. Hiking—South Carolina—Guide-books. 2.Trails—South Carolina—Guide-books. 3. South Carolina—Description and travel—1981—Guide-books. I. De Hart, Allen. South Carolina hiking trails. II. Title.
GV199.42.S58D4 1989
917.57—dc19

89-30588
CIP

Manufactured in the United States of America
Second Edition/Second Printing

To the volunteers who design, construct, and maintain the hiking trails in South Carolina.

Contents

List of Illustrations

List of Maps

IMPORTANT NOTICE

Map pages for each trail are <u>numbered</u> in the order they are to be used. Please observe the map number at the top of each map page.

Acknowledgments

When research began for the second edition of this book, I depended primarily on assistance from the South Carolina Department of Parks, Recreation and Tourism; the National Forest Service; and the officials in county and municipal government. In addition, I had counsel from directors and managers of private properties that offer recreational programs to the public.

In the state-park central operations, Joe Watson, chief naturalist, was my major resource person for the second edition. He was also helpful in the first edition, along with others such as Raymond M. Sisk, director; John E. Ransom, architect in engineering and planning; Charles Harrison, park operations; Kenneth O. Kolb, assistant director; and Mike Foley, chief historian.

Donald W. Eng, USFS Supervisor, has provided essential information in both editions, and William S. Craig, director of recreation, public affairs, and cultural resources, has assisted in the second edition. In the Sumter National Forest, I received assistance from district rangers Larry Cope, Enoree District (in both editions); R. Joel Gardner, Edgefield District; Don M. Bolinger, Andrew Pickens District; Michael C. Vinson, Tyger District; and John E. Cathey, and supervisory forester Carl Arnold, Long Cane District. In the Francis Marion National Forest, I received assistance from Carl D. Minehart, district ranger, Wambaw District.

Foothills Trail information was provided by Glenn Hilliard, chairman of the Foothills Trail Conference, and Charles Borawa, supervisor of project recreation, Duke Power Company, in both editions; and Walt Schrader, outdoor recreation activist, and George Kessler, forester of the College of Forest and Recreation at Clemson University, in the first edition.

Others who gave me material assistance in the second edition are: Christopher C. Revels, ranger, Kings Mountain

National Military Park; Eric K. Williams, chief ranger, Ninety Six National Historical Site; Ronald C. Snider, manager, Carolina Sandhills National Wildlife Refuge; Patricia E. Young, outdoor recreation planner, Savannah Coastal Refuges; Lewis Rogers, wildlife biologist, Webb Wildlife Center; Paul B. Ellis, III, parks administrator, City of Greenville; Charlene Rae Burns, public relations, Middleton Place; George P. Sawyer, professor of biology, Coker College; Allen Dean, ranger, Thurmond Lake, Corps of Engineers; the Reverend Clyde L. Ireland, director, Bishop Gravatt Center; Nita Swann, historian, Charleston Publishing Company; Robert W. McDonald, park leader supervisor, City of Columbia; Glen Bond, Jr., manager, Santee National Wildlife Refuge; and Betsy Veronee, director of public relations, Magnolia Plantation and Gardens.

Traveling, hiking, and researching across the state required long days and nights of work. I am grateful for those who gave me food, shelter, and general hospitality. They included Mr. and Mrs. Danny Outlaw, Camden; Mr. and Mrs. Mike Clarey, Easley; Capt. and Mrs. Roger Tucker, Charleston; Mr. and Mrs. David Phillips, West Columbia; and Duncan Hutchinson, Columbia.

Trail assistants from colleges, universities, and hiking clubs were essential for me to measure and describe the trails, to locate places to camp, to meet the officials, and to have shuttle service. In both adverse and pleasant weather, in time of fatigue and rest, the following hiking companions deserve recognition: Bob Brueckner, Kevin Clarey, David Colclough, Debbie Cooper, Steve Cosby, Jan Ewing, Jeff Fleming, Richard Galway, Sammy Gooding, Steve Harris, John Hayes, Tate Hayman, Greg Hippert, Dick Hunt, Bob Johnson, Robert Kistler, Lee Little, John Matthews, Ray Matthews, Walter May, Danny Outlaw, Les Parks, Linda Pressman, Scott Smith, Nile Spiegel, Eric Tang, Ryan Watts, Taylor Watts, Buster White, Travis Winn, and Mark and Kevin Zoltek.

Additionally, there is special gratitude to Sally Hill Mc-Millan, who, as former director of The East Woods Press, nurtured and promoted the first edition and gave her strong support to the second edition when The East Woods Press merged with The Globe Pequot Press.

Preface

"There is a peace the world can never give,
But nature grants it, joyous and profound . . . ."
—Archibald H. Rutledge,
"Love in the Wildwoods," *Deep River*

I have been walking and hiking and exploring the trails
of South Carolina since 1943. Each year I learn of new trails
with new views and mystery; and each year I visit some of
the old trails that have familiarity and classic charm. In
preparation for updating this second edition, I have rehiked
each trail described, or had those who maintain the trails
review my descriptions for changes or corrections. As a result
some obscure or closed trails are deleted, and new ones have
been added. A significant addition is the 19.6-mile eastern
extension of the Foothills Trail.

From the upcountry where editor Jim Clark invited us
to "vistas of unforgettable discovery," to the beaches where
poet Hervey Allen described the sound of the sea as being
"like a train among the hills, always passing but never gone,"
my adventurous expeditions have taken me to the heart of
the state's natural beauty and the hospitality of its people.

Among the state's poplars, pines, and palmettos I back-
packed and camped in the national forests; walked among
historic places in the Old Walled City of Charleston and
Magnolia Gardens; sank my boots in the swamps of the Congaree, Salkehatchie, and Hellhole Bay; fished and hunted in
the "Santee-Cooper Country;" rode horses in Hitchcock
Woods; canoed on the Edisto and the Saluda rivers; rafted
the wild Chattooga River; and bicycled on James Island. To
share these many outdoor activities with others has been an
unforgettable experience, and it is the purpose of this
guidebook to invite you to share it with us.

When I started serious research in 1980 to update information about the foot trails and to hike each mile of them,
it was like Euell Gibbons stalking wild asparagus in a salt

marsh. My most encouraging source of information was from the Recreation Division of the Department of Parks, Recreation, and Tourism (PRT) in Columbia, which was then planning a comprehensive study of state trails. Meanwhile, I contacted all county and city recreation departments, chambers of commerce, national forest offices, and a long list of outdoor sports enthusiasts. I followed the obscure Indian trails, fishing trails, old wagon trails, Boy and Girl Scouts trails, and the trails through the woods to Grandma's house.

Two years later it was of great assistance in my double-checking the trails inventory when the *Comprehensive Trail System Study* (of pedestrian, equestrian, bicycle, and ORV trails) was published for PRT by the Carter-Goble Associates, Inc., and Edward Pinckney Associates, Ltd., research teams. The state's primary study neither provided information on whom to contact for specific locations nor gave any trail descriptions; however, a corroborating study, *Trail Opportunities in South Carolina,* gave detailed map locations, addresses, and telephone numbers for about 50 percent of the land trails. (River trails had already been listed in *South Carolina River Trails,* published by PRT in early 1978.) Where you see differences in the Carter-Goble study and the second edition of this guidebook, they may arise because my research is more recent and I have measured all the trails with a measuring wheel. After honoring the requests of private trail owners who did not wish their trails to be listed, I have described a total of 207 land trails and provided resource information on the river trails.

Introduction

Types of Trails

South Carolina has classified its trails in five categories: pedestrian, equestrian, bicycle, river, and vehicular. They are usually described as scenic, historical, recreational, and nature—the latter emphasizing the flora and fauna. There are only a few vehicular trails; I describe the Florence Beauty Trail and the Laurel Hill Wildlife Drive as examples. Among the multiple-use hiking and equestrian trails in the national forests are Long Cane Horse and Hiking Trail (25.1-mile), Buncombe Trail (27.8-mile), and Jericho Trail (19.8-mile). The majority of the 500 miles of equestrian trails are on private property, and therefore are not described in this book. For information on stables, ranches, clubs, and equestrian events consult the South Carolina Horse Council, call (803) 734–4066, 776–1948, or 253–6318.

The state has six major bicycle touring trails that are routed to include natural and historic areas with stop-overs at state or commercial campgrounds. Routings are on designated roads with low traffic volume as much as possible. The north-south Carolina Connector Route (221.6-mile) is from McColl at the North Carolina state line to the Savannah River at the Georgia state line, near Garnett. The route goes through Sumter, Santee, and Branchville. Another route from North Carolina to Georgia is the Coastal Route (227.2-mile). It goes from Cherry Grove Beach on state roads through Conway, Andrews, the Francis Marion National Forest, Walterboro, and joins the Carolina Connector at Varnville. The other north-south route is the Central Route (169.5-mile) that begins at Kings Mountain State Park, goes through York, Chester, Batesburg, and Aiken to the Georgia state line near Augusta. Among the three mainly east-west routes, the Northern Crescent (334.9-mile) is the longest. Its west trailhead is at Fairplay near I-95 at the Georgia state line and follows the Crescent Foothills Scenic Highway

(SC 11) to Gaffney. From here it goes to Kings Mountain State Park, Rock Hill, and to Lancaster where it follows SC 9 all the way to the coast at Cherry Grove Beach. The Walter Ezell Route (288.8-mile) (named in honor of the leader who promoted the concept of the state bicycle routes) is a northwest-southeast route between Keowee-Toxaway State Park in the foothills through Clemson, Saluda, Santee, and the Francis Marion National Forest to end at McClellanville. From the Chattooga National Wild and Scenic River near Mountain Rest, the Savannah River Run Route (303.7-mile) generally parallels the course of the Savannah River. It passes through Walhalla, Calhoun Falls, Sumter National Forest, Aiken, Barnwell, Yemassee, Beaufort, and ends at the Hunting Island State Park. Bicyclists are subject to highway traffic laws by riding on the right side of the road with traffic flow and avoiding all controlled-access highways. The state provides a free bicycle touring guide-map available from PRT and the South Carolina Department of Highways and Public Transportation. The map is essential for bicyclists to have a list of bicycle clubs, resource addresses, color-coded highway routes, distance between road intersections, safety statistics, and a year-round climate chart. Write or call Recreation Division, PRT, 1205 Pendleton Street, Columbia, SC 29201, (803) 734–0142, or Department of Highways, P.O. Box 191, Columbia, SC 29202, (803) 737–1501. In addition it is advisable to request from PRT a free copy of the "South Carolina State Parks Camping and Other Facilities." Bicycle trails within the cities are most common in the urban greenways of Anderson, Charleston, Columbia, Florence, Hilton Head Island, and Rock Hill. Bicycling is also popular on the wide beaches of Kiawah Island, Sullivan's Island, and Isle of Palms. County parks with bicycle trails are described in Chapter IV.

For river trails the state has designated segments of the Ashepoo, Black, Congaree and Cooper, Edisto, Enoree, Little Pee Dee, Saluda, Santee and Wambaw, Savannah, and Tyger rivers for canoeists and boaters. Detailed descriptions and maps of these and seventeen other river trails are in Gene Able's and Jack Horan's *Paddling South Carolina: A Guide to Palmetto State River Trails,* Palmetto Byways Press, P.O. Box 50465, Columbia, SC 29250, (803) 787–6072. Also, the Walterboro-Colleton Chamber of Commerce, 213 Jefferies Blvd., Walterboro, SC 29488, (803) 549–9595, has a free map of the 56-mile Edisto River Canoe and Kayak Trail. A wild, untamed river with abundant wildlife, it is reported to be the "world's longest free flowing black-water stream."

Some of the land trails are in need of maintenance; others are manicured like formal gardens. They may be of asphalt, cement, gravel, sawdust, wood chips, pine straw, board, sand, or combinations. Some are eroded dirt, but most are of natural duff. Bridges are just as varied: relocated rocks, logs, steel, laminated or creosoted wood. The longest trail bridge is the nearly 200-foot suspension bridge at the Toxaway River/Lake Jocassee access. The longest trail is the Foothills Trail (85.2-mile), and the shortest is the Wells Park Trail (100-yard).

How to Use the Book

Trails are grouped in sections in five chapters: national forests; national parks, refuges, and Corps of Engineers projects; state parks, forests, historic sites, and wildlife management areas; county and municipal parks; and private, college, and university properties. Because the majority of the trails are in the national forests and the state parks, an introduction opens those chapters. For each recreational area the name of the county is listed in parenthesis to give you highway map orientation. On the first line of each trail description is its length, difficulty, topographic map, and general trailhead. And at the conclusion of each trail group within a recreation area, I have listed an address and telephone number for additional information. You will also find resource information in the appendix for government agencies, citizens' groups, trail suppliers, and a trail and general index.

Abbreviations

To save space and minimize repetition, the following abbreviations are used.

PRT (South Carolina Parks, Recreation and Tourism)
NFS (National Forest Service)
NPS (National Parks System)
FR (National Forest road)
USGS (United States Geological Survey
I-26 (Interstate 26)
US 301 (United States highway 301)
SC 6 (South Carolina primary highway 6)
SR 857 (South Carolina secondary road 857)
mi (mile, miles)
jct (junction or intersection)
km (kilometers)
rt (round trip, which may mean a backtrack)
ct (combined trails, which may mean a group of trails)
svc (service)
rec (recreation)
hq (headquarters)
cir (circumference)
sta (station)
fac (facilities)
mtn (mountain)
yds (yards)

Maps

Trail guidelines are overlayed on U.S. Geological Survey (USGS) contoured topographic maps for the state's longest trails in areas where backpacking and camping are more likely. To conserve book space they have been reduced to 64 percent. Because it would be impossible to include a map for every trail, many of which are short, the descriptions provide sufficient detail for you to locate the trailhead with a state or county map.

Following each trail heading is the standard USGS map title. It is a quadrangle map survey bounded by parallels of latitude and meridians of longitude covering 7.5 minutes at a scale of 1:24,000 (1 in = 2,000 ft). You can purchase these maps from a dealer in the state (see Appendix) or you can order from the Branch of Distribution, U.S. Geological Survey, Box 25286, Federal Center, Denver, CO 80225. As you must pay in advance for these maps, you may wish to request (free of charge) an Index Map of South Carolina and a price list. Expect two to four weeks for delivery. Topographical maps can be useful in unfamiliar backcountry and particularly so with a compass in swamps.

A state-highway map is free from the Silas N. Pearman Building, Room 536, 955 Park St., Columbia, SC 29202, or write to S.C. Department of Highways, P.O. Box 191, Columbia, SC 29202. From this address you can order county, city, outline, and traffic-flow maps. State-park maps are available (free) at the state parks, or you can write to PRT, 1205 Pendleton St., P.O. Box 113, Columbia, SC 29202. Maps of national forests are available (free) from the Public Affairs Office, U.S. Forest Service, 1801 Assembly St., P.O. Box 970, Columbia, SC 29201, and from District Rangers offices. The NFS also has more detailed maps (small fee). For catalogs of nautical charts and intracoastal waterway routes, write to Distribution Division (C-44), National Ocean Survey, Riverdale, MD 20840. For maps of the Santee-Cooper, Lake Marion, and Lake Moultrie area, write to Santee-Cooper Country, P.O. Box 12, Santee, SC 29142. For maps of Lake Moultrie, Lake Marion, and Cooper River, write to S.C. Public Service Authority, Project Land Div., Santee-Cooper, 223 N. Live Oak Dr., Moncks Corner, SC 29461. For Lake Murray information you may contact Lake Murray Recreation Association, P.O. Box 67, Silverstreet, SC 29145. Contact Duke Power Company, Corporate Communications Dept., P.O. Box 33189, Charlotte, NC 28242, for information on Jocassee, Keowee, and Waterlee lakes. Request maps for Lake Hartwell and Thurmond Lake from Savannah En-

gineer District, P   Affairs Office, U.S. Army Corps of
Engineers, P.O. Box 889, Savannah, GA 31402.

Trail Length, Time, and Difficulty

Each trail was measured with a Rolatape model 400 measuring wheel, known to my students as "clicker," "unicycle," "wheel barrow," "walking wheel," "running cane," "wheel of fortune," and "weed catcher." I have described the trails within the nearest 0.1 miles. If you can hike just one way on a trail by having a vehicle shuttle at the other end, only the mileage (mi) is listed under the name. If *rt* follows *mi,* it means you will need to backtrack or use a road or hike farther than a single linear distance. If a trail has *mi, rt*, and *ct,* it means the trail connects with other trails for a combined length.

No hiking time is listed, because walks on a trail vary. Saunterers may stop to consult a wildflower book. Photographers may be using stealth, and athletes may be jogging for a soccer team. The average hiker with a backpack could plan for two miles per hour on gradual contours. With a daypack and flat land, a hiker could easily average three miles per hour.

I have rated trails *easy, moderate,* and *strenuous* for difficulty. This is based on an average, healthy hiker, not a toddler or ridge runner. *Easy* means you can hike the trail without fatigue or exertion, as on the Edisto Nature Trail. *Moderate* means you may tire from the exertion and take an occasional rest. An example is the Buncombe Trail. *Strenuous* trails have steep or longer climbs, necessitating more frequent or longer rest stops, as on the Pinnacle Mountain Trail.

Animal and Plant Life

Space limitations made description of geological formations and plant and animal life impossible for every trail, but noteworthy details are included. For the best wildlife observation, leave your dog at home and go early in the morning or late in the afternoon to known watering holes. I have listed where and when you may see waterfowl and animals. Some plants are listed with both genus and species, which indicates the plant is rare, infrequent, or easily confused with a similar species. Oaks are often listed in the plural because a variety of species is present.

South Carolina has more pines than palmetto *(Sabal palmetto),* the state tree, so it is fitting that writers have accorded the pines more attention. Dr. Archibald H. Rutledge, naturalist, sportsman, and the state's first poet laureate, wrote about the pines as "parish pinelands sweet and old," or "splendor-coronetted pine" and about forest that "glimmers mystic, mute—veiled enchantress" in *Deep River* (The R.L. Bryan Company). Paul Hamilton Hayne in "Voice of the Pines" and "Aspects of the Pines" saw them as tall, "with dark green tresses," solemn, sombre, tranquil and luminous; and Henry Timrod, a lifelong friend of Hayne, wrote about the pines in *Ethnogenesis,* a moving reaction to the First Southern Congress at Montgomery in 1861: "And in our stiffened sinews we shall blend the strength of pine and palm!" Of the ten pine species in the state, the loblolly *(Pinus taeda)* and the short leaf *(Pinus echinata)* are the most common.

The following books are recommended as botanical and zoological references: *Manual of the Vascular Flora of the Carolinas* by Albert Radford, Harry E. Ahles, and C. Ritchie Bell (University of North Carolina Press); *Wild Flowers in South Carolina,* by Wade T. Batson (University of South Carolina Press); *Birds of the Carolinas,* by Eloise F. Potter, James F. Parnell, and Robert P. Teulings (University of North Carolina Press); *Amphibians and Reptiles of the Carolinas and Virginia,* by Bernard Martof, William Palmer, Joseph R. Bailey, Julian Harrison III, and Jack Dermid (University of North Carolina Press); and *South Carolina Mammals* by Frank B. Golley (Charleston Museum).

Support Facilities and Information

The excellent camping areas in the state include 31 state parks and more than 60 commercial campgrounds. For trails where camping is not allowed, I have listed the nearest (or most desirable) campground under **support facilities**.

A good book for the walker or hiker is *The Complete Walker* (Knopf, Inc.) by Colin Fletcher; and for campground locations *Woodall's Campground Directory,* published annually by Simon and Schuster, is helpful.

For information about hiking supplies, visit a trail shop (some addresses are in the Appendix) and subscribe to a hiking magazine such as *Backpacker,* Rodale Press, Inc., 33 E. Minor St., Emmaus, PA 18098.

Health and Safety

Concern for health and safety is always important on the trails. Fatalities or injury most frequently are the result of poor or risky judgment. Hypothermia, caused by the lowering of body heat, can be fatal even in temperatures of up to 45 or 50 degrees Fahrenheit. Sweaty or wet clothes are a common cause of hypothermia, and the victim often is not able to detect the problem. If someone shivers uncontrollably or speaks incoherently, take immediate action to warm the person.

Drowning, falling, and firearms misuse are other dangers. Deaths from poisonous snakes or electrical storms are rare, but watch where you walk, and do not lean against trees in storms. It has been said that to stay safe in the woods you must "use your head first and if things go wrong, remember to keep it."

Be sure to carry first-aid and snake-bite kits. Carry pure drinking water; if you must drink water you think is contaminated, use purification tablets such as Globaline or Potable-Aqua, or chlorine bleach (three or four drops per quart; shake and let stand for ten minutes), or boil for ten minutes. Though springs, wells, and running streams are listed, this does not mean any of them are safe for drinking. Use only water designated by a sign or brochure in national, state, or other parks and forests.

Wilderness Survival (Universe Publishers), by Bernard Shanks, is a good source of health and safety information.

Time to Go Hiking

We "never know when an adventure is going to happen," Christopher Morley told us, and John Burroughs advised us to "take the path you took yesterday to find new things." Whether you walk for adventure or discovery, you'll find that walking is "true magic, a psychological alchemy," "a muscular symphony," an aid to digestion, and a preventive to circulatory and respiratory disorders, as various authorities have claimed. It can transform the body and the mind. Sierra Club member Patricia Bagwell said hiking allowed her to hear herself think. Many years ago Fiona Macleod wrote in *Where the Forest Murmurs* that nature was so beautiful and complex "that the imagination is stilled into an aching hush."

Trails are like life—always changing, always offering surprises or new challenges. They are also like friends—there when you need their comfort and solace from the stresses of life. You will find many trails in this book that give you a sense of peace, of kinship with nature, and of a belonging to nature. I have described their locations and some of their secrets, but other secrets and inspiration await your visit. From the rugged and wild Chattooga River Gorge to the smooth sands of the Atlantic Ocean, there is a trail for everyone: long backpacking trails; short nature trails; or an urban greenway. They are yours, ready to be explored and enjoyed.

Welcome to the trails of South Carolina.

CHAPTER 1

National Forests

*"Kind Heav'n! whose wise and providential Care
Has granted us another World to share...the Shady
Forest...."*

South-Carolina Gazette
August 25, 1757

South Carolina has two national forests, the Thomas Sumter and the Francis Marion. Both were established in 1936 and named after South Carolina heroes of the Revolutionary War. Sumter, with 352,887 acres, has five districts: Andrew Pickens, Edgefield, Enoree, Long Cane, and Tyger. Marion, with 250,008 acres, has two districts, Wambaw and Witherbee. The national forests represent 0.3 percent of the state's land area. They are part of a 190 million-acre National Forest system in forty-four states and are administered by the National Forest Service (NFS), an agency in the U.S. Department of Agriculture.

At one time all the 602,895 acres of national forest in the state were privately owned. Almost all had been heavily timbered, and sections had been wasted from erosion and poor agricultural practices. Wildlife had disappeared or been severely reduced in these once magnificent forests and rich soils. As a result, state and local governments petitioned Congress to purchase land to support the sagging economy in the 1930s.

Congress directed that the forests be managed so that the five renewable forest resources—water, timber, forage, wildlife, and recreation—would be controlled for the maximum benefit and multiple use of the public. Multiple use objectives may vary from district to district, depending on needs for timber harvesting, reforestation, recreational facilities, and wildlife habitats.

Each national forest is required to develop and follow a forest-management plan—the Land and Resource Management Plan (usually called the Plan). The Plan is a product of forest personnel recommendations and public requests in planning and updating projects about every ten years. In addition, the Environmental Impact Statement (EIS) has to be prepared in detail.

During the 1990s some of the management projects are designed to allow natural processes to continue in the five wilderness areas; to inspect, repair, or replace hundreds of bridges, including 140 trail bridges; to maintain and rehabilitate existing facilities and trail mileage; and to have archaeologists survey approximately 13,000 acres to locate, evaluate, and protect significant prehistoric and historic sites.

The Plan also requires selected wildlife species to be protected, such as the red-cockaded woodpecker and the swallow-tailed kite. Many streams, lakes, and former borrow-pits are managed to produce trout, bass, bream, and catfish. All of these forest projects are in the Wildlife Management Area program and are managed cooperatively with the South Carolina Wildlife and Marine Resources Department. Sensitive plant species are protected, in an agreement between the Nature Conservancy and the NFS, by identification and management plans.

In 1988 visitors spent nearly one million visitor days using the resources of the Sumter and Marion national forests. (A visitor day is any combination of uses that totals 12 hours.) Estimates based on registration forms, traffic counts and ranger's reports show a wide range of activities. Visitor days totalled more than 208,000 for those who enjoyed "just riding around"; hunting, 164,000; fishing, 44,000; tenting and camping, 200,000; hiking, 47,000; and berry picking and wood cutting, 35,000. There were more than 100,000 visitor days for other categories such as picnicking, motor boating, rafting, kayaking, horseback riding, swimming, and water skiing.

Assistance in maintaining the trails and other recreational projects had been the work of the Youth Conservation Corps (YCC) and the Young Adults Conservation Corps (YACC) until the 1980s when the budgets were almost totally cut. "We are depending more on volunteers," said Enoree District ranger Larry E. Cope. Forest Supervisor Donald W. Eng said that the Senior Community Service Employment Program (SCSEP) crews have expanded and that their workers, plus volunteers, are assisting in a number of project areas. One of those projects has been that of locating, surveying, and protecting prehistoric and historic sites on 120,000 acres.

Timber management is a major responsibility of the NFS, but private timber companies contract and harvest the timber for the NFS because the NFS does not have harvesting equipment. The private contractors pay annually about $12,000,000 in revenue for the timber they harvest. Following the harvest, the contractors reforest by planting, seeding, or using natural methods. Where does the revenue go from the timber sales? The law requires that 25 percent of the funds collected go to the counties in which there is national forest to help pay for public schools and roads. "A portion is retained to insure reforestation, and the balance goes to the U.S. Treasury," explained Forest Supervisor Eng. A staff of about 215 manage the state's national forests.

Before you go hiking and camping in the national forests, know the following guidelines from the NFS:

1. Most of the developed recreation areas are open from late spring to early fall, and a few are open all year. Trails are open all year. Contact the appropriate ranger district to be sure of open dates.

2. Off-road vehicles (ORVs) and all-terrain vehicles (ATVs) are not allowed on hiking and horse trails. However, they are allowed on most forest roads unless posted otherwise. Traffic laws in the forests are the same as elsewhere in the state. Trailers and other RVs are permitted, but there are no water or electrical hook-ups in the Sumter or Francis Marion national forests.

3. Primitive camping is allowed only at designated campsites, and permits are required for camping elsewhere.

Free permits are available from ranger district offices and will usually be issued unless conflicts are anticipated.

4. Permits are not needed for campfires, but care should be used for fire prevention and only "dead and down wood" should be used.

5. Hunting and fishing in the forests require state licenses. Hunting on Sundays is prohibited. Hikers are advised to avoid the first few days when the hunting season opens—during either-sex deer hunts—and to wear bright clothing when using the forests during big-game hunting season. Seasons change slightly each year, the dates of which are shown in a publication by the S.C. Wildlife and Marine Resources Dept., available wherever licenses are sold.

6. "Pack it in—pack it out" is basic forest courtesy.

7. Be considerate. All of us have equal rights to the forest. However, if you see a violation of forest, local, state, or federal law, you should report it.

8. Park vehicles so they do not block gates, roads, or parking areas.

9. Numerous tracts of private land dot the forests like a crazy quilt. Avoid trespass; ask permission.

10. Horses are allowed on some of the multiple-use trails. Tie horses away from campsites to avoid damage to camp-area vegetation.

11. Protect water supplies from contamination.

12. Do not climb the waterfalls. The dangers are obvious.

13. Vandalism has increased—lock your car and hide valuables.

14. Request free brochures and maps from the supervisor's or district offices, or purchase one of the detailed "Forest Visitor Maps."

Sumter and Marion include segments of all the state's major areas of topography and natural resources, from the mountains to the sea coast, and they offer an extraordinary realm for recreation. There are more than 450 campsites; more than 150 picnic sites; wilderness, scenic, and swimming areas; thousands of acres of lakes and miles of streams; and more than 152 miles of hiking trails. In addition there are 76 miles of multiple-use horse and hiking trails, 64 miles of motorcycle trails, and 129 miles of canoe trails.

There are dark coves where sunlight never goes, cascades of clean water under giant hemlock and white pine, scenic rock outcroppings scented with azaleas, rolling hills of endless loblolly pine stands and jessamine gardens, and mysterious swamps with ageless bald cypress festooned with Spanish moss. There are trails in these great playgrounds; trails made and maintained by the staff of Sumter and Marion national forests: trails waiting for you.

For maps or information contact: Supervisor's Office, Strom Thurmond Federal Building, 1835 Assembly St. (P.O. Box 2227), Columbia, SC 29202; (803) 765–5222 (weekdays, 8:00 A.M. to 4:30 P.M.); or the district ranger's offices (addresses and telephone numbers are listed at the end of each section under **Information**).

FOOTHILLS TR
S.C.-N.C. STATE LINE

Sumter National Forest
SECTION 1
Pickens Ranger District (Oconee County)

The Andrew Pickens Ranger District, "gateway to the mountains," with 78,220 acres is the only mountainous part of Sumter National Forest. Elevations range from 800 to 3,400 feet. Its western boundary is the Chattooga Wild and Scenic River corridor, the state line with Georgia. At the northwest corner of its boundary with North Carolina is the Ellicott Rock Wilderness Area, and northeast is scenic 7,656-acre Lake Jocassee. Federal and private lands are interspersed.

Access to the district ranger's office is on SC 28, 6 miles northwest of Walhalla. There are 15 recreational sites in the district, six with camping facilities: Burrells Ford on FR 708 near the Chattooga River; Woodall Shoals on FR 757, south of US 76 near Long Branch, with secondary primitive campsites including tables, water, and restrooms; Cassidy Bridge Hunt Camp on SR 290; Cherokee Hunt Camp near Cheohee Lake; Pine Mountain Hunt Camp on FR 752-A in the southwest tip of the district, with primitive sites open during big-game season; and Cherry Hill on SC 107, with a campground for trailers and tents (but no hookups). Most of the NFS facilities are closed in November for the winter, but visitors may use the year-round camping facilities, including hookups, at Oconee State Park on SC 107. Primitive camping is allowed in the Ellicott Rock Wilderness or Chattooga River corridor anywhere that is more than a quarter of a mile from the road and 50 feet from a trail, stream, or river. Other campsites require a permit from the District Ranger. Camping is popular in the district because of fishing on the Chattooga River and on 16.7 miles of approach or main trails. The scenic slopes, gorges, and mountain tops are both a mental and physical challenge to hikers.

Picnicking areas are at Burrells Ford on FR 708 near the Chattooga River; Burrells Place on SC 107; Chattooga at the Walhalla Fish Hatchery west of SC 107; Cherry Hill

Campground on SC 107; Moody Springs on SC 107 near Cherry Hill; Rose Bud on SC 107; Sloan Bridge on SC 107, and Yellow Branch on SC 28 near the ranger station. Wildlife in the district is mainly deer, wild turkey, quail, grouse, rabbit, squirrel, raccoon, fox, and beaver. Brook, brown, and rainbow trout are north of the SC 28 bridge over the Chattooga River, and redeye bass are more plentiful south of SC 28.

Probably no place in the district is more popular with hikers or river floaters than the Chattooga River. This powerful, wild, blue-green river foaming with white turbulence drops nearly 2,500 feet in less than 50 miles (40 of which are in South Carolina). It was designated a Wild and Scenic River by Congress in 1974, and strict regulations protect the canoeists, kayakers, and rafters. If you plan a river trip with your hiking trip, know the safety regulations. You may contact one of the commercial rafting services listed in the Appendix or the district ranger's office listed at the end of this section.

The district has 13 trails, the shortest a round trip of 0.4 miles from the Chattooga River Information Station to Bull Sluice, and the longest (25 miles), the Foothills Trail, from Oconee State Park to the North Carolina state line. Rather than describe the Foothills Trail partly in this chapter and in other chapters, it is described here in its entirety. Other district trail descriptions follow. (Trails planned in this district are the Andrew Pickens Horse Trail with a rustic camping area and a trail for the physically handicapped.) For a small fee the district has a trail guide that is a folding map with trail directions and forest-facilities information.

Access: The Andrew Pickens Ranger District office is on SC28, 6 mi W of Walhalla and 10 mi E of the Chattooga River.

Foothills Trail
Length: 85.2 mi (136.3 km); **easy to strenuous;** USGS Maps: Tamassee, Satolah, Cashiers, Reid, Eastatoe, Table Rock,

Cleveland, Standingstone Mountain; trailhead: Oconee State Park.

The Foothills Trail is the longest trail in the state (85 miles); it is interstate (South Carolina and North Carolina); it is intercounty (Oconee, Pickens, and Greenville in South Carolina and Jackson and Transylvania in North Carolina); it is intrastate park (Oconee, Table Rock, Caesars Head, and Jones Gap); it is the most costly trail designed and constructed in the state from private sources (Duke Power Company); it is the only one about which an entire guidebook has been written (Foothills Trail Conference); it is the most spectacular in variety of topography, flora and fauna, water sources, and natural beauty (Chattooga River, Upper Whitewater Falls, Lake Jocassee, Toxaway River, Laurel Fork, Sassafras Mountain, Drawbar Cliffs, Raven Cliff Falls, and Middle Saluda River Gorge); and it is the most potentially adaptable for a network of other mountain trails (in the Mountain Bridge Recreation Area, Horsepasture River Gorge, Eastatoe Creek Gorge, and the Pisgah and Nantahala national forests).

The trail concept began in the 1960s as an idea for an upstate mountain trail. Discussions between the NFS, the Sierra Club, PRT, Clemson University Recreation and Parks Administration Department, and Duke Power Company led to planning and eventual construction. When Duke Power Company decided to build a trail of more than 40 miles to satisfy its Exhibit R (recreation plan) in fulfillment of the government requirements for the Bad Creek pumped-storage project, funds, dreams, and hard work came together to create a scenic ribbon through the former Cherokee nation (which they called "The Blue Hills of God"). It passes through rugged back country and through sufficient hiking space to once and for all silence the complaint that "South Carolina doesn't have any trails."

Although "it is entirely Duke's responsibility to maintain the trail (the section built by Duke Power Company) by itself or through cooperation with the Foothills Trail Conference or others," volunteer help will be encouraged, Charles Borawa, supervisor of Duke's project recreation, said. "We are working with the Foothills Trail Conference to assign groups to maintain segments of the trail."

Alfred Breedin, an associate recreation representative of Duke who assisted in supervising construction of the Duke portion of the trail, said "the project was worth the effort because you won't find a better hiking trail anywhere."

For additional information, the *Guide to the Foothills Trail* is published by the Foothills Trail Conference, Inc., P.O. Box 3041, Greenville, SC 29602; (803) 232-2681; or you can contact Project Recreation Supervisor, Duke Power Company, 422 South Church St. (P.O. Box 33189), Charlotte, NC 28242; (704) 373-4011. (As I had hiked the entire trail months before the Foothills Trail guide was published, the directions and descriptions which follow have not had the conference's materials, maps, or manuscripts for guidance. It is coincidental that the conference describes the trail from Caesars Head and Table Rock state parks to Oconee State Park, while I independently researched and hiked it from the opposite direction. I have hiked both directions, and I do not have a strong preference because some of the segments are more challenging, enjoyable, or scenic from one direction than the other.)

From Oconee State Park to SC 107 (6.1 mi)

From Oconee State Park campground my Chattooga River white-water friends took Lee Little and me on the cottage road to the Foothills Trail sign. At 0.4 mi we faced a jct R with the rust-blazed Tamassee Trail. We turned L and followed the white-blazed Foothills Trail sign through a mature forest, intercepting a few ravines with wildflowers and galax on a well-designed approach to the boundary of the Andrew Pickens Ranger District of the Sumter National Forest at 1.2 mi. We soon entered an open area with hardwood saplings, red cedar, birdfoot violets, and huckleberry patches. (A sign here said Bartram Trail, but that trail's eastern terminus remains in the planning stage.) Reentering the main forest, we skirted the E side of Long Mountain (2,080 ft), gradually ascending, and curving around the ravines. At 2 mi a trail sign post pointed to Oconee State Park, Long Mountain Lookout Tower, the Foothills Trail, and Bartram Trail. We took the spur of 0.1 mi to the firetower. We could see the mountains in Georgia and North Carolina, as the early sun cast shadows over in the Chattooga gorge. It was a May sky as blue as October, calling to mind Byron's description—"deeply blue, as someone somewhere sings about the sky."

Continuing ahead, we crossed an old road bed at 2.2 mi, then a small bridge over a stream where galax spotted the banks. Ahead was a timbered area with scrub pine. Reforestation had begun, but 0.2 mi of sunny open space is a haven for huckleberry, loosestrife, and bristly locust. At 2.8 mi we entered a tall pine forest and descended into a rosebay rhododendron thicket near a stream on the L. Beyond this was our surprise of the morning. Thousands of trillium covered the hillsides, many forming a display with fern crozier, fresh and wet green.

We crossed two small streams among white pines and mature hardwoods, fetterbush, running cedar, and pink lady slippers (*Cypripedium acaule*) at 3.5 mi, then veered L on a gentle ascent beside cascading Tamassee Creek at 3.7 mi. After leaving the low areas we ascended gradually. For the next 1 mi we saw evidence of the 1973 tornado and the April 7, 1978, Jumping Branch fire, which roared across SC 107 and destroyed more than 2,800 acres of the forest. In the open spots left by the fire grew gardens of bristly locust, thick patches of bracken, and scattered crested dwarf iris. A good view of Long Mountain firetower was at 4.2 mi. At 4.7 mi we reached SC 107 where a member of Lee's rafting team picked him up, and I hiked alone to Burrells Ford Campground.

Continuing E of the highway, I passed a tributary of Tamassee Creek on the incline to Dodge Mountain (2,380 ft). Skirting the E slope, I had excellent views at 5.6 mi. Flame azaleas were scattered in a mixed forest. At Tamassee Road, FR 710, was the first yellow blaze for the Bartram Trail. (See Bartram Trail in this chapter.) I turned L on the graveled road and at 6.1 mi reached SC 107. (It is 3.6 mi L on SC 107 to the entrance of Oconee State Park.)

From SC 107 to Burrells Ford (10.4 mi)

The trail continued across SC 107, entered a mature forest, and gradually descended. A cascading stream was on the L; buckberry was abundant, with rosebay rhododendron in spots. The trail entered a stand of large white pine and at 7.5 mi crossed a cul-de-sac of a fire road. Again it entered a stand of white pine where the duff was thick and soft. Log footbridges crossed Lick Log Creek banks and Pig Pen Creek; the remnants of a primitive cabin were on the L. At 8.4 mi I reached a jct with the Chattooga Trail. (From here on the L it is 4.5 mi to SC 28, though the sign has 3.7 mi. To the R it is 8.1 mi to Burrells Ford Rd.)

I turned R and, shouldering my backpack, ascended to a ridge crest at 9 mi. Soon I turned L on an old wagon road and descended but turned R from the road after 0.2 mi. I could hear the distant roar of the Chattooga River. Towering above were magnificent oaks, maple, and white pine, with buckberry and galax covering the earth. Scattered sourwood sought what sunlight it could find, like Kahlil Gibran's "slender reed and oak tree, side by side striving upward." At 10.5 mi I was on the E bank of the Chattooga, refreshed by its mist. Soon the trail was on a flat terrain providing excellent camping spots near the river. I went out on a spur trail to photograph the river. Upstream was a fishing party who invited me to share their noon-day meal, prepared over an open fire. "We would have fish if we had caught enough," said Ricky Baumgarner. Out on a broad shaft of granite was Will John Rogers, catching small- to medium-size rainbow trout. "I don't know how he is so lucky," Terry Simmons said. "It's his first time up here fishing . . . look at that smile on his face." They were all from the Walhalla Merchants Softball Team—Will John, Ricky, Ricky Pate, John Thompson, Robert Cowan, Tim Gillespie, Jess Neville, and Terry, the coach and manager. "It's peaceful here, only natural sounds," Terry said.

Continuing ahead, the trail ascended from and descended to the river occasionally on the sandbars or rocky, sometimes slippery, borders. Rivulets trickled down from the slopes and switchbacks cut through the *maximum* and *minus* pink rhododendron. The trail curved around Round Top Mountain to 12.9 mi where Big Ben Falls thundered over a 40-foot cascade before dropping in a 12-foot powerful hydraulic. The trail is about 100 vertical ft above the falls. Rocks and roots are usually slippery here.

At 13.7 mi is a jct with the rust-blazed Big Ben Trail. (The trail is 2.7 mi to Cherry Hill Campground; it also connects with Big Bend Road, FR 709, from SC 107). A footbridge crossed a stream with a flume on the L. After 0.2 mi I reached the river and hiked 175 ft on the river rocks. Yellow root, crested dwarf iris, and fetterbush grew near some excellent spots for a campsite. An exceptionally fine view was at 14.4 mi, with waterfalls, sandbars and huge rock formations. From here I ascended on switchbacks; some parts of the trail were steep and narrow—steep enough to prevent a motorcyclist, who had damaged the trail here, from going farther. I ascended on an old wagon road at 15.3 mi, and 0.3 mi farther, reached a jct veering R off the old road. (Straight ahead is Burrells Ford Campground.) At 16.1 mi I crossed a creosote and rail bridge over cascading King Creek. (On the R is a rust-blazed trail for 0.2 mi to the 80-foot King Creek Falls. To the L is the old wagon road to Burrells Ford walk-in campground.) The Chattooga Trail and the Foothills Trail go straight ahead after a turn from the wagon road, R. I ascended on a gradual incline to the Burrells Ford parking area at 16.5 mi.

From Burrells Ford to Fish Hatchery Road (3.8 mi)

On the second day I was joined by my white-water-river companions, Steve Harris, Steve Cosby, Robert Kistler, and Eric Tang. We were to hike the Foothills Trail to Sloan Bridge and shuttle back to complete the Chattooga Trail to Ellicott Rock and return on the East Fork Trail to the Walhalla National Fish Hatchery. This way we retained our campsite at Burrells Ford Campground for the second night.

From the parking area at Burrells Ford we crossed the graveled FR 708, ascended to a stand of exceptionally tall hemlocks, and crossed a creek with cascades at 16.8 mi. We crossed a rocky area in a dense section of rhododendron at 16.9 mi and reached the fork of the two trails at 17.1 mi. (The Chattooga forked L, 3.8 mi to Ellicott Rock.) We forked R on the Foothills Trail and ascended gradually on a wide ridge through mountain laurel. Undulating, we curved SE and NW on slopes to switchbacks at 19 mi. Ascending in tall hardwoods, we saw flame azaleas rising from the understory like large orange forest lanterns. At 19.3 mi we reached the ridge crest of Medlin Mountain along the boundary of the Ellicott Rock Wilderness area and began to descend gradually on the slope at 19.7 mi; at 20.3 mi we reached the parking area at the Walhalla Fish Hatchery Rd.

From Fish Hatchery Road to Sloan Bridge, SC 107 (3.3 mi)

Across the road, the trail entered a hardwood forest, ascending through rosebay rhododendron. At 20.9 mi we crossed a stream, the first of more than a dozen in the next 3 mi, and noticed disturbed earth, probably from an old homestead. At 21.5 mi we crossed a large rocky area with moss and lichens before reaching a small cascade on the R at 21.9 mi. Switchbacks in rhododendron and mountain-laurel thickets, then a stand of hemlocks, were followed by a power line at 22.8 mi. At 22.9 mi the trail went around a huge rock where we were sprinkled with spray from a waterfall. At 23.1 mi on the L was the East Fork of the Chattooga River, which we followed to Sloan Bridge Picnic Area and jct with the Fork Mountain Trail, L, at 23.6 mi. (A shuttle took us back to Burrells Ford to complete the Chattooga Trail. See Chattooga Trail, East Fork Trail, and Fork Mountain Trail in this chapter).

From Sloan Bridge, SC 107, to Whitewater River Bridge, NC 281 (3.9 mi)

The next day our white-water team had to return home and replacing them were Ray Matthews and Sammy Gooding. We continued on the Foothills Trail from the Sloan Bridge Picnic Area on SC 107 (0.5 mi N on SC 107 is the state line and 8 mi farther is Cashiers, N.C.) gently ascending on the slope of Chattooga Ridge to 25 mi at the state line. Here we left the Sumter National Forest and entered the Nantahala National Forest.

At 25.3 mi we began a switchback, reached a ridge crest for partial views of Lake Jocassee, and started a decline into coves on the E slope. At 25.7 mi the trail descended steeply, then ascended near large rocks on the L. The gap between Grassy Knob and Round Mountain was at 26.1 mi, with banks of ferns, rhododendron, buckberry, fly poison, and trillium. At 26.3 mi we entered an old road bed, turned R and crossed a small stream. On the R in a dense area of evergreens was a tributary to Whitewater River. At 27.3 mi the trail turned sharply R (ahead on the old road it is 100 yds to a campsite by the Whitewater River) and ascended to NC 281 (SR 171 in S.C.) at 27.5 mi.

From NC 281 to Horsepasture River (12.7 mi)

We crossed the paved road, climbed over the guard rail, and descended on a N slope by Whitewater River. The trail passed the "Big Tongue" on the R in a road bordered with fragrant rhododendron and wild hydrangea. At 28 mi was the overlook for the Upper Falls of Whitewater River, which cascades more than 400 ft (some descriptions have from 400 to 600 ft) into the gorge. (To the R is a paved trail 0.2 mi to a paved parking area and excellent views of Lake Jocassee.)

After the first 100 steps (in a series of 400) down into the gorge there was another superb view of the falls. A series of steps and steep treadway led to the river with huge boulders at 28.5 mi. We crossed the rapids by rock hopping and wading. (Now, there is a hemlock footbridge.)

Safely across the river, we crossed Corbin Creek on a hemlock footbridge. Extremely tall hemlocks were in this area; yellow root and fetterbush grew in clusters on the forest floor. It was "shady depths" like those described by John Muir, "where subdued light makes a perpetual morning." We joined an old wagon road and left it at 28.9 mi. We reentered South Carolina at 29 mi, leaving the Nantahala National Forest. A series of wooden steps, the first of thousands installed by Duke Power Company on the trail, began 0.2 mi after the state line. (Each step is 4 in x 6 in x 18 in with a 24 in rebar.) After the steps and stairs, there was a generally level area where we saw horse tracks (though horse traffic is not allowed on the trail). At 30.1 mi we reached a trail jct and campsite area by the Whitewater River. Here we met Carolyn and Jesse Hartley and their three children, Pam, Andrea, and Tiffany, from Greenville.

(Ray and Sammy had explored the cable bridges at the river, and I joined them on the blue-blazed trail on the W side of the river for a round trip of 2.3 mi. We followed a spur trail downstream to a graveled road at 0.1 mi and then 0.4 mi farther to view the Lower Falls of the Whitewater River. This area can be extremely dangerous when wet or slippery.)

Heading E, we entered a mature hardwood forest with scattered pines. At 30.3 mi we reached a ridge crest and ascended gradually, crossing a dirt road at a R angle at 30.5 mi.

A series of footbridges over ravines followed in an open oak-hickory forest; red clay showed in a sparse understory. At 31 mi we reached a gap, crossed over, and descended through a fern patch to an old wagon road, steep in parts. The trail followed an old road bed on the S slope of the mountain. We left the road at 31.4 mi and began a steep ascent to the North Carolina state line.

A ridge crest, rhododendron thicket, two streams, and timbered area followed, but we reentered the forest after a few yards. At 31.8 mi, we turned R at a locked gate, crossed a small stream, and followed a road R, into the forest, crossing a ridge and a small stream. An old road took us through mixed forest into the Thompson River gorge. At 32.8 mi we reached the exceptionally scenic Thompson River and crossed on a well-designed footbridge. (Rocky sections here on the trail require caution in wet or icy weather.)

(Duke Power Company has postponed the construction of a dam in the Coley Creek basin that would affect the original route of the Foothills Trail. However, you may see a N rerouting of the trail, temporarily or permanently, in this section between Thompson River and the Bearcamp Creek area. Any rerouting has not changed Duke's Bearcamp Creek Trail, a 0.7-mi spur route that is constructed upstream to a waterfall and pool.)

From here we ascended through rhododendron, holly, and oaks to a ridge, reached a jeep road, turned R and continued to ascend. At 33.4 mi we reached another ridge, turned on the crest, and followed a slope.

After crossing a rivulet and passing a rocky face on the L, we changed to the L side of the ridge and reached a timber road gate of the Crescent Land and Timber Corp. at 34.3 mi. After another gated road at 35 mi came a hardwood forest with an understory of mountain laurel, small hemlocks, locust, and dogwood. Cascades were audible on the R.

A footbridge crossed over a ravine, followed by two log bridges and an ascent to a ridge at 36.1 mi. From here we followed an old wagon road but left it to descend on a section of 100 steps. At 36.4 mi we reached Bearcamp Creek, where we camped under the hemlocks.

Here we met Wayne and Tonie Bell and their four children, from Lancaster. They had started at Table Rock and planned to go at least to the Upper Whitewater Falls parking area. "We have planned this trip for three months," Wayne said. "Tonie made our sleeping bags." "What do you think of this trip?" I asked Anthony, age 8. "Well, it is supposed to be a vacation," he said, "but I didn't know it was going to rain every day!" Megan, age 4, the youngest, said flatly that she was sleepy and ready for bed. It rained again during the night.

Back on the trail, for the next 0.7 mi we could hear Bearcamp Creek on the R, but we turned sharply and ascended to cross a ridge. An old road bed took us along a S slope. We climbed steep steps (unnecessary if the trail had been graded) and descended on more steps. At 39 mi large boulders were on the R. At an old road jct on a ridge, we turned L, reached an old road jct, and turned R to continue the descent.

At 39.5 mi we turned off the road on a steep climb L, crossing two footbridges over ravines. We crossed a ridge and followed a S slope. (At 39.9 mi is another example of unnecessary steps where a graded trail would have been better for backpackers.) At 40.2 mi we crossed a 50-foot suspension bridge over the scenic Horsepasture Creek Gorge. The edge of Lake Jocassee was on the R. The beautiful view was made possible by Duke Power Company engineering skill. (For boat shuttle to this and other points mentioned for Lake Jocassee accesses, contact Hoyett's Tackle Store in Salem, SC 29676; (803) 944–9016.)

From Horsepasture River to Toxaway River (6.7 mi)

We crossed a small stream heavily shaded by rhododendron and bordered with fetterbush, turned R on an old road, descended, then ascended to a ridge. More horse tracks. "They must bring in these horses with helicopters," we speculated. At 41.1 mi we turned R on a ridge road, then turned L from the road, crossed an old road and reached a much-used dirt road at 41.5 mi. Here was a fork road jct; the trail followed the second gated road on the L. We crossed Bear Creek on an excellent steel-bolted 30-foot bridge at 41.6 mi, reaching a hemlock forest, a good place to camp. After ascending to a plateau we met two backpackers, Mark Looper and Chuck Posey, from Easley. "We are going as far as our food lasts," Mark told us.

By now the sun had burned off the heavy fog and was shining against a bank, a good place to dry out our tent from the previous night's rain. After drying out we were on a ridge when we met two more backpackers—Tommy and Debbie Byers from Clover.

At 43.6 mi we crossed Cobb Creek in a rhododendron thicket near beds of Oconee bells (*Shortia galacifolia*), an evergreen with small white flowers. It grows only in a few mountain counties. We passed a landslide at 43.7 mi in a forest of pine and mountain laurel. From here we ascended on a ridge and for the next 2.5 mi undulated, following and crisscrossing old logging roads, and crossing small streams SE of Grindstone Mountain. One stream was at 45.2 mi, where rhododendron, galax, and Oconee bells were abundant. Continuing the descent, at some points steep, we turned R at 46.4 mi, crossed another small stream, and reached the edge of beautiful Lake Jocassee at 46.9 mi. This is Cane Break, a boat access to the trail.

From Cane Break, Toxaway River, to Laurel Fork Creek (5.8 mi)

Thunder shook the mountains and dark angry clouds moved in swiftly from the NW. Rain poured on us as we made a steep climb in the final approach to the spectacular view at the bridge. The rain made the rhododendron and Oconee bells shine as if they had been waxed. As sheets of rain fell, we crossed the extraordinary 200-foot suspension footbridge, which some say is the longest bridge of its type in the East. The bridge was designed and built by Duke Power Company. Across the bridge the rain suddenly stopped, the storm passed, and the sun came out. Camping

19

near the lake is allowed by the Crescent Land and Timber Corp. if you stay 1,000 ft from the shore.

We entered a hemlock stand with good views of the lake on the R. At 48 mi the trail went straight up the mountainside on more than 250 wooden steps. Some of these steps are too high for an ordinary step with a full backpack, and climbing them requires the exertion and patience of a Sisyphus. Almost at the top was a welcome "resting bench." At 48.1 mi we reached the ridge, followed it to a sharp turn L on a switchback, and descended to Rock Creek at 48.7 mi. We found a campsite under the hemlocks, sweetgum, and white pines, by a cascade. We walked down stream and took a swim in the lake.

The next day we followed the trail for 0.1 mi along the lakeside. Near the return to the South Carolina state line we began ascending on switchbacks at 49.1 mi. Rhododendron, beech, and hemlock were the major foliage on the mountainside. Galax was profuse. On an eroded red-clay road, the trail was steep. After a short plateau the trail ascended again, finally reaching a ridge crest at 49.6 mi. It took erratic turns, and the blazes were easy to miss. We hiked through patches of bristly locust, gold star, trailing arbutus, wild hydrangea, and calicroot (*Aletris farinosa*). At 50.7 mi, we exited from a gated road, turned R, followed a more recently used road to another gated road, and turned L at 51.6 mi. The roadside had large banks of blooming blackberry bushes, a feast for summer hikers. We changed roads, R, at 52.2 mi. A cascading stream was audible on the L. At 52.7 mi a spur trail came in from the R; it led to a Lake Jocassee access.

From Laurel Fork Creek to US 178 (8.4 mi)

The trail follows an old road, wide enough in its construction to have once been a public road. (A spur trail up a hill at 53 mi leads to an excellent view of Lake Jocassee.) The sound and views of Laurel Fork Creek Falls were impressive at 53.1 mi. At 53.2 mi a suspension bridge across

Laurel Fork Creek led to an ideal campsite, with evidence of former buildings in the area.

After leaving Laurel Fork Creek, the trail ambled from one side of the road and the stream to the other for 3 mi. Logging had altered the natural beauty in the area. Permanent bridges make it unnecessary to rock-hop. Forests of hemlock, white pine, oaks, and poplar included some virgin stands of hemlock. In addition to acres of rhododendron, there were borders of spice bush, witch hazel, and wild hydrangea, and beds of partridge berry, maiden hair and Christmas ferns, Oconee bells, and Indian pipe (*Monotropa uniflora*), a herbaceous perennial without chlorophyll. On one of the logging roads we met lumbermen hauling out large hemlocks; in some places timbering had caused erosion, and the trail was deep with red mud. "The trail corridor on Duke's section of trail is only 4 feet wide," Duke's recreation supervisor, Charles Borawa, said. At 56 mi a bench invited us to sit and observe a 60-foot cascade.

At 57 mi the trail crossed the last bridge before ascending S on a slope from Laurel Fork. Here we saw a copperhead, the first poisonous snake spotted on the trip. We climbed through dense rhododendron to a hilltop at 57.5 mi and descended in a deciduous forest to a small stream where, at 58 mi, there is a designated campsite area W of an old road. Boulders dominated the landscape at 59.2 mi. At 60.2 mi the trail made a horseshoe curve near a used graveled road and reached a parking area at 60.8 mi.

(At the parking lot is the yellow-blazed Eastatoe Gorge Trail [5-mi round trip], a spur that descends 2.5 mi to Eastatoe Creek in the Eastatoe Gorge Natural Area. From the parking lot walk up the road 0.2 mi and turn L on an old gated logging road. Follow it through a cut in a low ridge, turn L at a fork, and ascend through an area of grass, locust, and blackberry. At 0.7 mi cross Narrow Ridge, an area that has been clear-cut; follow signs and blazes to avoid side-logging skid roads. Here is a view of Roundtop Mountain, E. Descend gradually on old roads through a scenic forest of large poplar, hemlock, beech, birch, and oak. Fetterbush, rhododendron, ferns, and wildflowers are prominent. The area has a number of rare ferns, one of which is the Tunbridge fern, *Hymenophyllum tunbridgense*, which, according to botanist Richie Bell, is not found elsewhere in North America. At. 1.5 mi, L at a bench, leave the road, and descend on a foot trail. There is a campsite at Eastatoe Creek. Backtrack.)

We followed the graveled road to US 178, near the community of Rocky Bottom, at 61.1 mi. Laurel Valley Lodge was on the R, and as we filled our canteens the smell of home-cooked food tempted us to stay for dinner. We compromised and purchased tomatoes and cucumbers to freshen up our freeze-dried food menu. The motel is open all year, but in the winter the restaurant is usually open from Thursday through Sunday (803–878–4615). We returned to US 178. (Stores with groceries and gasoline are 7 mi R, down the mtn on US 178 to the jct with SC 11, and 8 mi L up the mtn on US 178 to Rosman.)

From US 178 to SR 199, Chimneytop Gap (2.0 mi)

At US 178 the trail crossed a bridge over Eastatoe Creek and ascended to Chimneytop Mountain. (Some hikers told us there was a campsite on the first knob at 61.4 mi, but we did not find it.) A massive rock formation and an excellent S view were at 61.8 mi. The trail skirted SW of the peak. Thunder drove us to camp in a flat area near an old roadbed, and as darkness descended, so did the rain.

From SR 199, Chimneytop Gap, to Sassafras Mountain (2.5 mi)

From Chimneytop Gap at 63.1 mi the trail crossed the paved SR 199, ascended steeply to an old road, and turned toward the N side of the slope. After a return to the ridge we climbed steeply, passing large rocks, good views, and pink lady slippers and twisted stalk blooming in a hardwood forest. Leaving the old road bed at 63.9 mi, the trail entered

23

an open forest with a profusion of New York ferns. We met Myron Aycock and Joel Dowis from Anderson on our climb.

We returned to the ridge at 64.2 mi and turned L on an old open grassy road. White pines bordered the trail, and a plump copperhead was enjoying the morning sun. The measuring wheel, "Clicker," nudged him out of the way. At 64.8 mi the trail led to a jct; we angled R and up. Three deer bolted down the old road to our L. Wild quinine (*Parthenium integrifolium*) grew on the banks of a paved road at 65.2 mi. After crossing it and climbing steeply, we saw locust, black birch, sassafras, witch hazel, and chestnut oak in a rocky area. Steps led to the top of Sassafras Mountain (3,554 ft), the state's highest peak, and a sheltered sign provided information on the trail routes. At the top of the firetower there was an exceptional 360-degree panoramic view. A paved road descended to the parking area at 65.6 mi. At the parking lot is an option to take the original Foothills Trail for 9.2 mi to Table Rock State Park, or to take the blue-blazed Foothills Trail for 14.2 mi to US 276 in Caesars Head State Park. (The Foothills Trail extends another 5.4 mi to Jones Gap State Park.) The original Foothills Trail is described first.

(If planning a vehicle shuttle from here to Caesars Head, there are two routes. The longest, all on paved roads, 29.7 mi, is down from Sassafras Mtn 4.2 mi to Rocky Bottom and the jct with US 178. A turn L on SC 11 from US 178 and another turn L on US 276 from SC 11 will take you to the trail jct at Caesars Head. The other route is approximately 20 mi, depending on which county road you take, and it is mainly in Translyvania County, N.C. One advantage of this route is the avoidance of the repetition of mtn ascents from SC 11. To follow it, descend from Sassafras Mtn but leave the paved road after 1.5 mi, R, at the first road, Glady Fork Rd, SR 1105, a gravel road that is 4.2 mi to East Fork Rd, SR 1107. Here you may go R or L on SR 1107 to reach US 276, but the road conditions are usually better to the L where it takes you through Connestee to US 276.

Either way, when you reach US 276, turn R. After you reach the S.C. line, S of Cedar Mountain community, it is 1.6 mi to the E trailhead.)

From Sassafras Mountain to Table Rock State Park (9.2 mi)

A few yds down the paved road the trail turned L on a slope, where some remarkably large pink lady slippers grew. Following an old roadbed among stands of mountain laurel and scattered holly, sourwood, and Virginia pine, it crossed a ridge at 66.6 mi. Here were large patches of trailing arbutus. At 66.8 mi there was an old homesite and what appeared to be an old mining area. Rhododendron thickets and large beds of galax grew nearby. We reached Hickorynut Mountain Gap at 67.3 mi where we saw cancer root (*Conopholis americana*), a yellow-brown parasite, at the base of oaks, and outstanding examples of downed American chestnut logs. At 68.5 mi a short section of the old Emory Gap toll road began, passing through a beautiful forest of both deciduous and evergreen trees. A footbridge crossed a small stream at 69 mi, where rhododendron and hemlock provided a heavy shade. The trail entered another open hardwoods forest with chestnut logs at 69.2 mi. Turning L on a ridge near boulders, it descended to a small bridge and a trickling stream. Legend has it that Marion Castles had a rock house there to hide from service in the Civil War; now there are campsites. A large rocky cliff is on the L at 69.4 mi. Rocks, streams, and picturesque topography make this area at 70.1 mi unusually attractive. On the L at 70.2 mi can be seen the "Lighthouse" on the lower area of the Drawbar Cliffs.

From here we followed an old roadbed among young poplars and through an open grassy area, turned L on another old road, and ascended to an exceptional view from Drawbar Cliffs at 71 mi. We could see Lake Keowee and the foothills beyond. We stayed an hour, observing the magnificent scenery and the plants on the outcrops.

Still ascending, the trail turned L on a ridge and took a S slope off the ridge at 71.1 mi. Mandrakes, cohosh, and Canada violets (*Viola canadensis*) grew in an open forest of large oaks.

At 71.4 mi we reached a jct with the yellow-blazed Pinnacle Mountain Trail and the boundary of Table Rock State Park. (The Pinnacle Mountain Trail is L for 0.2 mi to the summit of the peak, where, except in the winter, there are no views. See Table Rock State Park.) The Foothills Trail and the Pinnacle Mountain Trail turned R and descended to a magnificent view from a granite cliff at 72 mi. The descent from here was steep, narrow, and in some places eroded. At 72.7 mi were flumes and rhododendron; the trail descended on a precipitous area among rhododendron roots at 73.2 mi. At 74.1 mi are more flumes, cascades, falls, slides, and pools along Carrick Creek. At 74.7 mi the trail crossed a bridge at a waterfall and became paved before it reached the Nature Center at 74.8 mi. Across the road is a parking area. (Remember that camping is not allowed in Table Rock State Park except at the designated campgrounds, and the park superintendent must be informed if you plan to leave your vehicle parked overnight in the parking area. See Table Rock State Park in Chapter III, Sec 4, for support facilities.)

From Sassafras Mountain to Caesars Head State Park (14.2 mi)

This section of the trail is rugged, remote, and strenuous. It is partially footpaths and partially timber industry and pioneer settlers' roads. Deer, turkey, fox, raccoon, hawks, and songbirds frequent the route; wildflowers are prominent, including trailing arbutus, galax, orchids, Indian pipe, asters, and azaleas. Dense beds of wild berries and ferns are common, and the varied hardwoods make an unforgettable display of color in October. Blazes and markers are blue for the Foothills Trail, red for the Greenville Lake watershed boundary, and white for survey markers or private-property boundaries. Also, from here to Gum Gap, where the trail

leaves the state boundary, there are metal stakes that identify the state line—N.C. (N) and S.C. (S). Sometimes, markers are on the stakes.

Hiking this section with me were John Matthews, Mark and Kevin Zoltek, Nile Spiegel, Tate Hayman, and Greg Hippert. (Although this hike was later in the season, it was our continuous luck for it to rain all day, with a strong SW wind howling across the ridgeline.) We crossed the road from the Sassafras Mountain parking lot to a narrow dirt road that serves two radio towers. After passing L of the towers, we descended through a dense forest of oak, rhododendron, and hemlock to Sassafras Gap at 66.4 mi. (Here is evidence of the old Emory Gap toll road that ascends from Pickens County, S.C. to Transylvania County, N.C. There is a water source 0.3 mi N on the old road.) From here we ascended to skirt the N side of White Oak Mountain (3,297 ft) at 66.7 mi to find views of Glady Valley and the Blue Ridge Mountains beyond. After returning to the ridge crest at 67 mi, we followed, crossed, or paralleled a variety of old roads for 6 mi to Slicking Gap.

Along the way, at 67.9 mi, we passed through a former clear-cut where white pines were abundant, and at 68.5 mi we reached the top of Bigspring Mountain. After a gap and knoll, we descended steeply to a briar patch and wet area at 69.7 mi. Jane Cantrell Creek is L, and the N end of Little Table Rock Mountain is ahead. At 69.9 mi is a good campsite at an old logging road. To the L (N) at 71 mi, on Dolves Mountain, is an excellent view of the East Fork of the French Broad River valley. We reached Slicking Gap at 72.8 mi and began the climb on a timber road to the top of Slicking Mountain. At 73 mi there is a blue arrow painted on a flat rock to remind us that the trail follows R at the fork. At 73.6 mi are overlooks. Descending on switchbacks from Slicking Mountain we reached Gum Gap at 74.9 mi. (Here we left North Carolina and entered the preserved area of the S.C. Wildlife and Marine Resources Dept. Camping is not allowed on this or other properties for the remainder of this trail section.)

We climbed over the earthen barrier, R, and descended on a rocky (and closed-to-vehicles) road. Soon the trail paralleled Julian Creek until near its mouth, at 76.2 mi, where we rock-hopped Matthews Creek. After passing a gate we came to a curve in the road, L, at 76.9 mi. (To the R is a drain from the road and a 0.3-mile spur route [may be blue flagged] to the Upper Raven Cliff Falls. Views are spectacular; slick soil and rocks make the area dangerous. Backtrack.)

We continued on the road and at 78.1 mi we turned off the road, R, at a trail sign in Caesars Head State Park. We gradually ascended to a jct with the Raven Cliff Falls Trail at 78.4 mi. (To the R it is 0.8 mi to the observation deck for viewing the 420-foot Lower Raven Cliff Falls, a popular area for day hikers.) A turn L is 1.4 mi to the parking area at US 276, 1.1 mi N of Caesars Head State Park hq. (See more information under Caesars Head State Park, Chapter III.) For food, supplies, and services it is 14 mi N on US 276 to Brevard. South on US 276 it is 14 mi to Cleveland for groceries and gasoline. There is a snack bar at the Ceasars Head State Park hq.

From Caesars Head State Park to Jones Gap State Park (5.4 mi)

From the parking area on US 276, Nile Spiegel, Kevin Zoltek, and I continued on the completion of the Foothills Trail (which follows the Jones Gap Access Trail and the Jones Gap Trail) at its E terminus in the Jones Gap State Park. We descended to the Middle Saluda River at 80.5 mi, crossed a log bridge at 80.8 mi, and followed the old toll road, engineered and built by Solomon Jones in the midnineteenth century. Champion trees, ferns, and wildflowers garnish the trail. The river and its tributaries cascade over huge boulders and splash into numerous pools for nearly 4 miles in a drop of nearly 1,700 ft. At 83.1 mi we made a jct, R, with the Coldspring Branch Trail, and at 84.2 mi we crossed another log bridge over the river. Passing a number of designated campsites, we reached the Jones Gap State Park parking lot at 85.2 mi. (For detailed information on this section of the Foothills Trail, adjoining trails, and access descriptions, see Caesars Head and Jones Gap state parks in Chapter III.) Access to the E terminus is on the River Falls Road, 5.8 mi in from US 276/SC 11, 1 mi W of Cleveland.

Bartram Trail

Length: 6.9 mi (11 km); **easy**; USGS Maps: Satolah, Tamassee; trailhead: jct of SC 107 and FR 710.

The "unofficial" Bartram Trail in South Carolina overlaps the Chattooga Trail and the Foothills Trail, which are described elsewhere in this chapter. However, William Bartram and his travels are of such significance, perhaps the following information will stimulate new interest in extending the S.C. portion of the Bartram Trail.

William Bartram (1739-1823) of Philadelphia was the son of John Bartram (1699-1777), the first native American botanist to receive international recognition for botanical reasearch. William, who often traveled with his father, became renowned as a naturalist and writer, and his *Travels* (1791) greatly influenced English Romanticism. His explorations in the southeastern states included at least 14 counties in South Carolina; it is known that he traveled through Anderson, Pickens, and Oconee counties, but his route was mainly through valleys now covered by Hartwell Reservoir and Lake Keowee.

District Ranger Joseph Wallace told me the Bartram Trail "officially ends on the Georgia side of the Chattooga River." In the mid-1970s there was talk about extending the trail into the Sumter National Forest to "an unknown location east of the Oconee State Park." In preparation for that extension the district used the Chattooga Trail and Foothills Trail routes from the Chattooga River at SC 28 to SC 107 for 6.9 mi (13 mi if to the Oconee State Park).

MAP 2

Mill Mtn

Ridley Mtn ×2930

BM 2593

Big Bend Falls

Big Bend

Round Top ×2527

Moody Spring

CHATTOOGA

FOREST

BM 2273

Falls Cem

Cherry Hill Cem

CHATTAHOOCHEE

RIVER

×2363

NATIONAL FOREST

FOREST BOUNDARY

Crane Mtn

Rock Gorge

×2053

GEORGIA

SOUTH CAROLINA

Ford

RIDGE

Branch

WINDING STAIR

×2241

Pigpen

Cr

Lick Log Cr

Nicholson Cr

BM 2213

BM 1824

×1579

Mtn

Morton Mtn

Foothills Trail

TAMASSEE

LUMBER

Wash

ROAD

Crossland

N

Dodge Mtn

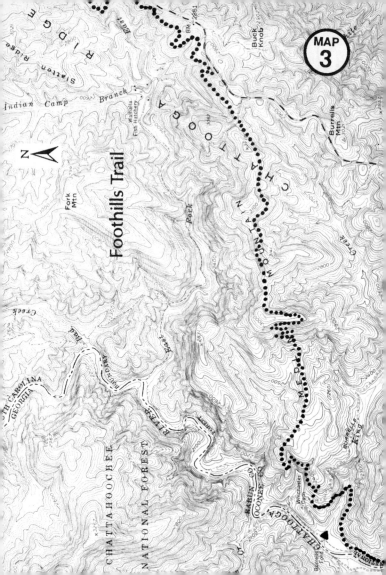

MAP
3

Foothills Trail

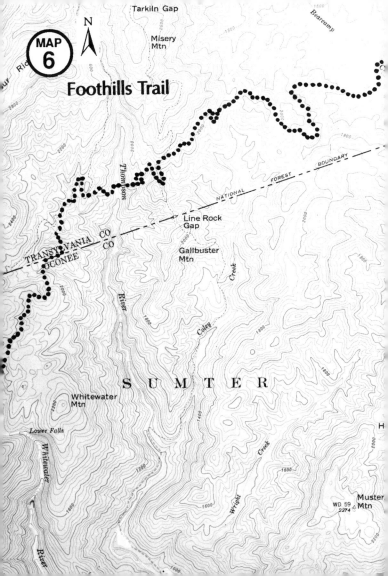

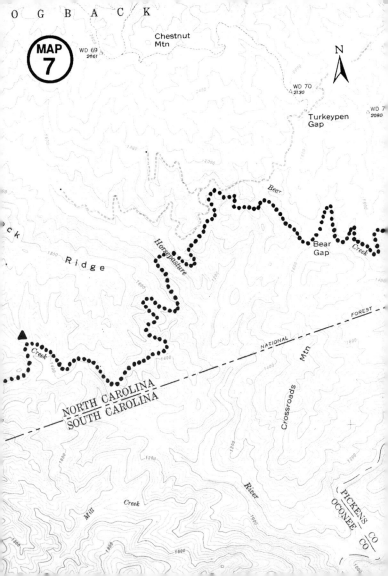

MAP
9

2741   2800

2600

TRANSYLVANIA CO
PICKENS CO

Standing Rock

Wild

Hog

Creek

Eastatoe

2000

Chestnut   Ridge   2800

2200

2000

67   2400

Flatrock
Mtn

2400

2600

BM

2200

2200

2000

1800

Creek

Laurel Fork
Gap

Side-of-Mountain Creek

Narrow   Ridge

1800

Cane Mtn

2200

2400

N

Foothills Trail

Long   Branch

2000

Diana   Mtn   1800   Laurel

Branch

Pine   Mtn   Creek   Cove

2000

1400

MAP
10

2400

Creek

Dogwood

TENNESSEE VALLEY

LOOKOUT TOWER
3554

Sassafr

Abner

2400

Chimneytop
Gap

Chimneytop

2000

2000

Caesars
Head

Chimneytop

2000

2000

2000

2200

MOOREFIELD

Creek

Rocky Bottom

Rocky   Bottom

BM R 23

Creek

1750

2000

2000

Roundtop Mtn

Rock Mt

1800

MEMORIAL

BM D 43
1962

Roundtop Mtn

2400

2000

Poplar Hollow

2600

3100

1800

HIGHWAY

1800

Creek

Cove

Mou

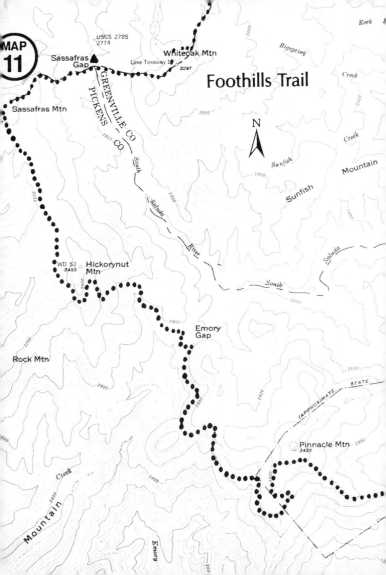

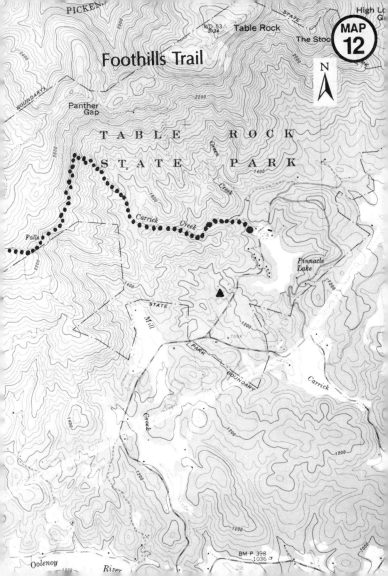

Foothills Trail

MAP 12

MAP
13

N

Sassafras Mtn

Sassafras Gap

PICKENS CO

GREENVILLE CO

SASS 2785

USGS 2785
0074

Sassafras Mtn

Laurel Fork Heritage

Wilson Mtn

Gowdy Mtn

Prong

TENN

Blassingim Mtn

VALLEY

Growling Spring Gap

DIVIDE

BLUE

Little Table Rock

Rocky Mtn

Cane Creek

Rocky Mtn

Laurel

Laurel

Rock Quarry

Table Rock

Mountain

Mtn. Park

Bursted Rock Mtn

MAP
14

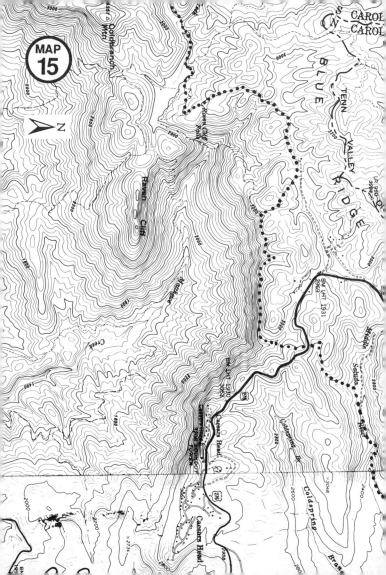

MAP
15

N

CAROL
CAROL

BLUE

RIDGE

TENN

VALLEY

Coldbranch Mtn

Raven Cliff

Middle

Creek

BM LHT 1931
2969

BM LHT 1910
2063

Saluda

Caesars Head

Coldspring Br

Coldspring

Caesars Head

Branch

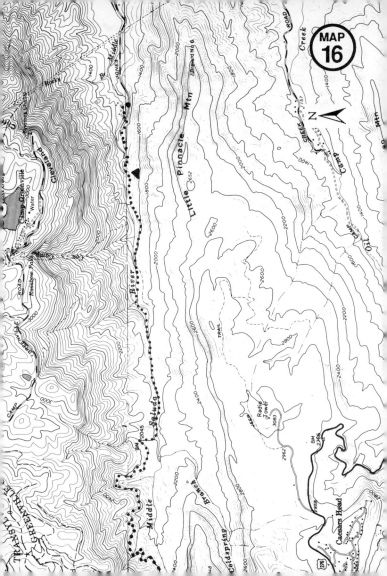

MAP
16

"We were never informed of the proposed turning-off point in our district," Wallace said. "We were told that the Department of the Interior was going to study the feasibility of locating the Bartram Trail in this area, but that department never gave us any recommendation."

In September of 1975 a meeting of parties interested in the "Bartram Trail in South Carolina" met in Greenwood and discussed 10 major localities, most of which were along the Savannah River basin and the Lake Keowee area. Their report stated that the trail across Sumter "from Oconee Station to the Georgia line was agreed upon." It was further stated that much of the "desirability" and "feasibility" would be "handled by local garden clubs and historic societies in a county by county study."

At present there are 75 mi of the Bartram Trail in Georgia, 37.6 mi on the S border of Thurmond Lake (formerly Clarks Hill Lake), and 37.4 mi from the Chattooga River through the Chattahoochee National Forest to the North Carolina state line, where over 81 mi of segmented sections extend through the Nantahala National Forest.

For information about the Bartram Trail in Georgia and North Carolina, read *The Hiking Trails of North Georgia*, by Tim Homan (Peachtree Publishers, Ltd., 494 Armour Circle, N.E., Atlanta, GA 30324), and *North Carolina Hiking Trails*, by Allen de Hart (Appalachian Mountain Club Publishers, 5 Joy St., Boston, MA 02108). Other information is available from the Bartram Trail Conference, 3815 Interstate Court, Suite 202A, Montgomery, AL 36109; (205) 277-7050; North Carolina Bartram Trail Society, Route 3, Box 406, Sylva, NC 28723; (704) 293-9661; and Georgia Bartram Trail Society, Highway 106, Box 803, Scaly Mountain, NC 28755.

Chattooga Trail (Sumter Section)

Length: 16.7 mi (26.7 km); **moderate**; USGS Maps: Cashiers, Tamassee, Satolah; trailhead: Russell Bridge, SC 28.

The total length of the Chattooga Trail is 36.9 mi, 20.2 mi of it in Georgia's Chattahoochee National Forest, and

16.7 mi in Sumter National Forest (4.3 mi are within the Ellicott Rock Wilderness Area). The Chattahoochee Section has termini at the US 76 bridge and the SC 28 bridge. The Sumter Section has termini at the SC 28 bridge and other trails in the Nantahala National Forest in North Carolina.

From SC 28 at Russell Bridge parking area E, the trail heads upriver. The black-blazed Chattooga Trail and yellow-blazed Bartram Trail markers led on a gradual slope through white pines. The trail is well designed and graded. At 0.4 mi it crossed a stream and wove in and out of coves. A rocky stream was at 0.7 mi. Wildflowers were prominent. In the spring, maidenhair ferns mix with wild geraniums, Indian cucumber root, trillium, and showy orchids. At 0.8 mi and at 1 mi I crossed streams in coves; at 1.8 mi the trail was on a slope, and I heard the continuous sound of the river.

The trail curved around Reed Mountain and came to an old road bed at 3 mi. Gradually descending, it approached the riverside and followed the river on an old road bed. At 3.4 mi it crossed Ira Branch, an area good for camping. Yellow root, galax, and pink lady slippers grew along the trail, and hemlocks reached silently into the sky, a haven for song birds. At 4.3 mi I saw a steep slope on the L, where Lick Log Creek fell with a roar into the Chattooga, and another Lick Log waterfall was ahead on the R. At 4.6 mi I reached the Foothills Trail jct (see Foothills Trail in this chapter).

I followed the black-blazed Chattooga Trail and the white-blazed Foothills Trail over a ridge and down to the Chattooga River again at 6.7 mi. At 9.1 mi was the 40-foot cascading Big Ben Falls. In a picturesque cove at 9.9 mi the rust-blazed Big Ben Trail turned R for 2.7 mi to SC 107. At 12.3 mi was the jct with a 0.2-mi spur trail up to 80-foot King Creek Falls. I reached Burrells Ford parking area at 12.3 mi.

With some Sierra Club friends I hiked from Burrells Ford parking area on the Chattooga Trail to Ellicott Rock. We passed the Foothills Trail jct at 12.9 mi and entered the Ellicott Rock Wilderness Area. We curved L at the headwaters of Spoon Auger Falls at 13.3 mi and descended gently to an old road bed with ferns at 14 mi. (A rust-blazed spur trail here is L to Spoon Auger Falls for 0.3 mi, and a total of 0.8 mi out to FR 708 at Burrells Fork Bridge.) Continuing upriver, we reached a jct with an old wagon road and, at 14.6 mi, sandy beaches by the river. A log footbridge with a cable crossed East Fork Creek; the East Fork Trail jct was at 15 mi. (The East Fork Trail gradually ascends for 2.4 mi to the Walhalla National Fish Hatchery and an exit to SC 107. See East Fork Trail in this chapter.)

From here we passed through a white pine stand. At 15.5 mi we saw what is claimed to be the state's champion white mountain camellia (*Stewartia ovata*). As two members of our team were bird-watchers, three were fishermen and another a wildlife photographer, the trail was providing something for all. At 15.6 mi the trail crossed Bad Creek, hugging the river as it stayed on a generally even contour upriver. At 16.4 mi on the R is the state-champion rosebay rhododendron (*Rhododendron maximum*), more than 2 feet in cir and 40 ft tall.

At 16.7 mi we reached Ellicott Rock. In 1811, when it was still Cherokee country, Andrew Ellicott surveyed and chiseled a marker "NC" to designate the tristate corner of the Carolinas and Georgia. A few feet before reaching Ellicott Rock is the true tristate intersection: Commissioners Rock, another chiseled marker on a rock that extends into the river. It bears the inscription LAT 35 AD 1813 NC–SC.

Upstream 0.1 mi into North Carolina is a campsite area and a jct L, with the 3.5-mile Ellicott Rock Trail that fords the river and ascends to FR 1178 at Ammonds Branch. To the R is the 3.1-mi Bad Creek Trail that ascends to SR 1100, 2.6 mi W of NC 107. On the Bad Creek Trail, after 1.2 mi, is the jct R with the 6.4-mi Fork Mountain Trail, described below. (Also see Chapter II in *North Carolina Hiking Trails*.)

Cherry Hill Recreation Area

The Cherry Hill Recreation Area has camping sites (but no hook-ups) for RVs and tents, picnic tables and grills, flush toilets, hot showers, drinking water, and sewage disposal. It is an excellent base point for short hikes, and it has a connecting trail to the long Chattooga Trail. The campground is usually open from May 1 through October.

Access: On SC 107, 5.8 mi N from Oconee State Park, and 7.5 mi N from the SC 107 jct with SC 28.

Cherry Hill Nature Trail

Length: 0.5 mi rt (0.8 km); **easy**; USGS Map: Tamassee; trailhead: Cherry Hill Campground.

We followed the trail signs at the far end of the campground through a thicket of rosebay rhododendron and New York ferns, crossed West Fork Creek on a footbridge, entered a stand of buckberry, and passed under large white pines. We recrossed West Fork Creek at 0.3 mi and returned to the point of origin.

Big Ben Trail

Length: 2.7 mi (4.3 km); **easy**; USGS Map: Tamassee; trailhead: on SC 107 near Cherry Hill jct.

From the jct of SC 107 and Cherry Hill Campground, we went S on SC 107 for a few yds to a rust-blazed trail entrance on the R. The trail descended in a hardwood forest to a crossing of Cane Creek in a forest of rhododendron, hemlock, and oaks at 0.1 mi. Ferns and galax grew along the stream. For the next 0.6 mi the trail paralleled the S side of Big Ben Road. At 1.2 mi the trail curved around the headwaters of Pig Pen Branch in a mixed forest and ascended to a jct with a spur trail, R, to Big Bend Road at 1.6 mi. From here the trail descended gradually to the E side of a stream with rhododendron and followed the stream to a jct with the Foothills Trail. We backtracked, but we could have hiked R on the Foothills Trail for 2.5 mi to Burrells Ford parking area for a vehicle shuttle.

Winding Stairs Trail

Length: 3.4 mi (5.4 km); **easy** to **moderate**; USGS Map: Tamassee; trailhead: corner of SC 107 and Cherry Hill Campground entrance.

Access: From the entrance of the Cherry Hill Recreation Area off SC 107, 5.8 mi N from Oconee State Park. We followed the rust-colored blaze through buckberry and blueberry in an oak forest. It was fall and the red oaks were reddish brown and the white oaks were golden. After crossing a smooth ridge Taylor Watts, Les Parks, and I descended to a trail jct at 0.2 mi. (The trail to the L goes to the Cherry Hill campground.) We turned R, following cascading West Fork Creek. Autumn colors were spectacular with ochre, orange, scarlet, and yellow in a generally open hardwood forest. There was a sharp L at 0.9 mi at a jct in the old road bed. On the L at 1.2 mi was the hypnotic sound of a gentle but high waterfall in a beautiful spot that would be a good campsite. We crossed trickling streams at 1.3 mi and 1.7 mi on a pleasant, wide, old road bed and rushing streams at 2.1 mi and 2.4 mi. At the 2.1-mi stream, many wildflowers bloom in the spring. At 2.4 mi Carolina lily and phlox grow. We heard cascading Comers Creek on the R at 2.8 mi. We surprised a wild hog in a wallow as much as he surprised us. After his fast disappearance we saw evidence of others in the area. Sheets of mica glistened along the old road as we approached an embankment and a stream; at 3 mi we were surrounded by fetterbush, papaw, sweet pepperbush, and ferns. At this point we began to hear West Fork Creek again. We reached FR 710, Tamassee Rd, at 3.4 mi. Our shuttle vehicle was there with Kevin Clarey and Dick Hunt. "What's that on your cap?" Kevin asked Taylor. Taylor had two hairy, yellow and brown orb-weaving spiders starting a new web on the bill of his cap.

Ellicott Rock Wilderness Area

There are 7,012 acres in the Ellicott Rock Wilderness Area. A section of the wilderness is in the NW corner of the state in the Sumter National Forest, in the NE corner of Georgia in the Chattahoochee National Forest, and in the Nantahala National Forest in North Carolina. Falling through this marvelous preserve is the rugged Chattooga Wild and Scenic River. This wilderness received its name from Andrew Ellicott, a famous land surveyor who completed the boundary between Georgia and North Carolina in 1811. (See Chattooga Trail described above.) The Foothills Trail follows the S edge of the wilderness boundary; the King Creek Falls Trail, Spoon Auger Trail, and part of the Chattooga Trail are near the Chattooga River. The East Fork Trail is completely in the wilderness, and the Fork Mountain Trail is about 80 percent inside the boundary. Although there are not any developed campgrounds in the wilderness, there are campgrounds and picnic areas on SC 107, near the E boundary of the wilderness. The Walhalla Fish Hatchery is also at the boundary. The nearest stores for groceries and gasoline are in Cashiers, North Carolina, 8 mi N on SC 107.

East Fork Trail

Length: 4.8 mi rt (7.7 km); **easy;** USGS Map: Tamassee; trailhead: Walhalla National Fish Hatchery parking lot.

From SC 107 (3.4 mi S from the state line), we drove down the Fish Hatchery Rd for 1.8 mi to the parking lot. After viewing the fish hatchery, which is open daily from 8:00 A.M. to 4:00 P.M., we saw the state-champion Eastern white pine (*Pinus strobus*) in the picnic area (more than 29 in in cir and 170 ft tall). Also in the picnic area is the state-champion mountain winterberry (*Ilex montana*), 1 ft in cir and 28 ft tall. The national-champion sweet pepperbush (*Clethra acuminata*) is also here. It is 11 in in cir and is also called white alder or cinnamon *Clethra*. Near the fish hatchery is another in the "big tree" league, the Eastern hemlock (*Tsuga canadensis*) with a 12-foot, 10-in cir and a 141 ft height. And 0.2 mi above the fish-hatchery trail is the national co-champ of the beautiful mountain laurel (*Kalmia latifolia*), growing 28 ft tall and 4 ft in cir.

We began the East Fork Trail on the R loop route through a tunnel of rhododendron and under tall hemlocks in the picnic area. We crossed East Fork on a bridge and continued R at a jct of the loop at 0.3 mi. We descended on an old wagon road and crossed a stream cascading from the R, with cement stepping stones for crossing at 1 mi. Hemlock, maple, oak, and hickory were prominent at 1.3 mi and rhododendron at 1.6 mi. The jct with the Chattooga Trail by the Chattooga River was in a stand of white pines at 2.4 mi. To the L it is 2.7 mi to Burrells Ford parking area, and to the R it is 1.7 mi to Ellicott Rock. (Backtrack, make a loop downriver, or use a shuttle for connecting trails upriver. If downriver, go 2.1 mi to jct with the Foothills Trail on L, and go 3.2 mi to Fish Hatchery Road. There turn L and hike down the Fish Hatchery Road for 1.7 mi for a total of 9.4 mi. If upriver, follow the Chattooga Trail for 1.7 mi to Ellicott Rock jct at the state line. Here you would have a choice of taking the 3.5-mi Ellicott Rock Trail out to Nantahala National Forest road 441F and 1178 to SR 1100 and SC 107 shuttle, or from Ellicott Rock taking E route on Bad Creek Trail for 3.1 mi to SR 1100 and SC 107 for shuttle. For another potential loop, see Fork Mountain Trail below.)

Fork Mountain Trail

Length: 6.4 mi (10.2 km); easy to moderate; USGS Map: Cashiers; trailhead: Sloan Bridge Picnic Area parking lot on SC 107.

This is a well-graded trail that weaves in and out of more than 20 coves. Robert Ballance and I began at the picnic parking area and hiked N 0.1 mi on SC 107 to cross the east Fork of the Chattooga River bridge to turn L into the forest at a trail sign. We followed a rust blaze upstream of the Slatten Branch in an outstanding virgin grove of rhododendron and laurel and crossed the branch at 0.7 mi. After entering an open hardwood forest, we crossed a ridge at 1.2 mi. At 2.5 mi we crossed Indian Camp Branch and

beyond entered a grove of large hemlocks before passing
through a fern glen. We entered an arbor of laurel at 2.8
mi. Crossing a ridge at 3.4 mi, we noticed large yellow poplar
and hemlock (near the N.C./S.C. state line) en route to the
dual forks of Bad Creek at 5 mi and 5.2 mi. Wildflowers,
such as pink lady slippers, are along the trail. At 6.4 mi we
made a jct with the Bad Creek Trail. (A loop can be made
here by descending on the Bad Creek Trail L, steeply, for
1.2 mi to the Chattooga Trail at the Chattooga River. The
Chattooga Trail jct with the Foothills Trail is 3.8 mi
downstream.)

King Creek Falls Trail

Length: 1.2 mi rt ct (1.9 km); easy; USGS Map: Tamassee; trailhead: Burrells Ford parking area.

Access: From SC 107 and FR 708, Burrells Ford parking
area. We followed the Chattooga River Trail S for 0.4 mi
to the jct with the Falls Trail. Here we turned L on the
rust-blazed trail for 0.2 mi to see the 80-foot King Creek
Falls. The area has large hemlock and white pines, as well
as dense rhododendron. Backtrack.

Spoon Auger Trail

Length: 1.2 mi rt (1.9 km); easy; USGS Map: Tamassee;
trailhead: Burrells Ford Bridge.

Access: From SC 107 jct with FR 708 Burrells Ford Rd.
Take FR 708 for 2.7 mi to the parking area on L. To approach this 0.1-mi trail, walk down FR 708 for 0.3 mi to
trail entrance on R. Follow the rust blaze to signs explaining the Ellicott Wilderness Area, cross Spoon Auger Creek,
and turn R at 0.2 mi for a 0.1 mi section of switchbacks to
the scenic falls. There are massive hemlocks in the gorge.
Backtrack. (A loop can be made by continuing upriver, where
there is evidence of beavers, to the jct with the Chattooga
Trail at 0.6 mi. Turn R and follow the Chattooga Trail back
to the parking area after a 2.5-mi round trip. Outstanding
views of large hemlock and white pine are on this route.)

Other Pickens District Trails

Bull Sluice Trail

Length: 0.4 mi rt (0.6 km); **easy;** USGS Map: Rainy Mtn; trailhead: Chattooga River Information Station.

Access: At the parking area on the E side of the US 76 Chattooga River bridge. The shortest trail in the district, this 0.2-mi walk to Bull Sluice is also the trail from which you can see the best white-water action. At the Information Station are large interpretive displays about the river and the general area, regulations, and other information. Follow the signs on a paved area through a forest of white pine, black gum, hemlock, and by a bank of galax to the outcroppings at Bull Sluice. The rapids are rated Class 5, the most risky of any on Section III of the Chattooga.

Tamassee Knob Trail

Length: 4.2 mi rt (6.7 km); **easy;** USGS Map: Walhalla; trailhead: Oconee State Park.

From the Foothills Trail sign in Oconee State Park (see Oconee State Park in Chapter 3), we followed the trail for 0.4 mi to a jct. The Foothills Trail forked L with white blazes, and the Tamassee Knob Trail forked R with rust blazes. Fall colors were excellent in a mature hardwood forest on this well-maintained trail. At 0.7 mi we entered an old wagon road into the Pickens Ranger District of the Sumter National Forest. Mountain laurel and rhododendron were prominent among locust and oak at 1.2 mi. At 1.3 mi we crossed a ridge to the SE side, where huge dogwood and redbud grew. In the springtime wildflowers are prevalent on the slopes. Some of the Solomon's seal were bending over with bright-red berries and golden leaves. We began a climb at 1.7 mi, reached a crest for a view of Tamassee Creek

Valley, and at a large rock saw a sign painted on an oak, "End," at 2.1 mi.

Yellow Branch Nature Trail

Length: 0.5 mi (0.8 km); **easy**; USGS Map: Whetstone; trailhead: SC 107 entrance.

Access: Yellow Branch Picnic Area off SC 28, 0.3 mi SE of the Pickens Ranger District hq, or 6 mi NW from Walhalla. Near the picnic area entrance, we followed the trail sign and descended through a large hardwood forest with mountain laurel and rhododendron understory. We crossed a stream at 0.3 mi and passed beds of galax and trailing arbutus by a cascading stream. Ascending, we passed large hemlocks and loblolly pines. On reaching the paved road, we turned R to the point of origin.

Information: Contact District Ranger, Andrew Pickens District, Star Route, Walhalla, SC 29691; (803) 638–9568.

Edgefield and Long Cane Ranger Districts
Edgefield Ranger District
(Edgefield, McCormick, Saluda, and Greenwood Counties)

The Edgefield Ranger District adjoins the Long Cane Ranger District on the west boundary, generally along Stevens Creek. On the south it borders Georgia and the U.S. Army Corps of Engineers property border at the Thurmond Reservoir. The north boundary extends to US 178 near Kirksey, and the east side is west of Edgefield. It has 63,130 acres, most of which is used for timber management. Hunting and fishing are allowed according to state and federal regulations. Four hunting camps, one of which (Key Bridge Hunt Camp) is a wildlife station, are in the district, and a major recreation area is at Lick Fork Lake. Backpackers who plan to camp out on the trails must have permission from the district office. (Hunting season for deer is from Oct. 1 to near the end of December; the district office suggests that this period is "probably not suited for backpackers or hikers." Hunting is not allowed on Sundays.)

Because of the hilly topography and sections of quartz and Carolina slate, hikers will find that this district has appealing scenery contrasts.

Access: Edgefield Ranger office is in Edgefield at the jct of SC 23 and Bacon Street. Turn on Bacon Street and go to the office on the L.

Lick Fork Lake

The Lick Fork Lake recreation area has facilities for camping, swimming, picnicking, boating, and hiking. Sanitary and shower facilities are also provided.

Access: From the ranger station take SC 23 W for 8.5 mi to jct with SC 230, Westside Volunteer Fire Dept. Turn L on SC 230 for 0.4 mi and turn L again on SR 263. After 2 mi turn R on SR 392.

Lick Fork Lake Trail

Length: **1.7 mi** (2.7 km); **easy**; USGS Map: Colliers; trailhead: parking area.

From the parking area I followed the trail sign on the well-maintained foot path through a young mixed forest. Wildflowers, including pink spiderwort, were prominent. I crossed a stream at 0.4 mi and Lick Fork at 0.5 mi. The fiddleheads of the Christmas ferns had recently uncurled on a moist bank, and on a slope I saw beech, oak, sourwood, pine, and hickory trees. At 1 mi I descended to a dam on the L through a dense cove with copious Virginia creeper and honeysuckle. I rock-hopped the stream at 1.1 mi to the jct with the Horn Creek Trail on the R. Turning L to complete the loop, I crossed a footbridge, reached a picnic area, crossed another footbridge and returned to the parking area at 1.7 mi.

Horn Creek Trail

Length: **5.4 mi** (8.6 km); **moderate**; USGS Map: Colliers; trailhead: parking area.

From the parking area I took the Lick Fork Lake Trail S for 0.6 mi to the jct with Horn Creek Trail. I followed the white-blazed trail downstream in a mixed forest to the graveled FR 640 crossing at 0.4 mi. I passed a spring and crossed a footbridge at 0.9 mi, then turned L away from the Lick Fork Creek. Where parts of the forest have been timbered, penstemon grew and jessamine was spreading. At 1.2 mi the trail ascended to a ridge top in a pine stand and crossed a graveled road, SR 263, at 1.6 mi. Here are blackberry patches and fire anthills.

I followed the trail through a young pine stand, parallel to FR 634 and reached Horn Creek at 2.2 mi. At 2.5 mi the trail crossed two footbridges. The forest was mature, tributary crossings were frequent, and the trail was wide. At 3 mi the forest floor changed. Dozers with KG blades had left their marks, and for 1.5 mi I had to crawl over or through brush left by the stingers. The selective cutting, however, provided some shade and trail-corridor direction.

I had circled the timber harvesters to recross SR 263 at 4.8 mi. Here I disturbed a box turtle eating a mushroom for lunch on a seeded road bed. Slightly descending, I reached the picnic area at 5.2 mi, turned R, and completed the loop at 5.4 mi (5.8 mi if counting the distance on the Lick Fork Lake Trail).

Jim Shaver, the park attendant, told me there was a colony of red-cockaded woodpeckers on SR 263, and I went to sit quietly and watch for this endangered bold bird with its black helmet.

Turkey Creek Trail

The two sections of the Turkey Creek Trail are excellent places to see flora and fauna any season of the year. Large stands of climax forest are in this area. Considerable design, planning, and work have gone into its construction. Unfortunately, the trail is segmented by the lack of a bridge at Stevens Creek and an upstream dead-end on the south section (satisfactory arrangements have not been completed with the owners of the property through which the trail must pass). Because the creek rises more than 15 feet during flood stage, a bridge over Stevens Creek would have to be more than 200 feet long, a costly undertaking, Forest Supervisor Donald W. Eng explains. (Perhaps an alternative would be to attach two strong guy-wires to sturdy trees for a foot support and hand guidance. Cuts in the NFS budget have greatly limited trail maintenance and reduced construction, and NFS officials say that, as a result, trail construction and maintenance is not a priority.)

North Section

Length: 11.9 mi (19 km); **moderate**; USGS Maps: Parksville, Clarks Hill; trailhead: parking area on SC 283.

To avoid backtracking I arranged a vehicle shuttle. I began at the N terminus on SC 283 between the Wine Creek and Turkey Creek bridges at a small parking area, following the white blazes through an open pine forest. Quartz and wildflowers were mixed with the honeysuckle ground cover. At 0.4 mi I heard the rocky Wine Creek on the R. Crows were noisy on the L in contrast to the towhees overhead. Brilliant pinkroot were at their peak along the creek bank; heartleaf, arbutus, and wood betony had already bloomed. A box turtle was breakfasting on a snail. Across Wine Creek there were wild azaleas and squirrel cups.

I crossed Mack Branch at 1.3 mi, with large beds of wood betony, more like those found in the mountains. The bottomland hardwood forest became more open, with only a scattered understory. At 1.8 mi there was a good campsite near a huge beechnut tree. High water had moved the footbridges at three ravines. At 2.3 mi I crossed a mudsoaked footbridge, evidence that the creek had risen surprisingly high. The trail continued on a slope, then descended to a floodplain. Cypress, papaw, hackberry, large grapevines, ironwood, and oaks grew along the river bank. One grapevine with a 25 in cir must be a champion.

The trail crossed a pipeline route and passed a stand of enormous cypress at 3.2 mi. At 3.7 mi switchcane, blackberry, and briars encroached on the trail. Hardwoods gave way to pine forest at 4.2 mi, where coreopsis and rattlebox had survived an earlier controlled fire burn. (The poisonous rattlebox, *Sesbania drummondii*, is being experimented with by the U.S. Department of Agriculture; the seeds may be an anticancer agent.) The trail reached SR 227 at the Key Bridge at 4.5 mi. It crossed the road, followed an old road bed briefly, then followed a high bluff by the river. At 5.3 mi the trail passed dead-end FR 618 on the R. I heard wild turkey calling ahead. Near a cement spring on the L at 5.7 mi was a good campsite. At 6.2 mi the trail crossed Coon Creek and for nearly a mile swung from cove to bluff. Turkey Creek tumbled over a row of river water bars. At 7 mi the air was cinnamon sweet with what local folk call wild mint, or mountain mint (although its fragrance was more like holy basil). Among buckeye and papaw and basswood, in one continuous path of beauty, the trail undulated. The river was dark and slow, brushing slightly against cypress knees. I crossed other tributaries at 8.6 mi and 9.1 mi, then abruptly the trail turned R. It had to: Ahead was the confluence of Turkey and Stevens creeks. Their silted silence concealed their power to make massive oak and cypress sink their roots deeper.

Eric Tang hiked in from the Stevens Creek trailhead to meet me. At 9.6 mi was a trail jct and sign. To the R was a spur 0.2 mi to the end of FR 617. We continued ahead to another jct at 9.8 mi where the trail forked. An alternate route turned L down the bank to Stevens Creek; the blaze was there, but the murky water was too deep to cross. The main trail continued ahead through thick grasses in bottomlands. We saw deer and wild turkey. At 11.5 mi we turned R and began an ascent to a more xeric area, to end at 11.9 mi.

From the trail's end at FR 617-A we drove to SR 138, turned L and went 1.3 mi to J. M. Price's water-ground enriched sifted white self-rising cornmeal grist mill at the Stevens Creek bridge and dam. John Henry Tolbert, who for 25 years has been the mill's operator, told us how "all that water comes down from Hard Labor Creek; in years back, can't say when, it washed away the mill . . . a cotton gin use to be here . . . I've seen the water up to the porch." Across the bridge on SR 138 it is 1.4 mi to US 221-SC 28.

South Section

Length: **11 mi** rt (17.6 km); **moderate**; USGS Maps: Parksville, Clarks Hill; trailhead: Modoc Bridge parking area.

(The center of this trail can be reached from US 221-SC 28 by taking SR 93 [east of Hamilton Branch State Park entrance] for 0.5 mi to FR 632, R for 2.1 mi to a cul-de-sac. FR 632-A is another route to within 0.2 mi of the trail's N dead-end.)

From the Modoc Bridge parking area at SR 23, 1.4 mi E of US 221-SC 28 in Modoc, Eric Tang and I followed the trail blaze upstream, crossing a footbridge, through a timbered area to a good campsite at 0.3 mi. At 0.4 mi we crossed a rocky area over Key Branch, followed by a stand of dwarf palmettos. Fire and timber harvesting had opened an area for the next 0.2 mi. We turned away from the river at 0.6 mi to avoid a floodplain and wet bottomland to curve back at 1.3 mi. Timbering on the L had increased the trail vegetation. After a slight ascent we reached a jct with a spur trail to the L for connecting FR 632 at 2.1 mi. We were on a bluff that became higher at 2.2 mi. It was refreshing to hear Turkey Creek splashing over rapids after 2 mi of hardly knowing it was there. Trees were tall upland hardwoods. We soon left the river and wound around another tributary from a ridge. At 2.6 mi and 3 mi, we could see the river after traversing a cove and ravine to follow a slope.

The best view of the river came at 3.2 mi. Here we could see the rapids through an open forest. At 4 mi we crossed a ravine where buckeye, papaw, and meadow rue grew. From here the trail twisted N, then W, then S, then W away from the river to cross a small stream. While we were looking at a garden of wildflowers, a buck came down the trail but bolted when I moved for my camera. In a clearing at 4.6 mi, sundrops, phlox, and wild mint gave color and fragrance. From here to the end of the forest boundary, we saw the river intermittently, probably best at 5.3 mi where a large patch of black cohosh grew. The trail dead-ended at 5.5 mi at private property. Dead-ends are frustrating, but we knew if we got through the briars and thistles there would be another dead-end at Stevens Creek. Looking on the bright side, Eric said, "I like to backtrack, we'll see what we missed."

Information: Contact District Ranger, Edgefield Ranger District, P.O. Box 30, Edgefield, SC 29824; (803) 637–5396.

MAP 1

Turkey Creek Trail (North)

MAP
2

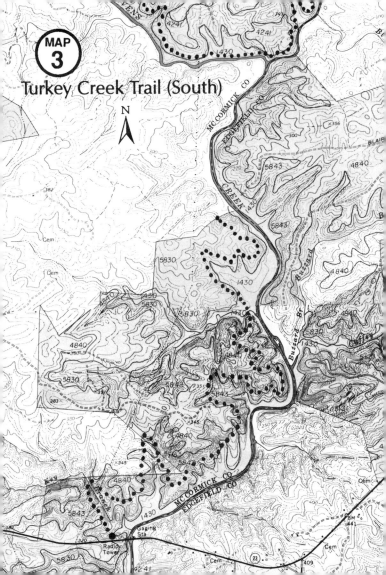

MAP 3

Turkey Creek Trail (South)

Bordering the South Carolina/Georgia state line at Thurmond Lake in McCormick County, covering the crescent in Abbeville County southeast of Abbeville, and including a southwest corner of Greenwood County, the Long Cane Ranger District has 55,084 acres, the smallest area of any of the districts in the state. Nonetheless, except for Edgefield Ranger District's Lick Fork Lake Recreation Area, it has the most complete recreational facilities, at Parsons Mountain Lake Recreation Area, of any of the districts. There is a paved road through the campground, lake-swimming facilities, picnic areas, a boat launch, sanitary facilities, hot showers, and sewage-disposal station. Visitors can hike to the firetower on Parsons Mountain or go backpacking (or horseback riding) on the 22.2-mile Long Cane Trail. The district also has the 650-acre Long Cane Scenic Area and some of the state's champion hardwoods. The park is gated, with continuous supervision by a resident NFS staff member. Wildlife in the area includes bobcat, deer, turkey, raccoon, squirrel, fox squirrel, quail, doves, copperhead, and highland cottonmouth mocassin.

Access: Long Cane Ranger Office is at the corner of Main Street (US 25 and 178) and Oregon Street, Rm 201, Federal Bldg (Box 3168), Greenwood, SC 29648; (803) 229–2406.

Parsons Mountain Trails

Length: 2.9 mi rt (4.6 km); **moderate**; USGS Map: Verdery; trailheads: parking area across the dam, or the picnic area.

Access to Parsons Mountain Lake Recreation Area is from Abbeville on SC 28 S to Rock Buffalo Church at SR 251. Turn L on SR 251 and go 1.5 mi to the park entrance on the R.

The access route to Parsons Mountain is from the Living on the Land Trail or from the campground area. The description below is from the campground area, near the boat ramp at the lake. At the trail sign we entered a forest of large hardwoods with an open understory. After 0.4 mi we passed at the lake. At the trail sign we entered a forest of large hardwoods with an open understory. After 0.4 mi we passed a small pond and descended to a small stream with a natural spring. We turned R through an area of large poplar, red and white oaks, hickory, and beech at 0.6 mi. Wildflowers are usually blooming in this area—fly poison, phlox, pinkroot, green-and-gold (*Chrysogonum virginianum*), black-eyed Susan, asters, indigo, and goat's rue. Among the flowering shrubs are papaw, dogwood, wild azaleas, redbud and New Jersey tea. To the R is a jct with the Audubon Trail, a 1.1-mile route to the Living on the Land Trail (described below). At 1.1 mi we crossed a gravel FR road and ascended steeply to the Civil War gold-mine shafts. From here we ascended to a ridge crest toward the top of Parsons Mountain (832 ft) and the 80-foot firetower at 1.45 mi. The mountain is named in honor of James Parson, a pioneer of the piedmont, who was granted the land from King George III in 1772. We backtracked to the parking area.

Living on the Land Trail

Length: 0.5 mi (0.8 km); easy; USGS Map: Verdery; trailhead: parking at swimming area.

From the parking area near the bathhouse, we entered the trail by a large trail sign. Twelve interpretive stations described the trees and animals and told how the pioneers lived off the land. Near the lake we noticed evidence of beavers. We turned R on a gradual incline to a jct with the Audubon Trail, or a loop back to the parking area.

Long Cane Horse and Hiking Trail

Length: 22.2 mi (35.5 km); **moderate** to **strenuous**; USGS Maps: Verdery, Abbeville E; trailhead: park campground.

This is a hiking and horse loop trail that twice crosses scenic Long Cane Creek and a number of its tributaries. About halfway in the loop is a 2.9-mile connector trail that can shorten the distance to 14.5 mi.

Dick Hunt, Bob Brueckner, and I took the Long Cane loop clockwise. We followed an old roadbed for 0.5 mi and crossed paved SR 251. We entered a young forest mixed with spots of pine barrens and gradually descended to SR 33 at 1.2 mi. After crossing the road we continued a slight descent to a sticky mud trail at floodplain level. At 2.3 mi we reached a jct (to the R it is 125 yards to the cul-de-sac of FR 530). To the L was the Long Cane Scenic Area boundary, an area many had hoped would be designated a Wilderness Area under the RARE II program. Within a few yards flowed the silent silted Long Cane Creek on its way to the Savannah River, and a steel bridge for hikers was slightly upstream from the horse crossing. River birch, sycamore, ironwood, and elm hugged the stream banks. When we crossed the bridge our noise sent two wild turkeys flying from the floodplain. We ascended to a ridge and then descended at 2.7 mi to a cove. The terrain and the hardwood forest were becoming more like the mountains than the piedmont. At 3.3. mi a sign indicated that the hardwoods in the cove were a holdover from the time when the Appalachian Mountains reached this far east; though the mountains wore down, this type of cove trees continued to grow. Sunlight was at a premium in this beautiful forest of tall poplar, oaks, elm, beech, maple, and hickory. Healthy patches of jack-in-the-pulpit and wood betony were between us and the floodplain. False downy foxglove bloomed on the drier slopes.

At 3.4 mi we saw the state's largest shagbark hickory (nearly 11 ft in cir and 135 ft tall). Other large shagbarks were on the slope. The next mile was on the floodplain, some of which was swampy. As we rounded a curve in the trail, a raccoon, ignoring his nocturnal habits, ran up a tree when he saw us. Dark clouds caused the forest to darken. Dick said that when he was a little kid he "thought all forests had scary walking trees with huge arms . . . ready to grab me, just like in the *Wizard of Oz*."

At 4.5 mi we left the Long Cane Scenic Area at FR 505. (After crossing the road, there is a jct, R, with the

2.9-mi connector that joins the main trail at the S side of Little Muckaway Creek. This connection shortens the distance from 22.2 mi to 14.5 mi. The trail descends to follow a natural gas pipeline and cross Curltail Creek in a flat area at 1.3 mi. It leaves the pipeline to cross Little Muckaway Creek before turning E.)

Continuing ahead on the main trail, we entered a small grazing field, then a pine forest that merged into a stand of hardwoods. There were more pines before we crossed FR 505 again at 5.2 mi. Cicadas were becoming louder and more sing-song as the heat of day increased. Patches of rose pink grew where we crossed a natural gas pipeline at 5.4 mi. At 5.5 mi we reached FR 505 again and turned L on the road to cross the Seaboard Coastline tracks. We continued on the road, originally the Old Charleston Road, for half a mile and entered a young pine forest on the R.

At 6.6 mi a number of white oaks had been splintered by lightning. After passing extremely large loblollies, we continued to descend through a mixed forest. Honey locusts and beauty bushes were near the trail, then a mixed forest at 8.4 mi and finally a stand of immense hardwoods similar to those in the Long Cane Scenic Area. Christmas ferns and rattlesnake orchids grew in a floor of honeysuckle. At 8.9 mi we crossed a small tributary to Big Curltail Creek and entered a clearcut, where trumpet vines and woodland sunflowers grew. We crossed FR 505 again at 9.2 mi and took what was apparently an older trail. In open forest in places, the trail was of excellent design and quality. Rocks, streams, slopes, small cascades, wildflowers, and even a cement bridge made this an ideal campsite.

We reached a jct of FR 505 and FR 506 at 10 mi. (To the L it is 1 mi to the Midway Hunt Camp where there is public drinking water.) We crossed the jct into a pine forest where the flash of a dove covey startled us. Prior timber harvesting had opened new grazing fields here for wildlife; as a result the trail had been relocated. We turned L on FR 506 and followed the road over two bridges of the Big

Curltail Creek and swamp to a red clay unnumbered FR at 11.7 mi. At 12.4 mi a huge white oak was on the R, and at 12.5 mi the Little Adams Cemetery was on the L. We counted some 20 gravesites, many those of children. One stone was that of Abraham Lits, born 1776, and another that of Jane Lits, born 1786.

At 12.8 mi the old road ended, and we walked under the Seaboard Coastline railroad to cross Gray's Creek. Emerging from the forest at 13 mi to a cul-de-sac of FR 509-C, we hiked it for 0.9 mi to the jct with FR 509.

From here we ascended through a pine forest on a gentle old jeep road and then gradually descended to Little Muckaway Creek at 15.2 mi. A good campsite, the stream was clear and rocky with sandbars, and papaw and wood betony grew on the banks. (After crossing the creek, there was a jct, R, with the 2.9-mi connector trail that joined the main trail near the edge of the Long Cane Scenic Area.) We passed a grazing field on the R and later entered a stand of cedar. At 15.7 mi we crossed FR 505, Curltail Rd. George Devlin Branch was at 16.3 mi, then a large grazing field, and we reached a fork at 16.7. (To the L it is 0.6 mi to Fell Hunt Camp, SR 47, where public drinking water is available.) We veered R, by an old farm building, and crossed a small stream. From a rocky area we ascended on an old jeep road to a plateau at 17.3 mi. At 17.7 mi we reached a parking area and cul-de-sac of FR 537, Rodgers Rd, in a piney area where sneezeweed, sumac, and honeysuckle grew. From here we hiked the graveled road to have a bridge crossing of Stillhouse Branch. After the bridge we turned R and came out to SR 33 near the Long Cane Creek bridge at 19.4 mi.

The trail turned R across the bridge and followed the paved road for 0.7 mi before turning L on FR 518, Candy Branch Rd. We passed a grazing field, turned R on a woods road and crossed a ravine in a hardwood area at 20.8 mi. After ascending and descending through the hardwoods we reached FR 515 at 21.8 mi where we saw the state-champion white oak (23-foot cir). From here we followed the trail to the campground.

Information: Contact District Ranger, Long Cane Ranger District, P.O. Box 3168 (Room 201, Federal Building), Greenwood, SC 29648; (803) 229–2406.

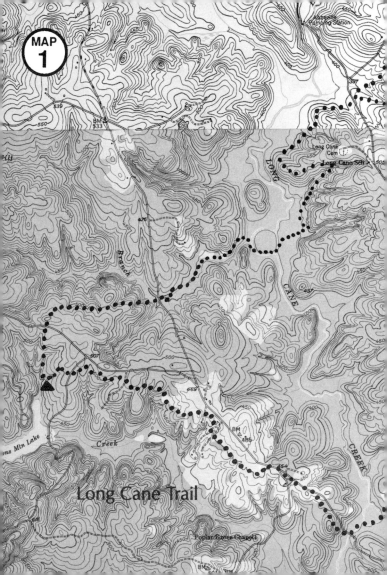

MAP
1

Long Cane Trail

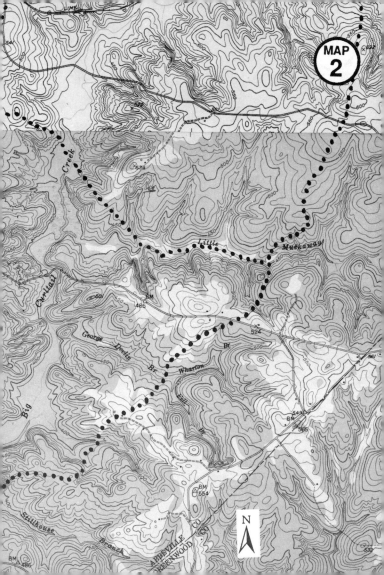

MAP
2

N

MAP
3

N

Long Cane Trail

Creek

x 486

F
O
R
E
S
T

865

Chauga

Cane

Grove

Mill

Creek

x 593

x 483

Little

Creek

Big Adams

Enoree District, with 78,310 acres, has two loop trails: a short trail at Molly's Rock, which is chiefly for nature study, and the long Buncombe Trail for hikers and equestrians. Wildlife in the area includes turkey, quail, dove, bobcat, deer, raccoon, red and gray fox, rabbit, fox squirrel, box turtle, and black snake. District Ranger Larry E. Cope said there are no poisonous snakes "to speak of—perhaps a copperhead every six years." The times I have hiked the trails, it must not have been the year of the copperhead: I have never seen one. There are no recreational areas here. "Everybody wants to go to the mountains or the coast," Cope said. "Here we are more private . . . I think you will find it a good place to hike."

Access: Enoree Ranger Office is on US 176-SC 121, 6.3 mi S from Whitmire and 10 mi N on SC 121 from Newberry.

Buncombe Trail

Length: 27.8 mi (44.5 km); **moderate**; USGS Map: Newberry NW; trailhead: Brickhouse Campground.

Access: The campground is 7.4 mi SW on SC 66 from jct with US 176 in Whitmire, or 3.6 mi NE on SC 66 from I-26 (exit 60), to Brickhouse Crossroads.

The Buncombe Trail was named for the Buncombe Road, an early road between Columbia and Buncombe (Asheville), North Carolina. At the historic Brickhouse Inn, it crossed another important early road, the Chester Road, which was the main route from Washington, D.C., to New Orleans. At the formerly busy intersection, the Brickhouse was built in 1832 as a "way station." The private home was constructed from local handmade brick. "The Brickhouse area saw a lot of history parade by," Cope said.

This trail has more equestrian use than hiker use, but its design and maintenance enable it to easily accommodate both. Trailheads could be established at a number of road crossings, but to describe the trail I have chosen the main

trailhead at the Brickhouse Campground. Here is the only source of drinking water approved by the Forest Service, and there are picnic tables, restrooms, and horse corrals. The trail has good campsites; a written permit is required from the district ranger. I hope that you will secure a permit to camp out in the general forest at least one night.

When Jeff Fleming, Bob Brueckner, and I arrived at the Brickhouse Campground it was a scorching 100-degree mid-July weekend. From the Brickhouse Campground near the water pump, we began a SW curve of the camp area. Some campers saw us through the woods. Hearing the clickety-click of the measuring wheel, one camper hollered, "Is everything measuring up?" On many other hikes I have thought about his question. The word *everything* means whatever exists; it sounds so philosophic, so permanent, but the question is a good one for the forest service and for forest users.

Through tall loblolly pines and an understory of maple, dogwood, redbud, and sweet gum, the trail passed a 1976 YCC granite logo, crossed a wooden bridge, and ascended slightly in a stand of hardwood at 0.5 mi. Along the way we noticed paint marks on the pines. These marks, in this case blue, were death signs—a timber company's bid for these handsome green towers.

The trail crossed a tributary of Headley's Creek and ascended on an eroded section to more level ground at 2 mi. Spots of wildflowers such as ironweed (*Veronia acaulis*), alum-root, butterfly pea, woodland sunflower, self heal, wild indigo, leopard's bane, and wild bean gave some color to the trail-border foliage.

At 2.5 mi at a jct with a motorcycle trail the trail turned a sharp L and descended to cross Drysachs Branch at 3.8 mi. An open skid road went through a clear-cut section and a young stand of pines for nearly half a mile. Midway through it was being attacked by kudzu, a fast-growing villous vine that thrives in heat and the poorest soil.

Near the edge of the field, I saw two bluebirds. This beautiful songbird "carries the sky on his back," Thoreau wrote. How appropriate that the trail was lined with beautyberry shrubs as we reentered the woods.

At 4.5 mi we began to hear I-26 traffic. At 5.9 mi we took a sharp L on an old logging road, crossed FR 359, and went L again. After crossing a small stream at 6.2 mi the trail undulated until leveling off at 7.5 mi where it crossed FR 359 again. We approached a damp area at 8 mi as we returned to FR 359 to cross Peges Creek. For 0.6 mi we hiked on FR 359 to the jct of FR 361, Bonds Rd, at 8.7 mi.

For 2 mi the trail zigzags in a young pine forest. At 10 mi the trail came within 50 yards of Indian Creek, and at 10.9 mi it paralleled Headley's Creek.

After crossing Headley's Creek on FR 361 bridges, we reentered the forest at 11.2 mi. Again the trail wove in and out of a timber harvest area where quartz shone bright in the sun and the hillsides simmered in summer heat. Occasionally the trail arced toward FR 361, but at 12.7 mi it headed NE in a pine forest. A small stream over rocks, large shade trees, and wildflowers made a spot at 1.7 mi an inviting campsite. After nearly 0.2 mi we entered an open field, exceptionally thick with blackberry and lespedeza, with featherlike leaves taller than our waists.

At Patterson's Creek we hoped we could find a rocky or sandy area other than the usual mud in which to take a bath, but we saw only mud. We crossed the wooden bridge, passed through a stand of extra-large poplar trees and ascended through a young forest of pine, oak, wild plum, and sumac for half a mile. Poison ivy and honeysuckle hugged the trail. At 15 mi we crossed FR 360. At 15.9 mi we reached a clear tributary of Patterson's Creek, with low cascades over mossy rocks and pools the size of a Roman bath—a fine campsite. Black cohosh, ferns, and climbing hydrangea were on the stream banks and enormous loblolly and poplar helped shade the area. The trees appeared to be the oldest we had seen on the trail. I longed to place a placard on the trail with poet George Morris's words: "Woodman, spare that tree! Touch not a single bough!"

The next day we crossed a stream on a large flat rock at 16.4 mi and came within sight of FR 420. Another good campsite was at 16.7 mi. We ascended through a pine forest to reach SC 66 at 17.9 mi, crossed the paved road, and took the L fork at 18.7 mi and again at 18.8 mi. At 19.5 mi the trail turned sharply R and descended toward Sandy Branch. Two deer ran ahead of us in patches of black-eyed Susan, ferns, wild ginger, and wild orchids. At the branch was a flat dry area near the bridge, another good campsite. After crossing the wooden bridge, we ascended to FR 363 at 20.1 mi.

Across FR 363, we noticed that trees with blazes were being cut down by a timber contractor. Near Mulberry Branch we saw deer and wild turkey at 21.5 mi. This branch also could be a campsite. From here the trail led up a gradual incline to FR 364, Duncan Road, at 22 mi. A local area resident drove up in his pick-up truck, his left jaw swollen from a wad of tobacco. "Whatcha doing, looking for horses?"

"No," Jeff said, "we are hiking . . . measuring the trail."

"My brother helped make that trail, and he helped measure it . . . on his Bronco . . . and it's 32 miles long," he said between spats.

After we crossed FR 364 and entered the woods, we saw the timber monsters. Bright yellow skins with yards of tentacles bound to their bellies. Gargantuan teeth and arms with powerful claws were motionless. Disordered cans of fossil fuel revealed their insatiable appetite. Lying beside them were their victims, 80-foot loblollies, their barks so scalped that the bleeding resin gave the forest the smell of sweet turpentine. But in the middle of this a lone rose pink (*Sabatia angularis*) near a tender pine offered an example of forest regeneration and succession. Within three years the area would be thick with new pines.

We crossed a wooden bridge at 22.4 mi and began a 2.5-mile winding path along the W side of Flannigan Branch. We saw and heard more wildlife in this area than anywhere else on the trail. Spicebush/swallowtail and metal mark butterflies were prominent, and sumac, beautyberry, phlox, horsemint, ironweed, button bush, and creeping bush clover flowered. In a quick turn around a corner of the trail, the thorns of a hawthorne spiked my hand just as a covey of quail flew up in my face. I thought I had been shot.

At 24 mi we passed an appealing area where the creek flows over smooth rock slabs. Soon we turned W, gradually ascending, and at 25.2 mi crossed FR 365, Fendley Road. For the next 0.6 mi in a pine forest we paralleled the gravel road; then we crossed SC 66. The understory was sourwood, holly, cedar, and small oaks on the way to FR 356 at 26.6 mi. We turned R and followed the blaze up the gravel road for 0.3 mi, turned L on FR 356-F, and reentered the woods on the R. A small cirque was on the L in a hardwood forest at 27 mi. We began to hear sounds from the Brickhouse Campground as we approached FR 358, crossing to the campground area and point of origin at 27.8 mi. Hot and dusty, the first thing we did was put our heads under the campground hand water pump. The cumbersome pump was slow; it singularly serves 23 campsites. "There are plans to drill a new well and install a different pump," promised Ranger Cope.

Molly's Rock Picnic Area

Molly's Rock Trail

Length: 0.7 mi (1.1 km); **easy;** USGS Map: Newberry E; trailhead: parking area.

Access: From US 176 (11 mi NE of Newberry and 3.5 mi N of SC 34) and FR 367. Turn onto FR 367 and go 0.5 mi to the parking area.

Molly's Rock Picnic Area had a shelter, sanitary facilities, nature study area, and hiking. From the shelter I followed the signs on a wood-chip loop trail around the lake to a mature mixed forest. At 0.2 mi I crossed a stream where there was elderberry, holly, dogwood, Hercules club (also called Devil's walking stick; *Aralia Spinosa*), sourwood, and ferns. At 0.3 mi there was a resting bench. The trail returned to the lake at 0.6 mi and crossed a bridge at the head of the lake to the picnic shelter. This is a peaceful area, and I saw or heard many birds—orioles, warblers, indigo buntings, nuthatches, blue jays, and meadowlarks.

Information: Contact District Ranger, Enoree District, Route 1, Box 179, Whitmire, SC 29178; (803) 276–4810.

Tyger Ranger District
(Union, Chester, and Fairfield Counties)

The Tyger Ranger District has 80,040 acres of forest, chiefly in Union County, but also in western Chester County from Lockhart to SR 51 in the northwest corner of Fairfield County. The district adjoins the Enoree Ranger District on the south. The two recreation areas in the Tyger Ranger District are Woods Ferry, on the east side of the Broad River; and Broad River, on the west side.

Access: The Tyger Ranger District office is on Duncan By-Pass, US 176 in Union.

MAP
1
Buncombe Trail

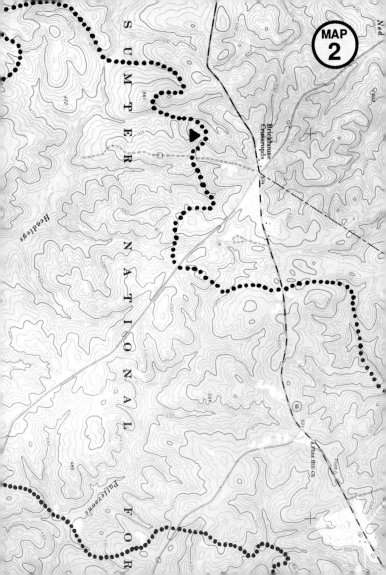

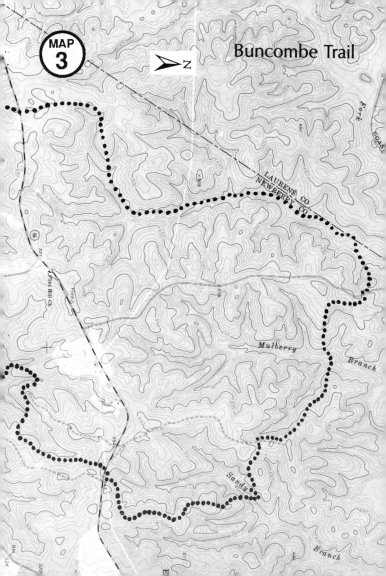

Woods Ferry Recreation Area

Facilities at Woods Ferry Recreation Area are a campground, picnic area, nature trail, boat ramp, restrooms, and showers.

Access: From jct of SC 121 and SC 72 at SR 25 (12 mi SW of Chester and 2.7 mi E of the Broad River), go 2.1 mi on SR 25 to SR 49 at Leeds. Continue on SR 49 for 3.7 mi to SR 574, and turn L on SR 574. Woods Ferry is 3.5 mi ahead.

Woods Ferry Trail

Length: 1 mi (1.6 km); **easy**; USGS Map: Leeds; trailhead: parking area.

From the picnic area, I walked to the bank of the quiet Broad River and went downstream to the uncleared forest, following the gray diamond blazes. The trail meandered through a dense hardwood forest of birch, oaks, gum, ash, poplar, and elm. Some dogwood and cedar were interspersed, and there were scattered loblolly pines. Mosquitoes ingored my insect repellent. After a 1-mile loop I returned to the parking area.

Broad River Recreation Area

This area is used mainly as a boat launch for fishing in the Broad River. The day I visited the park, two fishermen were trying to pull their boat out of the river at the ramp, but the pickup truck had sunk deeper and deeper into the sticky brown mud. Water was up to the tailgate. I drove to Union and called James Arthur Gibb, who in no time came to their rescue. Besides the boat ramp, facilities here are restrooms and a picnic area.

Access: From the jct of SR 86 and SR 389 (9 mi E of Union on SR 389), go E on SR 389 for 1.4 mi to the parking area.

Broad River Trail

Length: **0.6 mi** (1 km); **easy**: USGS Map: Leeds; trailhead: parking area.

Steve Harris and I followed the white-blazed trail upstream from the parking area. We crossed a small stream and went into a beautiful forest of gum, oaks, poplar, and birch. Some of the birch and elm leaned precariously over the river bank. At 0.3 mi we reached a steep embankment at the trail end and backtracked to the parking area.

Information: Contact District Ranger, Tyger District, Sumter National Forest, P.O. Box 10, Union, SC 29379; (803) 427–9858.

Francis Marion National Forest
SECTION 4.
Witherbee and Wambaw Ranger Districts (Berkeley and Charleston Counties)

The Francis Marion National Forest has two districts: Witherbee with 129,755 acres and Wambaw with 120,734 acres. A network of more than 575 miles of roads are maintained in the total 250,489 acres. In Witherbee there are two recreation areas: Canal, on US 52, south of McBeth by Lake Moultrie, and Huger, 3 miles north of Huger on SC 402. Both have camping, picnicking, and sanitary facilities. In Wambaw there is one recreation area, Buck Hall, which is 7 mi south of McClellanville on US 17 and FR 236. It has a campground, picnic area, boat launch, showers, and sanitary facilities. There are two sites on the National Register of Historic Places—The Battery, a Civil War–earthworks fortification on the Santee River, and the Sewee Shell Mound, on the Intracoastal Waterway.

Congress has designated four wilderness areas in the Francis Marion. These are Wambaw Creek (1,900 acres), Wambaw Swamp (4,850 acres), and Little Wambaw Swamp and Hell Hole Bay (2,200 acres). These areas are wet and swampy; enter with a compass and detailed maps. The Forest Service has designated Guilliard Lake on the Santee River (925 acres) as a scenic area.

The districts have two major hiking trails. The Swamp Fox Trail for hikers is in both districts, and the Jericho Trail is in the Witherbee District, for hikers and equestrians. The Wambaw District also has a 40-mi motorcycle trail with several loops. The trail is moderate to easy, accommodating all levels of riding skill.

Access: To Witherbee Ranger District hq at US 52, and SC 402 jct, E of Moncks Corner, take SC 402 for 3.6 mi and turn L. Go 6.2 mi on SR 171 to jct with SR 376. Turn L and go 0.6 mi to hq on R. To Wambaw Ranger District hq in McClellanville at the jct of US 17 and SC 9, Moores Corner, take SC 9 to hq on R.

hq in McClellanville at the jct of US 17 and SC 9, Moores Corner, take SC 9 to hq on R.

Huger Recreation Area

Swamp Fox Trail

Length: 20.8 mi (33.3 km); **moderate**; USGS Maps: Awendaw, Ocean Bay, Huger; trailhead: parking area on FR 251-F.

Designated a national recreation trail in 1979, this trail is well-maintained and clearly marked through sections of pine barrens, low mossy areas with hardwoods, and swamps with still and flowing waters. The trail is named for Gen. Francis Marion, the "Swamp Fox," whose brigade during the American Revolution would attack the British and then withdraw to the dense forests on Snow's Island. Colonel Tarleton said of the old fox, "the devil himself could not catch him."

I have hiked all sections of this trail a number of times, but I will describe a hike in early April when three of my students chose the Swamp Fox and the Jericho trails as a 40-mile weekend project. Huger Campground would be our base point because the hunting season was over and the camp would be quiet—so I thought. Straight muffler four-wheel-drives cruised the camp long after midnight, and loud radios announced the songs of Sneezy Waters.

Eric Tang and I began the hike at the Huger trailhead (0.8 mi E from the campground on SC 402 at jct with FR 251-F), and Jeff Fleming and David Colclough drove to the eastern trailhead in Awendaw. We would pass each other on the trail, and also provide a vehicle shuttle in the process.

Heavy rain had flooded a third of the first 10 mi. Jack Vines, assistant district ranger for the Witherbee district, told us springtime is the best hiking season; it's free of mosquitoes, though it can be wet. (Mosquitoes, ticks, and redbugs are numerous and voracious in the summer and early fall. Insect repellent is essential.)

For the first mile the forest was chiefly deciduous, with both young and mature oaks, beech, dogwood, and hickory. Fragrant wild pink azaleas and yellow jessamine were blooming—another reason for hiking in the spring. The crozier on the ferns uncoiled among spots of white violets, and waxy green partridge berries carpeted the path. At 1.2 mi we crossed twin footbridges in a swampy area and crossed SC 41 at 1.4 mi. Along the next 0.4 mi were patches of sweet pepperbush, bracken, pondberry, blueberry, gallberry, and fetterbush. The loblolly and pond pines were taller after we crossed gravel FR 170, Northampton Road; sphagnum moss was thick and spongy in low places. Boardwalks at 2.3 mi, 2.5 mi, and 2.7 mi crossed waist-deep water. At 3 mi we crossed FR 170 again and crossed a new dirt road at 3.5 mi.

An all-pine forest changed to mixed forest as we crossed three footbridges in a dark water flat properly named Muddy Creek. At 4 mi we reached paved Huger Road, SR 599. (A sign here said 4.2 mi to Dog Swamp Landing.) The trail skirted E of the headwaters of Muddy Creek, but we faced numerous wet areas as Dog Swamp swallowed the pathway. Underbrush was heavy. After 3 mi of Dog Swamp we crossed gravel FR 265 into an open pine forest, only to recross it after 0.2 mi. At 8 mi we crossed SR 133 (the highway between Huger and Awendaw).

Leaving SR 133 we crossed a boardwalk and footbridges over streams and canals, hiking on a long, straight old railroad grade. Past cypress stands at 9.1 mi, we crossed gravel FR 170-B; a road sign said Halfway Creek Campground, 4.5 mi, and Cainhoy, 14.8 mi.

After passing under a power line and crossing the neck of a small open pond, we met Jeff and David at 10.1 mi and ate lunch together. "How come you all are so dry?" I asked. "How come you all are so wet?" David answered.

At 10.6 mi was a mixed forest with wild azaleas, dogwoods, hollies, wild ginger, and violets. Two footbridges led across Harleston Dam Creek and swamp on sections of the old railroad grade. While on one of the bridges we heard mysterious noises downstream. Investigating, we discovered more than 20 white egrets.

Across paved SR 98 were the Berkeley/Charleston county lines and a parking area. An old woods road went into nearly 2 mi of the most scenic longleaf pine forest we had encountered. Paul Hamilton Hayne, a South Carolina poet who wrote a number of poems about pines (including "Under the Pine," in memory of his friend Henry Timrod), must have seen such forests when he wrote in "Aspects of the Pines":

> *A stillness, strange, divine, ineffable,*
> *Broods round and o'er them in the wind's surcease,*
> *And on each tinted copse and shimmering dell*
> *Rests the mute rapture of deep hearted peace.*
>
> *Last, sunset comes—the solemn joy and might*
> *Borne from the West when cloudless day declines—*
> *Low, flutelike breezes sweep the waves of light,*
> *And lifting dark green tresses of the pines. . . .*

We crossed an old road into a timbered area and reached the Halfway Campground at 14.8 mi. (From the parking area there is an exit to SR 98, Halfway Creek Road, R to jct 133. At the jct it is 7 mi L to Huger and 5 mi R to Awendaw.) We drank from the pump and refilled our canteens. Following an old railroad grade, we headed for the drainage area of Cooter Creek on the R and Wambaw Swamp on the L. In open spots the sweet glue from the sundews sparkled in the sun. (According to folk medicine the sundew, a scopose herb with saponia, reduces coughing.) At 16 mi we passed under a Boy Scout sign, Troop 4. The trail followed graveled FR 224 at 16.6 mi for 0.6 mi to cross a stream from Wambaw Swamp. Jessamine bloomed fragrant and golden along the road, hanging from cypress, maple and oak. Leaving the road, we entered an area where tall pines were being harvested, crossed FR 202 at 17.6 mi, and entered a long, straight trail on the old railroad bed. The forest was mixed, with sensitive ferns. We reached SR 1032 at 19.2 mi. Across the road we continued straight, crossing a small stream and a larger bridge over Steed Creek at 20 mi.

Across graveled FR 217, honeysuckle, jessamine, blackberry, ferns, fresh budding hardwoods, and shiny green pine needles displayed leaf variety as we came to the eastern trail terminus parking lot in Awendaw. (Although the trail can be hiked in a day, my preference is to take a more leisurely pace and camp out at the Halfway Campground.)

Jericho Trail

Length: 19.8 mi (31.7 km); **moderate**; USGS Maps: Huger, Bethera, Ocean Bay, Schulerville; trailhead: corner of Irishtown Road, FR 251-F, and SC 41.

We knew that parts of this loop trail would be flooded, or covered with standing water, so we dressed accordingly. (In recent years this trail has been used more frequently by equestrians than by hikers or backpackers.) We parked at the jct of Irishtown Road, FR 251-F, and SC 41, 1.1 mi from the western trailhead of the Swamp Fox Trail. ·

Following notes I had taken from a conversation with the ranger office and the NFS outline map, we hiked on the old railroad bed for 0.3 mi to flooded Turkey Creek. If there had been a bridge, it had washed away. Confused, we looked around for another passage and saw the blaze dipped L into Rock Hole, a swamp with entrenchments, cypress knees, and streaks of angry, cold, brackish water. We waded in, following the blazes until they ended at Turkey Creek's main artery. "No way we can get across," Jeff said. We sank an 8-foot stick into the turbulence. It did not hit bottom. We turned around and sloshed back through an area made sinister by the early-morning fog.

Starting over, we hiked SC 41 for 0.4 mi to cross the highway bridge over the dark, swollen Turkey Creek. At 0.5 mi we turned L at a parking area and followed a white blaze to the old railroad grade at 0.6 mi. (Straight ahead leads 0.2 mi to the other side of the creek we had tried to cross.)

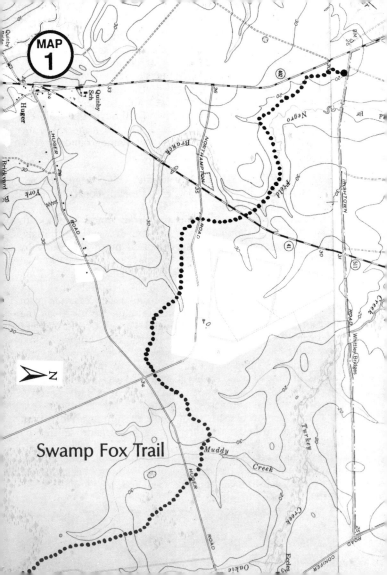

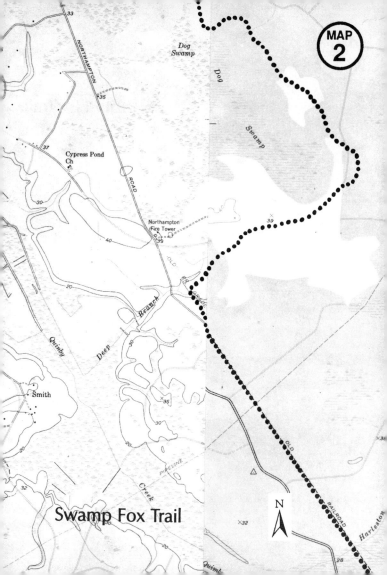

MAP
2

Dog
Swamp

Dog

Swamp

NORTHAMPTON

35

37

Cypress Pond
Ch

ROAD

30

Northampton
Fire Tower
35

39

40

OLD

20

Branch

Deep

30

Quinby

Smith

35

30

20

PIPELINE

20

Creek

N

Swamp Fox Trail

32

32

OLD

RAILROAD

Harleston

28

Quimb

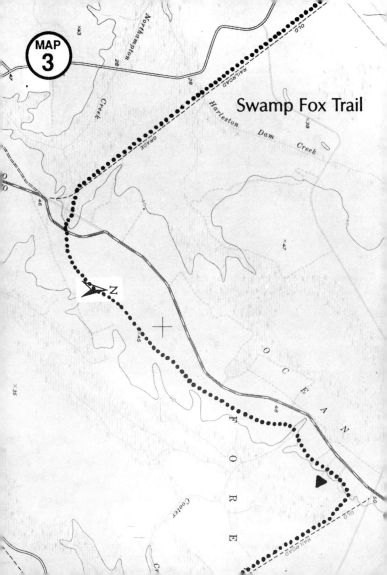

MAP
3

Swamp Fox Trail

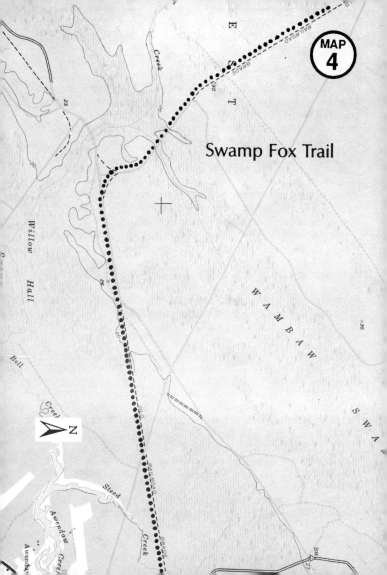

MAP
4

Swamp Fox Trail

Turning R, we followed the railroad bed to FR 251-H at 1 mi. Beech, wild azaleas, cancer root, pine, white-starred atamasco lily, and switchcane grew here. After crossing bridges over Fox Gully Branch, we moved on to cross FR 159, Yellowjacket Road, at 1.6 mi; FR 258, Summerhouse Road, at 2.3 mi; and FR 166, Conifer Road, at 3 mi. Water cascaded over the road at Nicholdson Creek bridge at 3.3 mi and at the Greentree Reservoir where Russell Tyler, forest technician, was cleaning out debris from the overflow pipes.

Leaving the reservoir we entered a total clearcut at 3.4 mi and walked through mud for 0.2 mi before entering the forest again. Fetterbush and gallberry bordered partial trail relocations. A bridge crossed Fourth of July Branch and Jericho Branch, a drainage stream from Boar Bay at 4.8 mi.

We veered R at 4.9 mi, where a sign indicated it was 1.7 mi to SC 41. At 5.1 mi was a primitive campground to the L in a generally open, pine forest. (From this campground and parking area on SR 48 it is 0.4 mi NW to the Hell Hole Trading Post in Bethera crossroads.) At 5.6 mi we turned R on an old sawmill road and reached the site of Jericho Plantation. Huge live oaks shaded the vanished homestead. To our L was a grazing field for deer, turkey, and other wildlife. We continued ahead, skirting N of Jericho swamp to SC 41 at 6.6 mi. For the next mile the trail was partly on an old road bed and dike, formerly Big Island Motorway, in a timber harvest area.

Low evergreens and blueberry patches were prominent as we entered a pine forest at 7.6 mi. Across graveled Hellhole Road, FR 158, the trail curved L and then R into a pine forest that had been damaged by fire.

We waded through a Cook's Creek tributary at 8.8 mi in a hardwood stand and came out in a drier area with fire anthills around us. Two deer fled into a more dense forest to the L. At 9 mi we reached graveled FR 165. Walking on the road, we crossed three culverts diverting Hell Hole Swamp to Cook's Creek. The trail left the road to go through grazing fields and young forests of longleaf pine. Fire anthills were numerous in the wide trail. Sundews were prevalant. At 9.8 mi we saw deer grazing in a field near a well-mowed trail. Seeing deer, wild turkey, chameleons, and songbirds, and smelling fragrant jessamine in the fresh, quiet air made it a pleasant hike. At 11 mi we entered a Wildlife Management Area, and on FR 159 we crossed the wide Nicholdson Creek bridge.

Here we turned L onto FR 158, a new road, and followed it to a R turn through more wet lands, crossing graveled FR 167, Burned Cane Road, at 13.1 mi, and skirting Kutz Creek Swamp on the R. After passing more grazing fields on the L, we entered another attractive longleaf pine forest at 14 mi. We hiked the edge of a timbered area, and at 14.4 mi crossed FR 167-A. The trail entered a pine forest, then a timbered area, and at 14.7 mi a forest of extra tall pines. After crossing graveled FR 166 we came to a magnificent pine forest. "Too beautiful to ever cut," said Jeff.

At 15 mi we reached our second crossing of Turkey Creek. The swamp was flooded, and a small bridge built by the YCC was inundated. Although this crossing was nearer the headwaters, we had some trepidation about sinkholes beyond the bridge. Eric, a Malaysian, had an additional anxiety; he associated all swamp water with numerous snakes. Grouped close together we cautiously maneuvered our way through the dark, rushing water. As the water became more shallow, we saw dwarf palmetto, gallberry, fetterbush, and small cypress, and, on dry ground, blueberry bushes.

At 16.1 mi we crossed FR 174. From here the trail made a horseshoe curve toward FR 265 and crossed FR 174 again at 17 mi. On the S side of Turkey Creek, out of the swamp, we passed through a deciduous forest of large oaks, poplar, sweet gum, maple, hickory, beech, ironwood, and holly. In a nearby flood plain were dwarf palmetto, dense fern patches, mandrake, wood sorrel, wild ginger, and numerous other wildflowers. At 17.9 mi a bridge crossed muddy Muddy

Creek; we left the hardwood area at 18.8 mi. We faced an open drainage canal at 19 mi. A footbridge crossed over the canal, and the trail turned R, into the forest. After 0.4 mi we reached graveled FR 251-F; another 0.4 mi to the L on FR 251-F to SC 41 and the hike was over.

Guilliard Lake Scenic Area

Guilliard Lake Trail

Length: **0.6 mi** rt (1 km); **easy**; USGS Map: Jamestown; trailhead: parking area.

Located on the S side of the Santee River, this 1,000-acre forest was established to preserve some of the ancient trees, particularly cypress. Perforated limestone outcroppings are in the area on Dutant Creek. Camping is limited here to six sites; fresh water and activities such as picnicking, fishing, birding, and nature study are available. You can reach it from Jamestown by taking SC 45 SE for 3.6 mi to FR 150 and turning L. Go 1.6 mi on FR 150 and turn L on FR 150-G. Go another 1.7 mi to the picnic area.

When Scott Smith and I routinely checked the facilities at Guilliard Lake, the site of the former town of Jamestown, we were not prepared for the surprise we got. The trail went upstream and crossed a small stream to follow the river's edge. Huge trees, some contorted and convoluted, were around us. Ash, cedar, elm, loblolly, and live oaks were intertwined, seized by long snake-like Alabama supplejack, coiling, curling, twisting, crawling, hanging over limbs, and dangling over the trail—a route into *Raiders of the Lost Ark*. The vines were smooth, damp, shiny from the junglelike moisture. The ferns and partridge berry were so thick a moccasin could have slithered up my trouser legs before I could have untangled myself from the vines. Before we turned back we lowered ourselves into a floodplain where the dark earth was dry enough for us to see 8-foot-tall cypress knees. They were scaly, or glazed, but always damp, alive, ready to pulsate, like creatures from *Alien*. A base of what I think was

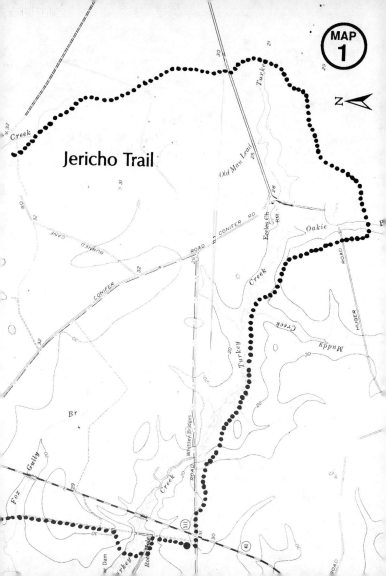

MAP 1

Jericho Trail

MAP
2 Jericho Trail

N

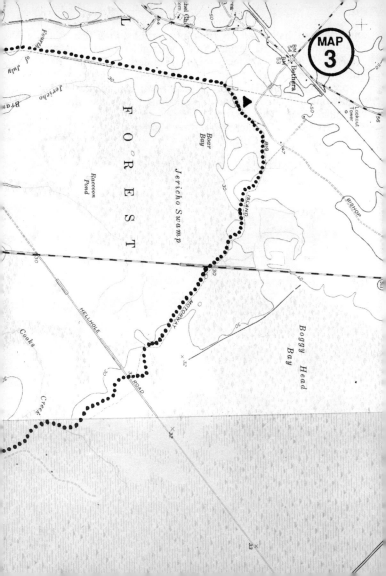

an ash had ballooned to such proportions that five adults could stoop to walk inside. Some unfamiliar birds squawked raucously overhead where the trail ended at 0.3 mi. Back through the cypress, I thought of Beatrice Ravenel's words: cypress roots "at the edge of the swamp as roughly fluted, age-wrinkled, have budded their rufous knobs like dim and reptillian eyes. That Watch."

Information: Contact Witherbee Ranger District, HC 69, Box 1532, Moncks Corner, SC 29461; (803) 336–3248. Wambaw Ranger District, P.O. Box 788 (S. Pinckney St), McClellanville, SC 29458; (803) 887–3257.

CHAPTER II

National Parks, Refuges, and U.S. Army Corps of Engineers Projects
SECTION 1. National Parks
Congaree Swamp National Monument (Richland County)

"That in order to preserve and protect for the education, inspiration and enjoyment of present and future generations an outstanding example of a near virgin southern hardwood forest situated in the Congaree River floodplain . . ." began public law 94-545, passed by the 94th Congress in October 1976. It was the result of 26 years of research and efforts by such groups as the Audubon Society and Sierra Club in Columbia, and of the formation of Congaree Action Now (CAN) to preserve this majestic natural heritage.

Comprising 15,135 acres, the monument is the state's largest natural area for floodplain study. More than 325 vascular flora have been located, including 7 species of wild orchids and 16 species of ferns. Several national and 19 state-record-size trees are here, and 64 trees have reached 80 percent of the national record. Wildlife is abundant, with 41 species of mammals, 24 species of reptiles, 130 species of birds (including 20 species that are endangered), and 52 species of fish. Poisonous snakes are the cottonmouth moccasin, copperhead, and canebreak rattler. Fishing is allowed according to state laws. Permits are necessary for camping.

About 10 to 15 percent of the monument is perpetually covered by water, and 90 percent of the park is inundated from up-river flooding an average of ten times each year. My first visit to the park was a March day when flooding had occurred. Ranger Fran Rameta was my guide, and we drove on a roadbed that was covered with water. Although a trailhead at an old hunting lodge was on high ground, the water surge prevented passage farther into the forest. On a subsequent visit when the floodplain was dry, ranger Rameta led a group of us on an unforgettable hike to the heart of the swamp.

In addition to land trails, there is a marked canoe trail on Cedar Creek. Access is on SR 1288, off SR 734, from SC 48 at Gadsden. (You must furnish your own canoe and life-saving equipment.) Reservations may be made at the ranger station for a guided canoe route. A permit from the ranger station is required if you plan to camp overnight on a canoe trip. One advantage of canoeing is that you can explore areas of the swamp that are inaccessible by land trails.

Access: From downtown Columbia at the jct of US 21/176/378 and SC 48, take SC 48 SE for 12.2 mi to a fork. Take the R fork, SR 734, which is Old Bluff Road. (If you are on I-26, take I-326 to SC 48 for the fastest route.) Follow Old Bluff Road 4.6 mi to the Congaree Swamp sign. Turn R on Simms Rd, a dirt road, and go another 0.8 mi to the ranger station. (If arriving from the E, it is 11.3 mi from US 601 at Wateree on SC 48 to Gadsden, L on SR 1288, and R on SR 734 to the park entrance.)

Bluff Trail, Boardwalk Trail, Weston Lake Trail, Kingsnake Trail, Eagle Trail, Oak Ridge Trail, and Congaree River Trail

Length: 19.3 mi rt ct (30.8 km); *easy*; USGS Map: Gadsden; trailhead: parking area.

The Congaree Swamp trails are multiple loops that extend from the ranger station to the Congaree River. Colored markers and a map board provide directions, and a hand map is available at the ranger station. On each Saturday at 1:30 P.M., a park naturalist offers a guided tour; other group tours may be prearranged on other days. The routes provide a classic example of tree heights—emergent, the highest; high canopy; second canopy; and the understory trees and shrubs.

The 1.3-mi Bluff Trail circles the ranger station and has a primitive campsite on the E section of the loop. From this trail and at the parking area is the 0.7-mi Boardwalk Trail, where you meet a typical wet element of the swamp. The Boardwalk Trail connects with the 3-mi Weston Lake Trail. It was on the Weston Lake Trail that we saw an overcup oak, a monumental national champ rising 16 stories high and over 22 ft in cir near Cedar Creek. Nearby is a loblolly pine champ, about 300 yrs of age, which is more than 16 ft in cir and 170 ft tall. Along the trail papaw grows in profusion, but fruit is scarce because of the perpetual lack of sunlight from the forest canopies.

From the Weston Lake Trail there are two footbridge crossings of Cedar Creek. The southeast bridge is a route to the 3.3-mi Kingsnake Trail loop and the 0.8-mi Eagle Trail loop. At the southwest bridge is a route to the 3.7-mi Oak Ridge Trail loop and the 6.5-mi Congaree River Trail loop.

We followed the Congaree River Trail counterclockwise, and after 3.3 miles reached the north bank of the Congaree River. We turned L, downstream, and passed through a dense forest of giant sweet and black gums, cypress, sycamore, and ash. Among the understory plant life were scattered water elm, spicebush, ironwood, and switchcane. After leaving the riverside, we turned L along Boggy Gut to complete the loop and return to the Oak Ridge Trail jct.

Information: Contact Superintendent, Congaree Swamp National Monument, Gadsden, SC 29052; (803) 776–4396. (Also, Suite 607, Strom Thurmond Federal Bldg., Columbia, SC 29201; (803) 765–5571.

Cowpens National Battlefield (Cherokee County)

Gen. Daniel Morgan, considered by military historians to be one of the superior battlefield tacticians in the American Revolution, hurriedly deployed his 900 men on a slope in Hannah's Cowpens. It was the afternoon of Jan. 16, 1781. That morning their breakfast had been interrupted when they heard that "Benny (the British) is coming." Leaving their camp near Thicketty Creek, they would make a stand against Lt. Col. Banastre Tarleton and his 1,100 infantry and cavalry on a frontier pasturing ground.

A pitched battle ensued about daybreak on Jan. 17, 1781. In about an hour it was all over. The British suffered 110 dead, more than 200 wounded, and 500 captured. Revolutionary losses were 10 dead and 60 wounded. To illustrate the significance this British defeat had on the Congress, a bill was passed on March 9, 1981, awarding 3 of the 12 Revolutionary War–hero medals to officers of Cowpens: Brig. Gen. Daniel Morgan, Lt. Col. William Washington, and Lt. Col. John E. Howard.

The 842-acre park, established March 4, 1929, has an interpretive center, wayside exhibits on the trails and the tour road, picnic area, the Robert Scruggs House, and a U.S. Memorial Monument. Lee Price, park technician, told me that "if we can receive help like the former YCC's we will open the three-mile Nature Trail." On your visit ask park staff if the trail, near New Pleasant Baptist Church, is open.

Access: From the jct of SC 11 and SC 110 go E on SC 11 0.2 mi to park entrance. It is 2 mi E from Chesnee on SC 11 and US 221A and 8.5 mi N of Gaffney on SC 11 from I-95.

Cowpens Battlefield Trail

Length: 1.2 mi (1.8 km); **easy;** USGS Map: Cowpens; trailhead: Visitor Center.

This loop trail of ten exhibit stations is paved from the Visitor Center to the Green River Road (the site of the British formation march). (Another 0.2-mi paved trail also leads to this point from the tour road, Battlefield Overlook. This is an easy route for the physically handicapped.) The other half of the trail follows the Green River Road, a well-maintained dirt route to the lawn of the Visitor Center. Among the vegetation on the trail is wild cherry, Virginia pine, maple, cedar, sweet gum, sourwood, oaks, dogwood, sumac, mulberry, New England tea, and elderberry. Wild-flowers bloom in the open fields.

Information: Contact Superintendent, Cowpens National Battlefield, P.O. Box 308, Chesnee, SC 29323; (803) 461–2828/7077.

Fort Sumter National Monument (Charleston County)

There are two short trails, each approximately 0.5 mi, where leaves and tree limbs never fall, but whose historic paths receive the salty mist of Charleston Harbor. Each year thousands of visitors walk on the cement and turf and climb the stone steps at two national monuments: Fort Sumter, "where the Civil War began," and Fort Moultrie, across the channel, site of the first decisive American victory in the Revolutionary War.

Fort Moultrie, on Sullivan Island, has undergone a number of stages of development and reconstruction. The first fort was built in 1776 to protect Charleston from the British. After the Revolution the second Fort Moultrie, an earth-and-wood five-sided battery, was built, but a hurricane destroyed it in 1804. A brick fort was built in 1809 but was not used in the Civil War. After 1885 a new battery of concrete and steel was constructed. On your walk, which should include Cannon Walk and Battery Jasper, you will go back in time, from WW II Harbor Entrance Control to the palmetto-and-sand fort of 1776.

The U.S. Government began building Fort Sumter in 1829 and had almost completed the structure on a harbor shoal by 1860. Designed for a garrison of 650 men and 135 guns on three tiers, only 85 men and 60 cannon were there when, on Aug. 12, 1861, a Confederate battery at Fort Johnson on the shoreline opened fire. The shelling lasted for 34 hours, and on April 14, Maj. Robert Anderson, the fort's commanding officer, agreed to evacuate. On April 15 President Lincoln began mobilizing the U.S. militia. For four years, "the longest siege in warfare," the Confederates held the fort and never surrendered to Union attacks.

Visitors' hours at the forts are 8:00 A.M. to 5:00 P.M. (closed on Christmas Day). Access to Fort Moultrie (administered jointly with Fort Sumter) is on W Middle Street on Sullivan Island. From US 17, take SC 703 and follow the signs. Access to Fort Sumter is by boat only. In Charleston turn onto Lockwood Drive from US 17 and go to the Municipal Marina (Near W end of Calhoun Street). For the boat schedule contact Fort Sumter Tours.

Information: Fort Sumter Tours, Box 59, Charleston, SC 29402, (803) 722–1691; and Fort Sumter National Monument, 1214 Middle St., Sullivans Island, SC 29482; (803) 883–3123.

Kings Mountain National Military Park
(Cherokee and York Counties)

Established in 1931 by the U.S. War Department and transferred to the National Park Service in 1933, Kings Mountain National Military Park has 3,945 acres of rocky clay soil, on which an oak-hickory forest and scattered pines grow. Named after an early settler, the area was farmland, grazing fields, and timberland. A small outlying spur of the Blue Ridge Mountains, its highest elevation is 1,045 ft at Browns Mountain. An exceptionally significant war shrine of the American Revolution, it commemorates a band of 910 frontiersmen whose speed, courage, and marksmanship defeated 1,104 Loyalists led by British Maj. Patrick Ferguson on Oct. 7, 1780. "It was the greatest victory of the Southern militia," wrote historian Wilma Dykeman in *With Fire and Sword*. (See Overmountain Victory Trail for more information.)

The park has considerable exhibit material in the Visitor Center for interpreting the history of the area and the battleground. An interpretive Battlefield Trail with visual displays circles the ridge crest from the Visitor Center. The park has 4.8 mi of the 15-mile Kings Mountain National Recreation Trail, which loops through the Kings Mountain State Park. Another significant trail (mainly a tour-road trail) is the Overmountain Victory Trail, which has its southern terminus here. The park is open daily 9:00 A.M. to 5:00 P.M., except Thanksgiving Day, Christmas Day, and New Year's Day. Each year at 3:00 P.M. on Oct. 7, the park has a simple ceremony after the Overmountain Victory Trail marchers arrive.

Access: From I-85 near the North Carolina state line, turn at park sign on SC 216 to the park entrance.

Kings Mountain Battlefield Trail

Length: 1.5 mi (2.4 km); easy; USGS Map: Grover; trailhead: Visitor Center terrace.

To get the most out of the trail, first see the interpretive film and displays in the Visitor Center. Then exit on the terrace and go R. The entire loop is paved with asphalt to aid the physically handicapped. Visual displays are along the route.

After 0.3 mi we passed a small stream on the R where button bush, ostrich fern, mountain laurel, wild ginger, and trailing arbutus grew. At 0.5 mi we passed a spring on the L, the spot where the frontiersmen tended to their wounded. At 0.7 mi on the R is a spur trail to the place where President Hoover spoke to 75,000 people on Oct. 7, 1930, in celebration of the Sesquicentennial of the Battle of Kings Mountain. At 1 mi we passed the centennial monument in honor of the "officers and others," and at 1.2 mi we passed an obelisk erected in 1909, which lists all the Patriots who died or were wounded in the battle. Descending from the ridge we passed the rock cairn where Major Ferguson was burried in a raw cowhide. Some historians believe that Virginia Sal, one of two women with Major Ferguson during the battle, was buried beside him. The battle, which was fought from 3:00 to 6:00 P.M. on a Saturday, pitted Americans against Americans—Patriots against Loyalists. The only Englishman was Major Ferguson. An example of the Patriots' desire for revenge was the murder of some Loyalists after they had surrendered. Patriot losses were 28 killed and 62 wounded; and Loyalist losses were 225 slain, 163 wounded, and 716 taken prisoner. Major Ferguson's decision to ensconce his troops on a hilltop where he could be surrounded was a deadly mistake, even though he had said "God could not drive him from it." The trail returns to the Visitor Center at 1.5 mi.

Kings Mountain Hiking Trail

Designated a national recreation trail in 1981, this excellent trail for hiking and camping is 15 miles long, with 4.8 mi in Kings Mountain National Military Park and the other 10.2 mi in Kings Mountain State Park. (See Kings Mountain State Park.)

Please observe park regulations if you plan to camp on the Kings Mountain Hiking Trail. Hikers must use only the Garner Branch campsite in the park, must register at the Visitor Center, and must register any vehicle left overnight in the parking area. No pets, horses, or ORVs are allowed on the trail. Firearms and fireworks are prohibited. Basic trail courtesy requires that you pack out what you pack in. (Other campsites are available in Kings Mountain State Park.)

Overmountain Victory Trail (Park Section)

Length: 2.3 mi (3.7 km); easy; USGS Map: Grover; trailhead: Kings Creek.

The Overmountain Victory Trail, also called the Overmountain Victory National Historic Trail (as amended by the National Trail System Act of 1978 and 1980), is a 313-mile motor route from Craig's Meadows in Abingdon, Virginia, to Kings Mountain National Military Park battlefield in South Carolina. Short segments—about 12 mi—of the route involve federal lands in Cherokee National Forest in Tennessee; Pisgah National Forest, Blue Ridge Parkway, and W. Kerr Scott Reservoir in North Carolina; and Cowpens and Kings Mountain battlefields in South Carolina.

The route simulates as closely as possible the route taken by the overmountain frontiersmen in September and October of 1780 to accept the challenge made by Major Ferguson.

He had threatened that if they continued to oppose British rule and arms he would march into the mountains, "hang their leaders, and lay their country waste with fire and sword."

For a number of years, members of the Overmountain Victory Trail Association have been traversing the route. They and thousands of other hikers, equestrians, and motorists celebrated the 1980 bicentennial with a march from Abingdon to Kings Mountain. The organization strives to identify and protect the "historic route and its historic remnants and artifacts for public use and enjoyment." Three major publications on the history, management, and mapping of this trail are published by the Regional Office, National Park Service, 75 Spring St., S.W., Atlanta, GA 30303; (404) 221-5185.

Chris Revels, lead park ranger at Kings Mountain, showed me the trail route for my first hike. I drove W from the Visitor Center to the park boundary and turned L on paved SR 86. After 1.7 mi I reached a jct with SR 85, first on the R and ahead on the L. I parked on the L and began hiking L, almost parallel with SR 86 for 0.4 mi back to Kings Creek, the beginning of the trail into the park. After wading the shallow stream, I followed Houser Road to the Henry Houser homestead (1803) on the L. Continuing ahead to a powerline jct, I turned R at 0.4 mi, ascending and descending to a power-line jct at 0.6 mi. I turned L, then R into a hardwood and scattered-pine forest. Leaving the old forest road at 1.4 mi, I turned R on the graveled park road, Yorkville Road, and approached SC 216 at 1.8 mi. Across the highway I took graveled Shelbyville Road and went 0.2 mi to a gated fireroad. I turned R on the fireroad, which has first a R and then L jct with the Kings Mountain Hiking Trail. The trail continues straight ahead at both jct and reaches the Battlefield Trail at 2.3 mi. I stopped in the area where young Maj. William Chronicle died while leading his men up the hill. Nearby there was a sign: "Within the hour a blow will be struck for liberty."

Information: Contact Superintendent, Kings Mountain National Military Park, P.O. Box 40, Kings Mountain, NC 28086; (803) 936–7921.

Ninety Six National Historic Site
(Greenwood County)

Several romantic legends explain how Ninety Six got its name. One tells of a Cherokee maiden, Cateechee, who rode 96 miles on horseback from Keowee to save the English trader she loved from an impending Cherokee attack at the British fort. A more prosaic story is that as early as 1737 there was a trading post here on the famous Cherokee Path, a trade route from Charleston through Camden to the Cherokee Indian village of Keowee, 96 miles ahead.

Designated a historic site in 1976, the 989 acres are on the S edge of the town of Ninety Six, a town with a number in its name, its name in its zip-code number and in its post-office-box number. Its named was changed in 1785 to Cambridge, at the wish of the settlers, but it was renamed Ninety Six in 1852. Between Greenwood, the "Emerald City," and beautiful Lake Greenwood, the town and the park are in the heart of the Old Ninety Six District. The park is open daily except Christmas Day and New Year's Day. There is a visitor center, and video tapes with historical information are available. No camping is allowed in the park.

Access: From downtown Ninety Six at the jct of SR 248 and SC 34, go S 1.7 mi on SR 248 to the park entrance on the L.

Ninety Six History Trail

Length: 1 mi (1.6 km); **easy**; USGS Map: Ninety Six; trailhead: parking area.

"The greatest thing about this park is the Star Fort," Park Superintendent Robert Armstrong will tell you. I entered on a wide paved trail with a border of honeysuckle and periwinkle in a young mixed forest, crossed the Island Ford Road, and made a loop around the siegeworks of the British Star Redoubt. Along the trail are exhibit signs that fully explain the battle events. Here the University of South Carolina has made extensive archaeological study of the earthworks where Gen. Nathanael Greene ordered an assault on June 18, 1781. The attack failed because Lord Francis Rawdon sent 2,000 British regulars to protect the fort. But soon afterward Lord Rawdon ordered the post burned and abandoned. After the earthworks at 0.5 mi, I passed in a grassy field "a real country town" (c. 1769–1781), where, signs explain, there once were "12 dwellings, courthouse, and jail." I examined the stockade fort and nearby, where a sign read:

> *James Birmingham*
> *Volunteer*
> *Long Cane Militia*
> *Killed here*
> *on November 19-21-1775*
> *The first South Carolinian to give*
> *his life in the cause of freedom.*

Information: Contact Park Superintendent, Ninety Six National Historic Site, P.O. Box 496, Ninety Six, SC 29666; (803) 543–4068.

SECTION 2. Wildlife Refuges
Cape Romain National Wildlife Refuge
(Charleston County)

The Cape Romain National Wildlife Refuge is among the three wholly in South Carolina, and more than 400 in the nation. They were created by Congress and are administered by the U.S. Fish and Wildlife Service of the Department of the Interior.

The refuges provide a natural environment for the protection of all species of wildlife, including those species that are endangered or threatened, and recreational facilities that are environmental or wildlife oriented.

Poet laureate James Dickey has said that the "prettiest beach" he has seen anywhere in his travels is Pawley's Island, "except perhaps for the eastern beach of Bull's Island . . . a landscape out of Rimbaud."

Bull's Island is wild, free of people, and, as restless French poet Arthur Rimbaud, who wrote in *Le Bateau Ivre,* said, "I have bathed in the poem of the sea . . . devouring the green azures."

This island is indeed a refuge from the noise and stress of highways and offices. But you can retreat there only for a day now; camping has been forbidden since 1978. And well it should be, because Bull's Island (named in honor of Stephen Bull, a colonial leader) is part of the Cape Romain National Wildlife Refuge. This refuge is recognized by many naturalists as the most significant wildlife area on the East Coast and is known for its wide range of waterfowl. More than 260 species of birds, some extremely rare, have been recorded there. Ornithological studies indicate that 107 of the general species nest on the refuge.

More than 35 mammal species have been identified in the refuge. On Bull's Island there are fewer species, but among them are white-tailed deer, raccoon, otter, bottlenosed dolphin, southern fox squirrel, marsh rabbit, and a number of bat and mice species.

Among the amphibians are green tree frog, spring peeper, squirrel tree frog, and southern leopard frog. Reptiles include eastern mud turtle, yellow-bellied turtle, diamondback terrapin, Atlantic loggerhead turtle (an endangered species), Kemp's Ridley turtle, and alligator. Although both the southern copperhead and the eastern cottonmouth are in the refuge, the cottonmouth is the only poisonous snake identified on Bull's Island. At least eight other species of snakes have been catalogued within the refuge.

A treasure in the coastal environment, this 64,229-acre refuge has 34,229 acres of land, salt marshes, tidal creeks, and barrier islands. An additional 30,000 acres of open water provide a sanctuary for migratory waterfowl. Established in 1932, the refuge includes three major barrier islands: Cape Island, Raccoon Key, and Bull's Island, called "gem of the Barriers" by Alexander Sprunt, Jr.

Bull's Island, the largest of the three, has 5,108 acres, of which 900 comprise eight impoundments of freshwater. It is approximately 6 miles long and 2 miles wide. In the interior there are 1,500 acres of maritime live oak, loblolly pine, and cabbage palmetto forest. Botany-oriented hikers will see an understory of red bay, yaupon, wax myrtle, holly, jessamine, muscadine, supplejack and pepper-vine. Ferns and wildflowers complete the landscape. Aquatic plants include banana waterlily, sago pondweed, bulrush, giant foxtail, wild millet, and spike rush.

A monthly calendar of wildlife events is provided by the refuge headquarters. In January and February oystering and clamming peak, and ducks such as scaup and scoters are abundant in the open water before they move into the tidal creeks. Pelicans return in February. Saltwater fishing for channel bass is at its best in March, and the freshwater fishing season opens on March 15. In April, loggerhead sea turtles mate in the bays and tidal creeks. Alligators and loggerheads begin nesting on Bull's Island in May. Floundering in the shallow waters is best in June. July brings pelican, heron, egret, and shorebird fledglings; they begin flying in

August. Wood ibis and black-crowned and yellow-crowned night herons are plentiful on Bull's Island in July. Dowitchers and herring gulls arrive and blue-winged teals leave in September. The freshwater fishing season ends on Sept. 30. Migrating waterfowl arrive in large numbers for wintering in October. The fall channel-bass run peaks in November, and the local Audubon Society conducts its annual Christmas Bird Count on Bull's Island in December.

Travel to Bull's Island is by boat; once there you travel on foot. A charter boat is operated by John Pryor (803–884–0448).

You should go first to the refuge hq at Moore's Landing for information on changes in restrictions, fishing regulations, or other visitor information. Here are restrooms, drinking water, and a boat ramp (usable only at high tide). Other boat ramps are at Sewee Camp Resort, Buck Hall, and McClellanville, all northeast of Moore's Landing (off US 17). Water distance to the island is about 3 miles. Headquarters hours are weekdays only, 8:30 A.M. to 4:30 P.M.

Take everything you will need for the day hike: food, hiking shoes, rain gear, sun protection, and insect repellent. Near the information exhibit on the island are a rain shelter, restrooms, picnic tables, and drinking water.

Access: To the refuge hq leave US 17 (15 miles N of Mt. Pleasant and 3.8 mi S of Awendaw) on Sewee Road. Go 3.5 mi and turn R on Bull's Island Road; go 1.6 mi to Moore's Landing, the Intracoastal Waterway and the refuge hq.

Bull's Island Wildlife Trail

Length: 2 mi (3.2 km); **easy;** USGS Maps: Sewee Bay, Bull Island; trailhead: near information exhibit on Bull's Island.

From the dock follow the service road for 0.4 mi to the information exhibit and trail sign. Made a National Recreation Trail in February 1982, the trail is designed to give a cross section of the various wildlife habitats and flora representative of the southern barrier islands.

With me on this late-March hike were David Colclough, Jeff Fleming, Eric Tang and our boatsman, Henry Kerr. At 0.5 mi we crossed a service road in the forest and followed a levee between Upper Summerhouse Pond on the R and Lower Summerhouse Pond on the L. Alligators often sun on the grassy banks. "This is sago pondweed and this is widgeon grass," Henry said, pointing his finger at the marsh. Coots were swimming nearby. "They bob their heads like a cork most all the time," he said.

The Fish and Wildlife Service had been clearing out some of the marshes, leaving mud that looked like ebony clay. "Now to get rid of sand gnats," Henry said, "you mix rubbing alcohol and Avon's Skin-so-Soft." At 1.4 mi we turned L on a service road, where a fox squirrel and a raccoon, busy with their daily chores, ignored us. We reached Beach Road, turned R, passed the refuge personnel building, and returned to the trailhead.

Sheepshead Ridge Loop Trail

Length: 3.7 mi (5.9 km); **easy**; USGS Maps: Sewee Bay, Bull Island; trailhead: near information exhibit.

We set out on the Sheepshead Ridge Road (on which passage is difficult after a heavy rain) through pines, palms, wax myrtle, and bullis vines. At 1.3 mi we turned R to cross a levee in Jack's Creek Pool and a short mound in an open area. At Lighthouse Road there was a photo observation blind at 1.7 mi. Canvas back ducks were numerous. David nearly stepped on a 5-foot Southern black racer. We returned to the Beach Road at 2.6 mi, and turned L to hike 0.2 mi out to the beach. Sand dollars were prominent on the wide beach. Huge banks of logs looked as if a tidal wave from the movie *Green Dolphin Street* had hit the refuge. We returned on the Beach Road to the shelter for a loop of 3.7 mi.

Old Fort Loop Trail

Length: 6.6 mi (10.6 km); **easy**; USGS Maps: Sewee Bay, Bull Island; trailhead: near information exhibit.

We turned L on Old Fort Road in front of the refuge personnel building and hiked through the forest to the remains of the old tabby wall, thought to be a fort or lookout for pirate ships in Bull's Bay, at 2.2 mi. After a clockwise loop around Jack's Creek Pool, we reached Lighthouse Road and the photo observation blind again at 4.9 mi. We followed the road back to Beach Road, turning R, and completed the loop at 6.6 mi.

Other hikes are on the beach, going NE for 4 mi to Boneyard Beach or SW to the south end (4 mi from the shelter). As no camping is allowed in the refuge, hikers may wish to consult the South Carolina Wildlife Department about camping on Capers Island, which adjoins Bull's Island. A permit is required. Information: (803) 795–6350.

Support Facilities: Buck Hall Campground (Sumter National Forest) is approximately 10 mi N of Moore's Landing. Access is off US 17 (7 mi S of McClellanville), E on FR 236 for 0.2 mi. No hook-ups or showers, but flush toilets, picnic tables, and grills. Open all year. Telephone Wambaw Ranger District (803) 887–3311.

Information: Contact Refuge Manager, Cape Romain National Wildlife Refuge, 390 Bulls Island Road, Awendaw, SC 29429; (803) 928–3368.

Carolina Sandhills National Wildlife Refuge
(Chesterfield County)

An example of what 45 years of excellent natural-resources management can do for 45,601 acres of destroyed forest, impoverished soil, and vanished wildlife is the Carolina Sandhills National Wildlife Refuge. Established in 1939 as a wildlife-management demonstration area, it has become a diversified environment of restored forest with timber management, 30 ponds (335 acres) and 1,100 acres of open field habitats. Deer and beaver have returned. Other mammals are raccoon, mink, otter, skunk, red and gray fox, bobcat, fox squirrel, gray and flying squirrels, muskrat, and rabbit. More than 190 species of birds, 40 of which are rare, have been catalogued. Migratory ducks, including mallards, black ducks, widgeons, pintails, and ringnecks, as well as Canada geese, take refuge here in the winter months. It has one of the nation's largest populations of the endangered red-cockaded woodpecker.

The refuge is on the Fall Line, with gently rolling sandhills between the piedmont plateau and the coastal plain. Its forest is chiefly longleaf pine and turkey oak. Scattered hardwoods are more prominent near streams. Open for daytime use only, the refuge has auto-tour routes to observation decks and nature study, picnicking, and hiking. Hunting and fishing are allowed according to refuge regulations.

Access: On US 1, 11.5 mi S of Patrick and 3.5 mi N of McBee, enter at the refuge entrance sign. The refuge hq office is on the L.

Woodland Pond Trail

Length: 0.9 mi (1.4 km); **easy**; USGS Maps: Angelus, Middendorf; trailhead: parking area.

From the refuge hq on US 1, go 1 mi on the refuge road to Pool A, L, on the N side of Little Alligator Creek to the parking area. Follow the sign at the woods edge, and at 0.1 mi you will cross a footbridge over the edge of the lake. Some evidence of past beaver activity is here. At 0.5 mi cross a footbridge over a stream, then take a boardwalk, and return to the paved road. Turn L by the dam, and return to the parking area. Vegetation includes pines, poplar, oaks, and red bay.

Whitetail Trail

Length: 4 mi (6.4 km); **easy**; USGS Maps: Angelus, Middendorf; trailhead: Martin's Lake boat ramp.

From Woodland Pond Trail go another 3.2 mi N on the paved refuge road to a sign at Martin's Lake on the R. Follow the gravel road for 1 mi, passing a parking area on the L at 0.6 mi on the way to the boat ramp.

Scott Smith let me out at the boat ramp so I would not have to backtrack. From the boat ramp I entered the trail and saw Carolina buckthorn, witch hazel, trailing chinquapin, pineweed, juniper, pines, bayberry, mosses, and ferns. At 0.5 mi I reached the observation deck from which I could see across the lake to fields of grain for the migratory birds. After another 0.4 mi I reached the wildfowl photography blind; then the blazed trail continued to a deer crossing at 1.3 mi. Deer tracks were numerous. I crossed the refuge paved road to the SW side of Pool-D. Plants in the area included rattlebox, dwarf papaw, false indigo, sumac, camphorweed, wooly mullein, snakeroot, titi, pink spiderwort, bonamia, and alder. Here as elsewhere the state flower, yellow jessamine (*Gelsemium sempervirens*), grew in profusion. More than 125 species of plants grow in the trail area.

I entered the woods again at 1.8 mi on an old logging road, turned R at 2 mi, and crossed a wood bridge over a creek. On an old road at 2.9 mi I reached a jct with a loop trail around Lake-12, but noticed another jct with the loop trail at 3.2 mi. after crossing a footbridge over a creek. The trail now entered a partial hardwood area before its exit at 3.4 mi. on SC 145 (from here S to US 1 on SR 145 it is 6 mi). I continued across the road to the Lake Bee dam and at the other side turned R on a trail without blazes. Pool-H and a refuge road were at 4 mi, where Scott was waiting to pick me up.

Support Facilities: The nearest campground is Cheraw State Park, 18.5 mi N on US 1. (See Cheraw State Park in Chapter III.)

Information: Contact Refuge Manager, Carolina Sandhills National Wildlife Refuge, Route 2, Box 330, McBee, SC 29101; (803) 333–8401.

Santee National Wildlife Refuge (Clarendon County)

Established in 1941, the Santee National Wildlife Refuge has four management units—Bluff, Dingle Pond, Pine Island and Cuddo—bordering on Lake Marion, a hydroelectric reservoir. The refuge has 15,095 acres (1,425 acres of cropland, 2,350 acres of forest, 9,000 acres of open water, and 2,320 acres of shallow impoundments, ponds, marsh, and swamp), with 25 miles of canals.

Approximately 30,000 ducks and 1,500 Canada geese winter at the refuge, and more than 200 species of other birds live there or visit. Mammals include bobcat, deer, raccoon, squirrel, mink, otter, and fox. More than 100 species of fish there include chub, shiner, sucker, sunfish, largemouth bass, perch, sturgeon, gar, shad, pike, catfish, silverside, crappie, neddlefish, mullet, bowfin, striped bass, white bass, and carp.

January is the peak month for Canada geese and mallards. In February there is an increase of wood ducks, purple martins, and bluebirds. Alligators have been seen sunning on some of the canal edges in March. April and May are excellent months for fishing. In August the summer warblers begin to migrate south, but September is the peak month for migratory songbirds. Ruby-crowned kinglets, white-throated sparrows, finches, cormorants, hawks, and bald eagles are seen in October and November. February is good to fish for largemouth bass, catfish, and striped bass. Sport fishing is permitted year round, but specific waters are closed from Nov. 1 through Feb. 28. (Check with the refuge manager for fishing regulations.) Camping, overnight mooring of boats, swimming, open fires, and firearms are not allowed in the refuge.

The trails are in the Bluff, Dingle Pond, and Cuddo units. (Consult the refuge manger before hiking the 12-mile dike road in the Cuddo unit.)

Bluff Unit

The Visitor Center, open Monday through Friday, is located here, as are the maintenance complex, observation tower, a wildlife foot trail, and Fort Watson, the first post in South Carolina retaken from the British on April 15, 1781.

Access: From I-95 (exit 102), and jct with US 15-301, follow the signs N on US 15-301 for 0.3 mi, and turn L on SR 803. Go 0.3 mi on SR 803 to the Visitor Center on L, and another 0.7 mi to Fort Watson.

Santee Wildlife Trail

Length: 1.1 mi (1.8 km); easy; USGS Maps: Summerton, Vance; trailhead: parking area.

This trail is also called Wrights Bluff Nature Trail. From the parking area Clive and Sonyie Rassow and I entered the forest to cross a boardwalk at 0.1 mi. The trail was wide and covered with pine straw; it was surrounded by pine, wax myrtle, grapevine, English ivy, sweet gum, Devil's walking cane, sensitive fern, and the unisexual perennial herb with fragrant nonpetaled soft white flowers, the stinging nettle (*Cnidoscolus stimulosus*, not to be confused with another stinging nettle, the *Urtica dioica*.) At 0.4 mi we entered a young hardwood forest with Spanish moss hanging from the oaks. After crossing another boardwalk, we turned R to an observation deck at 0.6 mi. As we neared a gravel service road, we heard dozens of doves. They were in such abundance and cooing so loudly we stopped to listen. "Perhaps they are making love," Clive said. "St. Augustine said that 'doves show love when they quarrel with each other,'" Sonyie added. At 0.8 mi we passed over an elevated boardwalk with a view of a lake. Pickerel weed and sweet-scented water lilies loomed over their watery foundation. We reentered a pine forest before an exit in an old field near the parking lot.

Dingle Pond Unit

Southeast of the Bluff Unit is the Dingle Pond Unit, which allows fishing, nature study, canoeing, and hiking.

Access: From I-95 (exit 102) and SR 400 jct, go E by the Santee Resort Club for 0.3 mi and turn L (R is SR 390). Follow SR 400 for 1.7 mi to gated road on R.

Dingle Pond Trail

Length: 1.8 mi rt (2.9 km); **easy;** USGS Maps: Summerton, Vance; trailhead: gated woods road.

Along the woods roadbed, we heard ducks and frogs before we saw the swamp and lakes area. On each side of the trail were wax myrtle, pine, and Devil's walking cane. At 0.3 mi water from the western lake flowed into the more eastern lake. Water lilies and cattails grew thick with other marsh plants. Ferns bordered the banks. We continued on the old roadbed through a pine forest with Spanish moss. We heard or saw catbirds, cardinals, towhees, and mockingbirds. At 0.7 mi we reached the end of the gated road, but another 0.2 mi led us to SR 390 (the KOA road from the fork with SR 400). We backtracked, seeing much we missed on the way in.

Information: Contact Refuge Manager, Route 2, Box 370, Summerton, SC 29148; (803) 478-2217.

Savannah National Wildlife Refuge (Jasper County)

The seven Savannah Coastal Refuges span 100 miles of coastline with a total of 53,340 acres. Five of the refuges are in Georgia—Blackbeard Island, Harris Neck, Tybee Island, Wassaw, and Wolf Island. Pinckney Island is located entirely within South Carolina; portions of Savannah Refuge, the largest of the coastal refuges, lie in Georgia and South Carolina.

In this low-country, and especially on the barrier islands, which the Spanish called "Golden Isles," the diversity of fauna and flora has attracted such naturalists as Alexander

Wilson, Mark Catesby, John James Audubon, and William Bartram. Contemporary naturalists and the public in general continue to find this area appealing for the same reasons. Here you will see freshwater marshes, tidal rivers and creeks, and river-bottom hardwood swamps. The former rice fields of the colonial period have been impounded for waterfowl management. Each year some 20,000 migratory ducks, representing more than 12 species, winter on Savannah Refuge from November through February. Wood ducks, purple gallinules, and king rails are regular nesters. You will see alligators from March through October, and bird-watching for the more than 200 species is at its best from October through April. Fishing is permitted in the freshwater pools from March 15 to October 25. Group tours can be arranged by contacting the refuge hq in Savannah at (912) 944-4415.

Access: From the jct of I-95 (exit 5) and US 17 in Hardeeville, go S on US 17 for 8 mi to refuge entrance.

Laurel Hill Wildlife Drive and Cistern Trail

Length: 6.3 mi rt ct (10 km); easy; USGS Maps: Limehouse, Savannah; trailhead: parking area.

At the wildlife-drive entrance sign on US 17, Scott Smith and I turned at the refuge gate to the parking area. A large sign indicated that we were permitted to observe the wildlife for photography or nature study; to hike, picnic, and fish (in season and if using boats with electric motors only). Prohibited were camping, swimming, the use of firearms, fireworks, open fires, and the collection of plants or animals.

We had a choice of walking the Laurel Hill Wildlife Drive (open from sunrise to sunset) or driving around the loop route. We chose the walk because it was January, and we could see more of the migratory waterfowl. The earthen dikes separate management pools (formerly rice fields tended by slaves) from old hardwood hammocks. At 1.1 mi we reached the Cistern Trail, a short 0.2-mi loop that passed an old cistern. Vegetation here includes live oaks, cabbage palmetto, hackberry, and mulberry. At 3.4 mi there was a dike on the L and another at 3.6 mi. We photographed mallards, pintails, ring-necked ducks, and a few herons and egrets. At one point, near a dike on the L at 4 mi, we had an excellent view of a great blue heron. We reached US 17 and were back at the parking area at 6.1 mi.

Information: Contact Refuge Manager, Savannah Coastal Refuges, P.O. Box 8487, Savannah, GA 31412; (912) 944-4415.

Formerly Clarks Hill Lake, Thurmond Lake (named for Sen. Strom Thurmond) is the nation's largest U.S. Army Corps of Engineers project east of the Mississippi River. Completed in 1954 as part of a comprehensive development plan for the Savannah River Basin, it serves more than eight million visitors annually. Nine Corps recreation areas (five in South Carolina and four in Georgia) and 13 campgrounds (four in South Carolina and nine in Georgia) are provided. Six state parks are also located on Thurmond Lake (three in each state).

The lake is 39 miles long with 1,200 miles of shoreline and 70,000 acres of water. Fishermen enjoy catching large-mouth bass, crappie, catfish, hybrids, stripers, and bluegill. The large expanses of water offer excellent opportunities for sailing, skiing, boating, and swimming.

Hydroelectric energy is one of the Corps's commitments to the public. At Thurmond Lake seven generators can each produce 40,000 kilowatts of power at any given time. Visitors are welcome to tour the power plant and other facilities, but should first visit the Visitor Center on US 211 near the dam on the South Carolina side. (On the Georgia side of the lake, at the edge of the dam, is where the yellow-blazed Bartram Trail begins. It meanders through wooded bottomland and gentle slopes around the lakeshore for 22.9 mi in trail section I and 14.7 mi in trail section II to the Little River bridge on GA 47. Picnic and camping areas are available along the way.)

Below Dam Fishing Pier

This recreation area has a boat ramp, picnic grounds, and a Vita-course exercise and hiking trail.

Access: Near the Thurmond Lake Visitor Center on US 221, take the driveway across from the Center to the parking area at the fishing pier.

Clarks Hill Trail

Length: 1 mi (1.6 km); **easy;** USGS Map: Clarks Hill; trailhead: parking area.

Begin in an open field and follow a former exercise loop trail. There is an old tramway bed that serves as an additional route for a nature trail to the Savannah River. Tall gum, oaks, sycamore, poplar, locust, ash, and river birch are part of the forest on this trail.

Modoc Campground

Facilities here consist of a campground with or without hook-ups, group campground, boat ramp, picnic ground, comfort station, drinking water, amphitheater, playground, showers, and two hiking trails. There is a year-round campground caretaker.

Access: Campground entrance is located 0.5 mi S of Modoc on US 221.

Modoc Nature Trail

Length: 1.5 mi (2.4 km); **easy;** USGS Map: Clarks Hill; trailhead: parking area.

We began the trail across from the main shower house and meandered through loblolly pine, sweet gum, oaks, dwarf palmetto, and ferns. Muscadine grapevines and jessamine shared space with wisteria. We read interpretive markers along the way. Boy Scouts had been maintaining the trail. A loop brought us back to the point of origin.

Modoc Walking Trail

Length: 0.8 mi (1.3 km); **easy;** USGS Map: Clarks Hill; trailhead: parking area.

We began this hike behind the main shower house and roughly followed the shoreline. The high bluffs overlooking the lake provided excellent views. Hiking clockwise, halfway on the trail we crosssed two gravel roads. At 0.5 mi the view of the lake was magnificent. Boy Scouts help maintain this trail, too.

Information: Contact Resource Manager's Office, P.O. Box 10, Clarks Hill, SC 29821; (803) 333–2476 or (404) 722–3770.

Hartwell Lake
(Anderson, Oconee, and Pickens Counties)

Hartwell Lake, with 56,000 acres of water and a shoreline of 962 miles, was constructed by the U.S. Army Corps of Engineers between 1955 and 1963 as a hydropower and flood-control project on the Tugaloo, Seneca, and Savannah rivers. The dam was built across the Savannah River from Hartwell, Ga., and rises 204 feet from the river bed. Much of the area's history is now under water, but the stories and legends of the Cherokee Indians, William Bartram, Andrew Pickens, John C. Calhoun, and Revolutionary War heroine Nancy Hart (for whom Hartwell is named) will always be above water.

The recreational areas for this massive impoundment (ranked among the ten most-visited Corps of Engineers projects in the nation), where clean power produces over half a billion kilowatt-hours annually, are expansive: 20 in Georgia and 28 in South Carolina. Twelve of the 19 campgrounds are in the state. Other facilities include more than 25 commercial marinas, state and municipal parks, and accesses. The Visitor Center on the Georgia side provides an extensive program of living history, tours, nature study, energy interpretation, and safety projects.

Hartwell Dam Recreation Area

Hartwell Lake Beaver Trail

Length: 0.7 mi (1.1 km); easy; USGS Map: Hartwell Dam; trailhead: parking area.

On US 29 SW of Anderson go to Hartwell Lake and watch for the Beaver Trail sign on the L, opposite the sign of Hartwell Dam Recreation Area. After parking at the designated space, we entered an interpretive, well-maintained, wide trail of wood chips in a field of blackberry and honeysuckle. Spots of cedar, wild cherry, wild plum, and hackberry rose above the berries. We entered a forest of oaks, gum, and poplar at 0.2 mi, crossed a pond on a footbridge at 0.3 mi, and walked on a grassy carpet decorated on each side with pokeberry, elderberry, sumac, and honey locust. At 0.4 mi we crossed a footbridge near a beaver dam. Fresh greenery and saplings with partially chewed bark had been crocheted on the dam rim by the beavers. (This trail may be closed temporarily for a new design.)

Information: Contact Resource Manager, Natural Resources Management Center, Lake Hartwell, P.O. Box 278, Hartwell, GA 30643; (404) 376–4788.

State Parks, Forests, Historic Sites, and Wildlife Management Areas
State Parks

There are more trails in South Carolina state parks than in any other system in the state. Of the 52 properties, 44 are operational parks (eight are not developed for public use). Only 11 do not have designated foot trails. From the beginning of the parks in 1934, when the state legislature passed a bill to give the responsibility of the system to the Commission of Forestry, a "Nature Trail" was considered standard in the planning and development of a park. Currently there are 66 named foot trails with more than 120 miles. Camping facilities are provided in 31 of the parks.

The system developed from a grass roots desire of the citizens to have more recreational facilities. An example was a donation of 706 acres from a group of citizens in the Cheraw area to the state in early 1934. Myrtle Beach donated 1,067 acres. Then Sumter County donated 1,000 acres for Poinsett State Park, followed by 1,235 acres from the Charleston Water Works for Givhans Ferry State Park. Kings Mountain State Park with 6,141 acres came from federal donations in the fall of 1934. In 1935 there were five more—Edisto Beach, Paris Mountain, Table Rock, Lee, and Oconee. That same year the Sesqui-Centennial Commission in Columbia donated land for the Sesquicentennial State Park. It was a chain reaction across the state, and on July 1, 1936, Myrtle Beach State Park opened to the public as South Carolina's first state park. Since then the public's demand for recreational facilities has resulted in one of the best state-park systems in the Southeast.

An unfortunate closure of Edisto Beach State Park for some years came during the 1950s Civil Rights movement.

In a 1961 class-action suit to have the parks open to all citizens, a U.S. District Judge in Greenville required all parks to obey the Civil Rights Act of 1954. Rather than comply, the state attorney general "advised the State Commission of Forestry that all parks would be closed on the evening of September 8, 1963." After a year the will of the people prevailed on the state legislature and government officials to begin the process of reopening the parks (though the federal ruling did not require the parks to be reopened). First came a partial reopening, and by 1966 all parks were serving the public again.

The system continued to grow, and it became too large for supervision by the Forestry Commission. In 1967 responsibility was transferred to the Division of State Parks and Recreation under the newly created Department of Parks, Recreation and Tourism (PRT). Attendance soared, and by 1968 the General Assembly provided new life for the parks with a $6-million bond issue.

Since then the park system, through its plans, development, and expansion, has become one of the state's major attractions for local citizens and tourists. This has required outstanding leadership, and Ray M. Sisk, director of the Division of State Parks, has been there to provide it. His and other staff reports in *Park Lites* (the official publication of PRT) indicate growth in new parks, recreational services, and facilities, as well as protection of natural and cultural resources in all the parks. The total acreage of parks and historic sites is more than 85,000, and the total attendance annually is nearly 9,000,000.

The park service has a dozen parks with seasonal-programs staff, but parks with year-round full-time interpretive-programs staff are: Charles Towne Landing, Caesars Head, Cheraw, Hickory Knob, Hunting Island, Huntington Beach, Kings Mountain, Myrtle Beach, Poinsett, Rose Hill, Santee, Sesquicentennial, Table Rock, and Woods Bay.

A number of new parks are under construction or in the planning stages. Some of them are the 6,239-acre Lake Russell/McCalla, off SC 81 near Calhoun Falls; the 422-acre Lake Warren, W of Hampton off US 278; and the 442-acre Jasper, off I-95 near Ridgeland. For a progress report, call PRT, (803) 734-0157.

The Division of State Parks has divided the 46 counties into three regions and ten planning districts. In the Piedmont Region are three districts—Appalachian, Catawba, and Upper Savannah—with 16 counties. In the Midlands Region are four districts—Central Midlands, Lower Savannah, Santee-Wateree, and Pee Dee—with 20 counties. In the Coastal Region are three districts—Waccamaw, Charleston-Berkeley, and Low Country—with 10 counties. In keeping with this structure, the following parks are listed alphabetically within each region.

SECTION 1. PIEDMONT REGION
Andrew Jackson State Park (Lancaster County)

Andrew Jackson State Park is the state's only historic park honoring a U.S. president. Donated to the state by Lancaster County in 1953, the 36-acre park has a museum that features the farm and household life of the nineteenth-century piedmont settlers in an area formerly belonging to the Waxhaw Indians. The park has a 25-site campground near a seven-acre lake that has bass, crappie, bream, and catfish; a children's playground; a boat dock; a "meeting house" for groups and organizations; a primitive campground; a picnic area; a replica of an old schoolhouse, and a nature trail.

In a manicured meadow is the park's impressive focal point: an equestrian statue of the young Andrew Jackson, a gift from sculptress Anna Hyatt Huntington (Huntington Beach State Park is named in honor of her and her husband). Children from around the state gave nickels and dimes for the purchase of the base. An inscription explains: "We, the children of Lancaster County, South Carolina, are interested in a youthful statue of Andrew Jackson because he was born among the red clay hills of our county and here he spent the formative years of his life. . . ."

Sixth grade, H.R. Rice Elementary School
Nancy Crockett, Teacher and Principal
May 15, 1967

Although it is not certain in which of the Carolinas Andrew Jackson was born, historians agree that after young Andrew's father died, he spent his boyhood in South Carolina living with his mother's Scotch-Irish relatives, the Crawfords. By the time he was 14, he showed an interest in the development of the nation. He rode with Maj. Willie Richardson Davie's troops in the American Revolution and was captured by the British but returned to his family because of his age.

Access: From Lancaster go N on US 521 for 8 mi; or from Rock Hill at I-77, go E on SC 5 for 11.9 mi and L on US 521 for 0.6 mi to park entrance.

Andrew Jackson Nature Trail

Length: 1.1 mi (1.8 km); **easy**; USGS' Map: Van Wych; trailhead: parking area.

From the parking area Steve Harris and I passed the "meeting house," a chapel-like structure in the pines, dedicated to Viola C. Floyd (1901-1978) for her service as historian, teacher, and community leader. The trail meandered over a ground cover of reindeer moss under pines and cedars. After passing a picnic area at 0.3 mi we entered an open space at 0.6 mi where blackberry and honeysuckle competed with young sweet gum. A doe and fawn, partially in a patch of lespedeza, were ahead of us. At 0.9 mi we crossed the park road again into bunches of lyre-leaf sage, ragwort, and Queen Anne's lace before we returned to the "meeting house" and parking area.

Information: Contact Superintendent, Andrew Jackson State Park, Route 1, Lancaster, SC 29720; (803) 285–3344.

Baker Creek State Park (McCormick County)

In 1967 the state leased 1,305 acres for 25 years from the U.S. Army Corps of Engineers to establish Baker Creek State Park. With rolling hills of clay and quartz, and pines bordering Thurmond Lake (formerly Clark Hill Reservoir), the topography is so ideal for camping, fishing, and relaxing, it is a model for a natural park. It has 100 campsites with electricity, water, comfort stations, and hot showers. There are picnic areas, a boat dock, a tackle store, a playground, carpet golf, a pavilion bathhouse, a swimming area, a primitive campground, and trails for hikers and equestrians.

Access: From downtown McCormick take US 378 SW for 3.7 mi to jct with SR 329 on R. Follow SR 329 for 2 mi into the park.

Wild Mint Trail

Length: 0.8 mi (1.3 km); **easy**; USGS Maps: McCormick, Willington; trailhead: between campsites 56 and 57.

From Camping Area #2 between campsites 56 and 57, I descended to the edge of the lake and followed the trail sign. I read the trail brochure, but campers had removed some of the posts at the 14 stations, and at other locations the plant specimen had vanished. But there was more to see than the listed species. Along the trail were buttonbush, holly, redbud, wild plum, wild cherry, sweet gum, persimmon (from whose heartwood golf-club heads are made), loblolly and shortleaf pines, mulberry, dogwood, and indigo. At 0.3 mi I crossed a paved road and immediately smelled that familiar odor of cloves; it was wild mint, thus the name of the trail. After a loop curve on the hilltop, I returned to cross the road again and complete the loop.

Baker Creek Walking Trail

Length: 0.7 mi (1.1 km); **easy**; USGS Maps: McCormick, Willington; trailhead: picnic area #1.

I began this loop around a picnic area at the sign near an electric meter, uphill from the boat ramp. The forest was mostly pines and oaks with scattered ash, cedar, and dogwood. Jessamine and *vaccinium* were prominent; indigo, sticky fox glove, and wild onion provided spots of color. After crossing the road at 0.4 mi, I returned to the point of origin.

Information: Contact Superintendent, Baker Creek State Park, Route 1, Box 219, McCormick, SC 29835; (803) 443–2457/5886.

Caesars Head State Park (Greenville County)

Caesars Head State Park has 7,467 acres covering a chunk of pristine mountain beauty in the northwest corner of Greenville County. It is the heart of the Mountain Bridge Recreation and Wilderness Area. Park facilities are limited; it is basically a natural, undeveloped, dense, and partially impenetrable forest, and many state naturalists hope that it stays that way. Only a country store with a snack bar, ornaments, gifts, and maps; a large picnic shelter; interpretive center; and a gardenlike trail to the head of Caesar have been artificially created. The park presents programs of nature, mountain music, crafts, and arts at the top of Caesars Head (3,266 ft), a rock cliff from which you can see Table Rock, the Dismal (a gorge between the mountains), and the mountain ranges of North Carolina—even the Georgia mountains on a clear day.

One explanation of how Caesars Head got its name is that the cliff looked like Julius Caesar (students of Roman sculpture would have to use considerable imagination for this), and another is that a hunter's dog named Caesar plunged to his death in a fox-chase accident there. Some visitors say the cliff looks like a sheep's or ram's head.

In addition to the mountain top scenery, the park has trails so outstanding the park could well have been named for any of them. The Raven Cliff Falls Trail leads to a spectacular view of a rugged wild area, and the Jones Gap Trail on the Middle Saluda River goes through a chasm of resplendent beauty, and the Coldspring Branch Trail descends to a cascading stream that joins the river. (The Foothills Trail connects with these trails; see Chapter I.) One unusual feature of the park is that a specified number of primitive campsites are set aside, along the Middle Saluda River, in a joint project with the Jones Gap State Park.

Access: From the jct of SC 11 and US 276, take US 276 and go 6.3 mi to the park entrance. From Brevard, N.C., take US 276 S, and at the state line go 2.8 mi.

Caesars Head Trail

Length: 130 yds rt (0.6 km); **easy;** USGS Map: Table Rock; trailhead: parking area.

From the parking area walk to the garden path, which leads to a view over and under Caesars Head. Here are superb vistas of the Matthews Creek valley below, the Greenville Lake, Table Rock, and smaller foothills toward the piedmont, and high mountains west, such as the Pinnacle and Hickory Nut Mountain.

Raven Cliff Falls Trail

Length: 4.6 mi rt (7.3 km); **moderate**; USGS Map: Table Rock; trailhead: parking area on US 276.

From Caesars Head Park hq we drove 1.1 mi N on US 276 to a parking area on the R. (The Foothills Trail follows the Raven Cliff Falls Trail for the first 1.4 mi. See Chapter I.) We walked across US 276 to the trail entrance and descended on a wide roadbed. The forest floor was covered with New York ferns and buckberry. After crossing the site of an old dam, we ascended gradually on a S slope to the end of the roadbed at 0.6 mi. After curving across a ridge with a rock outcropping, we descended to a ravine before ascending steeply. At 1 mi we turned L on an old woods road that led us to a jct with another old road, R. (To the R, the Foothills Trail continues on its route for nearly 77 miles to Oconee State Park.) We continued ahead on the S side of the slope, but shifted to the northern side at 1.7 mi. The old jeep road ended at 2.2 mi, where we descended on a short steep trail to an observation deck. From here we had a magnificent view of the five major falls and multiple cascades that drop 400 ft until the white water disappears below. Framing all this scenery were large oaks and hemlocks and banks of mountain laurel. (A sign cautioned us not to descend farther because of the risk of falling and for the protection of the natural environment.) We backtracked to the trailhead.

Jones Gap Access Trail, Jones Gap Trail, and Coldspring Branch Trail

Length: 8.1 mi ct (12.9 km); **moderate** to **strenuous**; USGS Maps: Table Rock, Brevard, Cleveland, Sandingstone Mountain; trailheads: (See below.)

Access to the W trailheads is at the Raven Cliff Falls parking lot on US 276, 1.1 mi N of Caesars Head State

Park hq, and 2.8 mi S of Cedar Mountain. Access to the E trailhead is at the Jones Gap State Park parking lot at the end of Jones Gap Road and SR 97, River Falls Road, 5.8 mi from US 276/SC 11. To locate River Falls Road, look for the road jct on US 276/SC 11, near the Hi-Way Grocery, 1 mi W of Cleveland and 4.9 mi E of the W jct of US 276 and SC 11.

At the Raven Cliff Falls parking lot are two options for the hike into the Jones Gap gorge. One is a loop of 5.9 mi and the other is a linear route of 5.4 mi to Jones Gap State Park parking area. We began our hike on the N side of the parking lot on the 0.7-mi Jones Gap Access Trail (also called Miller Trail and one of the alternate routes of the Foothills Trail). Through hardwoods, first on a ridge and then on its nose, we made a steep descent to a grove of hemlock and rhododendron by the Middle Saluda River (a small stream at this point). At 0.7 mi we made a jct, R, with the Jones Gap Trail, the old Jones Toll Road. (To the L it is 0.7 mi to US 276, the route formerly used for the W entrance of the Jones Gap Trail. You may notice that the park personnel have built rock water bars to prevent erosion.)

The famous Jones Toll Road operated from 1848 to 1910 and was engineered by Solomon Jones (1802–1899), "roadmaker of the mountains." Born in Flat Rock, N.C., this tall, mild, blue-eyed mountaineer married Mary Hamilton at the age of twenty and later served on the Hendersonville Public Health Commission. He is best remembered by the road that bears his name. Lacking engineering instruments, he used his natural talent and sense of contour grades to begin the road in 1840. Eight years later, without slave labor, it was completed. Mrs. Hattie Finlay Jones, a descendant who lives in Greenville, told this story about Solomon's road: "He turned loose a pig and followed it five and a half miles up the slope." The state of South Carolina permitted Solomon to install a tollgate at the foot of the mountain, near River Falls and Drakes Inn. (In addition to Solomon receiving a toll, his daughter and heir, Mrs. June Jones Cox, received

143

$50 a month from the state for the project for a number of years.) The toll fee was 1 cent each for hogs and cattle, 15 cents for a one-horse wagon; 25 cents for a two-horse wagon or one-horse buggy, and 50 cents for a two-horse buggy. (As far as I know, hikers got through free.)

In 1851 Solomon built a home on 4,000 acres in the nearby Oil Camp region and for about 20 years, beginning in 1870, he sold real estate. Later he moved to the summit of Mt. Hebron. On his gravestone is this epitaph:

Here lies Solomon Jones
The Roadmaker, a True Patriot
He labored fifty years to leave
The world better than he found it.

We followed the blue-blazed Jones Gap Trail and at 0.3 mi crossed the stream on a footlog. Near here is the state's largest reported yellow birch with a cir of more than 8 ft and the largest witch hazel, more than 8 in in cir. Below us were cascades, flumes, and pools of clear water, examples of a splashing river that drops 1,680 feet through 4 mi of the gorge. On our L were the slopes toward the Tennessee Valley Divide on the S.C./N.C. boundary and Little Rich Mountains. To the R was the steep ridge E to Little Pinnacle Mountains. For the next 0.4 mi is one of the best examples of Solomon's engineering. He constructed a switchback that would pass, except for the short curves, for a railway grade. Wildflowers were prominent—trillium, crested dwarf iris, Solomon's seal, bloodroot, and fringe tree. At 1.1 mi we entered a deep cove. For the next mile we crossed numerous streams plunging down the slope. At 1.5 mi is the state's largest reported mockernut hickory (more than 10 ft in cir) and the state's cochampion Fraser magnolia (more than 5 ft in cir). A yellow poplar stand afforded some sunlight on the road at 1.9 mi. At 2.5 mi we reached a jct, R, with the 2.7-mi Coldspring Branch Trail (described below).

Continuing downstream, we followed the path to the L, paralleling the river and noticing deer, turkey, and raccoon tracks. There are a number of good campsites in this area. At 3.7 mi the trail has been rerouted, R (to the L an old trail leads to the Cox Camp stream and N about 0.7 mi to Rainbow Falls), to cross the John Reid Clonts Bridge. The trail rejoins the old trail at 4 mi. We passed campsites along the river and at 4.4 mi crossed an insignificant drainage. But to the R of it, in a grove of saplings, is an enormous landslide that exposed a spectacular rock face of Little Pinnacle Mountain. At 4.7 mi we arrived at the Jones Gap State Park parking lot. (Backpack camping is allowed at specific sites along the river, but a permit is required from Caesars Head or Jones Gap state parks. See Jones Gap State Park later in this chapter.)

To hike the orange-blazed Coldspring Branch Trail, we crossed the Middle Saluda River on a log footbridge, crossed an old wagon-road intersection, and began a gradual ascent. Maple, poplar, hemlock, fetterbush, and wildflowers were prominent. After rock-hopping the branch six times, we turned away from it at 1.3 mi. We ascended on a wagon road to a ridge crest at 1.9 mi, turned L, and arrived at US 276 at 2.6 mi. A R turn onto the highway was 150 yds from the parking lot.

Information: Contact Superintendent, Caesars Head State Park, 8155 Geer Highway, Cleveland, SC 29635; (803) 836–6115/7438.

Chester State Park (Chester County)

Chester State Park has 523 acres of a mixed forest, which includes a 160-acre lake. Deer, raccoon, squirrel, and dove have a sanctuary in the forest, but it is a different story for the bass, crappie, bream, and catfish that abound for the anglers in the lake. Fishing boats may be rented at the boat dock (private boats are not allowed in the park). The park was purchased by the state in 1934 from the Lake View Corporation and other landowners. Facilities include a community recreation building, picnic area, 25-site campground, equestrian arena, field-archery range, primitive campground, and hiking trail.

Access: From the jct of SC 9 and US 321 Bypass and SC 72 in Chester, go S on SC 72 for 2 mi to park entrance.

Caney Fork Falls Trail

Length: 1.3 mi (2.1 ki); **easy;** USGS Map: Chester; trailhead: parking area.

From the parking area I followed trail signs at the boathouse and entered a young mixed forest on a well-maintained and well-graded trail. Coreopsis, wild pink, five finger, wild larkspur, deerberry, and silverberry were in bloom. At 0.3 mi I passed a picnic area where the majority of trees were hickory, elm, oak, sycamore, and hackberry. After passing the campground at 0.7 mi, the trees were much larger and the trail became wider. Leaving the forest, I crossed the dam and returned to the parking zone by the picnic area and falls at 1.3 mi.

Information: Contact Superintendent, Chester State Park, Route 2, Box 348, Chester, SC 29706; (803) 385–2680.

Croft State Park (Spartanburg County)

In 1949 Croft State Park, with its 7,088 acres, became the state's second largest park. With this acreage the facilities can be expanded as urban development in the vicinity increases. Among the present facilities are an Olympic-size swimming pool, a boat dock for fishing, paddle boats, a 50-site campground, picnic areas, a horse arena (the home of the Spartanburg Horseman's Association), and multiple-use trails.

The park is rich in history; Cherokee Indian mounds, old Antioch Church grave sites and other graveyards, and foundation sites of early settlers' homes. During World War II this area and other properties adjoining the park boundary were used as Camp Croft for more than 20,000 troops and as a recruiting and induction station for selectees from western North Carolina. Park Superintendent Ray Hayes and

Ranger Phil Tyner told me the park is "getting to capacity, according to government environment regulations...we may have to build another swimming pool."

Little Sycamore Nature Trail

Length: 1.5 mi (2.4 km); **easy**; USGS Map: Spartanburg; trailhead: behind the swimming pool.

Following the trail sign at the entrance behind the swimming pool, I descended into a mature hardwood forest to a stream with rock formations, beech, ferns, and wildflowers at 0.2 mi. I ascended on a gentle grade to a ridge and turned L at 0.8 mi. A slight grade descended to a picnic area near the swimming pool for a loop of 1.5 mi. Plant life along the trail included oaks, poplar, pines, a variety of *hypericum*, jessamine, reindeer moss, sourwood, wild orchids, and spicebush.

Croft Jogging Trail

Length: 0.5 mi (0.8 km); **easy**; USGS Map: Spartanburg; trailhead: opposite the campground entrance.

From the corner of the campground and boathouse roads, I followed the signs. This was a good jogging trail, and the ten physical-fitness stations make it an exercise trail. The trail was smooth and wide, a good place for observing wildlife and plant life. It was in a mixed forest, and wisteria and silverberry were prominent.

Lake Johnson Trail

Length: 5.5 mi (8.8 km); **moderate**; USGS Map: Spartanburg; trailhead: parking area at horse stables.

The park has this trail listed as a "horse trail," but the park superintendent said that hikers also used the trail. He said the trail could be made into a 25-mile loop bordering Edwin Johnson Lake.

Jeff Fleming and I drove 0.5 mi from the campground to the trail entrance on the road by the horse arena to the horse stables and parked. We entered the posted roadbed on the R. As the park map is not clear on this trail, we assumed we were right because of numerous horse tracks. Silverberry fringed the old road as we hiked through a mixed forest. After 0.4 mi of gentle terrain we came to a jct. "Which way?" asked Jeff. I didn't know. We agreed to first explore the R trail. After 0.2 mi we were on the banks of the Fairforest River. There was evidence that ORVs and horses had crossed the river, but we would have to wade if we crossed. We decided to backtrack to the jct. There we turned R and crossed a steel bridge over Kelsey Creek. Ahead was a gradual climb on an old roadbed in a mixed forest. At 1.7 mi we reached the ridge top in a pine forest. Here the park boundary extended E where an old road showed more horse and ORV use. (From here on the E route a rider or hiker could hike another 1.5 mi to SR 681 and on other private roads.) Ahead, the forest changed to a mixture of pine, oak, hickory, mulberry, cedar, dogwood, and redbud. White asters and purple-blossom sensitive briar patches were on the road banks of red and yellow clay. A huge stand of poplar was on each side of the road at 2.8 mi, a few yards before our ascent on a treadway of silver-brown dirt.

Suddenly out of the trees rose the WRET-TV tower of the South Carolina Education TV Network, which the park superintendent had told us was on the trail. We had climbed 3 mi. After 0.1 mi we passed a locked firetower, its metal rusting, its wood steps feeble, its window panes shattered. Like so many of these sentinels of the past, it is no longer needed, replaced by scheduled surveillance from helicopters. Twelve horseback riders and a lone hiker approached us. They assured us that our loop needed to be on the paved SR 295 for a short distance before we were on the return route. After hiking 0.3 mi to a rusty gate at the park boundary, we turned L onto an old roadbed bordered with periwinkle and draped with wisteria. A deer bounded away from our L. At 4.9 mi we passed a long, open shelter and then descended to an open clay embankment. Reentering the woods, we noticed the Foster cemetery had been restored by Boy Scout Troop 102. Did this troop have relatives here we wondered, or did they see the need to preserve the memory of those whose gravestones were being covered by nature's forest blanket?

At 5.4 mi we were crossing the dam of Lake Johnson when the sound of motorcycles broke the tranquility. We hardly had time to jump aside in the briars before three cyclists dressed as yellow jackets, with the name "Hell's Yellow Jackets" on their costume, roared past us. The hot dust from the trail billowed up in clouds as they disappeared. Soon we heard the grind of the engines as they spun in the clay dust of the embankment we had passed. At 5.5 mi we returned to the horse stables parking area.

Information: Contact Park Superintendent, Croft State Park, 450 Croft State Park Rd, Spartanburg, SC 29302; (803) 585–0419/583–2913.

Hanging Rock Battle Monument (Lancaster County)

This scenic Revolutionary War-battle area is maintained as a state historic site. It has a 0.5-mi hiking-auto trail encircling a hillside of enormous weather-rounded and split-granite boulders. One huge rock balances precariously over another in a stand of white oaks. From the summit of the rocks is a view of Hanging Rock Creek flowing through a hardwood forest. Here among these boulders on Aug. 6, 1780, Col. Thomas Sumter defeated British Maj. John Carden of the Prince of Wales American Regiment. The area is on the Heath Springs USGS Map.

Access: From the jct of US 521 and SR 15 in Heath Springs, go 1.7 mi on SR 15 to the sign of the James Ingram Home (where George Washington spent a night in 1771), and turn L on SR 467. After 0.8 mi turn R on a dirt road, the Hanging Rock Battle Trail.

Information: Contact Parks Recreation and Tourism, Suite 110, Edgar A. Brown Bldg., 1205 Pendleton St., Columbia, SC 29201; (803) 758–3622.

Hickory Knob State Resort Park (McCormick County)

They cleared all the hickories off this knob when they created this deluxe country club–style resort park. But there are plenty of hickories for those who love them around the lake's edge and golf courses and in the rich forest. There are 1,090 acres here, leased from the U.S. Army Corps of Engineers in 1969. It has everything for vacationers who "are looking for the right place . . . one that is removed from the hectic pace of everyday living . . . accessible and economical," as their advertisement says.

On top of the knob is the lodge complex with motel, restaurant, swimming pool, and tennis courts. Another motel and a conference building are near the lake, close to the marina. All this can easily accommodate 300 guests. In a crescent from the knob are 18 cabins complete with color TV and telephone. The park also includes a playground, a large boat dock, a tackle shop, a fishing pier, a boat ramp, a skeet and trap range, a putting green, an archery course, rental bicycles, equestrian facilities for 50 horses, kennel facilities for 80 dogs, and show rings. And the 6,560-yard championship golf course, with full service, designed by golf architect Tom Jackson, gives this beautiful park its country-club atmosphere. There is a 75-site campground with all the usual conveniences for tent campers and RVs, as well as a nature trail.

Access: From McCormick take US 378 SW for 5.8 mi to SC 7. Turn R on SC 7 and go 1.5 mi to the park entrance.

Turkey Ridge Trail

Length: 0.3 mi (0.5 km); easy; USGS Map: Willington; trailhead: near parking area at the Lodge Complex.

After parking at the Lodge Complex, I walked to the edge of the forest where there is a trail sign. I followed the 18 trail numbers, with signs that acquaint you with the flora and fauna. At 0.2 mi the trail curved by the lake where almost silent ripples were sequins from the sun. Tall loblolly stood silent. "When the pines tranced as by a wizard's will, doth some lone Dryad haunt the breezeless air," wrote Charleston poet Paul H. Hayne in "The Voice of the Pines." Silent as the pines was the understory of sweet gum, oaks, dogwood, and wild cherry, some heavy with trumpet creeper (*Campsis radicans*) and twining honeysuckle. Only the sourwood had a sound from swarms of honeybees seeking clear nectar from the fragrant urn-shaped flowers. This was a place of peace.

Information: Contact Superintendent, Hickory Knob State Resort Park, Route 1, Box 199-B, McCormick, SC 29835; (803) 443–2151.

Jones Gap State Park (Greenville County)

The 3,346-acre Jones Gap State Park is among the state's most recent parks. Although located at the E end of Middle Saluda River Gorge, it is named for Solomon Jones, a mid-nineteenth-century mountain road builder. Jones constructed a five-mile toll road from the park area to the top of the gap near the S.C./N.C. state line. His achievement remains a scenic and historic route on what is now the Jones Gap Trail and the easternmost section of the Foothills Trail (see Caesars Head State Park for information on Solomon Jones and the Jones Gap Trail). The park acreage is the former eastern section of Caesars Head State Park.

Looking N from the park entrance is Cleveland Cliff, a towering 1,400-ft wall from the river, and on the S side is the Little Pinnacle Mountain, almost as high, but not visible. In a joint arrangement with the Caesars Head State Park, the parks have designated a specific number of primitive campsites along the Middle Saluda River. Permits are necessary from either park. As you enter the park, the office is on the L, and the gorge parking lot is at R. USGS maps are Cleveland and Standingstone Mountain.

Access: On US 276/SC 11 (1 mi W of Cleveland near the Hi-Way Grocery) go 5.8 mi on SR 97, River Falls Rd and Jones Gap Rd to the park entrance.

Information: Contact Superintendent, 303 Jones Gap Rd, Marietta, SC 29661; (803) 836–7122.

Keowee Toxaway State Park (Pickens County)

Keowee Toxaway State Park, which opened in 1970, has one of the state's most unique features—an emphasis on the heritage of the Cherokee Indians. Displays are in the interpretive center, orientation building, and four kiosks.

Highways 11 and 133 intersect in the center of the 1,000-acre park, and Keowee Lake is on the north boundary. Facilities include a 24-site campground, a primitive camp, a picnic area, Lake Keowee for boating and fishing, trails, and a meeting house.

Access: Park entrance is on SC 11, 7.1 mi W from the jct of SC 11 and US 178, 1.2 mi E from the Keowee Lake bridge on SC 11.

Cherokee Interpretive Trail

Length: 0.3 mi (0.5 km); **easy;** USGS Map: Salem; trailhead: Interpretive Center.

From the parking area S of SC 11, I went up to the Interpretive Center and Museum for information on the trail, then followed the sign to the orientation building, where "Prehistory to 1500" told about the environment and the Archaic Indians and ancestors of the Cherokee. At the first kiosk, "Cherokee Culture 1500-1700" told of their dress, agriculture, games and dances, medicines, structures, and social/political systems. "The Coming of the Traders 1700-1745," at the second kiosk, emphasized the impact of English goods and trade problems. At the third kiosk, the theme was the "Cherokee War, 1745-1761"; subthemes were trade problems, Creek War, conferences and treaties, and Fort Prince George. Near the end of the loop trail was the fourth kiosk, "End of an Era, 1761-1816," about the Treaty of 1761, the coming of the settlers, the Revolutionary War, the Hopewell Treaty of 1785, and the "Trail of Tears" in 1816.

Writing about the "Trail of Tears," the removal of the Cherokee from South Carolina, Rev. Evan Jones described the exodus first hand. "Multitudes were allowed no time to take anything with them, except the clothes on their backs. Well-furnished houses were left prey to plunder . . . stripping the helpless of all they have on earth."

Raven Rock Hiking Trail and Natural Bridge Nature Trail

Length: 4.2 mi rt ct (6.7 km); **moderate** to **strenuous**; USGS Map: Salem; trailhead: parking area by the chapel.

Across SC 11 from the Interpretive Center is a parking area near the chapel. (Primitive camping is allowed for $1.00 per person per night.) We began our hike here, to the R of the chapel, and followed a narrow blue-blazed trail through an oak forest. Blueberries, Bowman's root, and mountain laurel were part of the understory and ground cover. At 0.3 mi we went L on an old farm road with profuse bracken and Indian plantain. After descending 0.6 mi into a mature forest, we crossed an underground stream in a rocky scenic area.

To the L, at a sign, is the Natural Bridge Nature Trail. It is a short, scenic connector trail, about 100 yds through mature rhododendron, to the return route of the Raven Rock Hiking Trail. (The connector provides the option of a loop to the L for another 0.5 mi back to the parking area.) Rosebay rhododendron and phlox were near a cascade and pool. From here we followed a steep, twisting trail among large boulders with scattered pines and mountain laurel. Occasionally we saw a light blue or white blaze. For the next mile the trail ascended and descended among ridges and ravines, twisting as if planned for an obstacle course. At 1.8 mi on McKinney Mountain (1,182 ft) the trail made a sharp turn L for the loop, but we continued ahead to reach the campsite. We descended steeply on a blue-blazed trail to an excellent campground on a peninsula of pines in Keowee Lake at 2.2 mi.

On the return, we followed a blue-blazed trail R, along the lake to a fine view from a rocky bluff. Beyond this point we found the remnants of an old whiskey still and a small stream. (The blue blaze may be confusing here; turn back to the bluff and hike up the ridge to regain the main trail.) After we returned to the bluff and followed the ridge to rejoin the main trail, we descended steeply on a ridge to reach a cascading stream at 3.3 mi. Wake robins, wild geraniums, ferns, and hemlocks made this a most attractive area. We were so attentive to the plants that Steve Harris, my hiking companion, nearly ran the measuring wheel over a copperhead coiled in a sunny spot on the trail. At 3.6 mi we ascended away from the stream; the trail switched back and forth on an old logging road to connect with the Natural Bridge Nature Trail, at L. We crossed another stream a number of times and began our final ascent on an old logging road at 4 mi. At 4.1 mi we turned R off the road, and reached the parking area.

Information: Contact Superintendent, Keowee Toxaway State Park, Sunset, SC 29685; (803) 868-2605.

Kings Mountain State Park (York and Cherokee Counties)

In 1934 the U.S. government donated to the state of South Carolina 6,141 acres for the development of a state park with recreational facilities adjacent to the Kings Mountain National Military Park. As part of the Kings Mountain range of low foothills, the park is an oak-hickory hardwood forest with scattered pines. Numerous springs and clear streams are between the slopes of clay and quartz. Lake Crawford, an 8.3-acre impoundment with swimming and pedal boating, is the center of the park's activities. Adjacent is a campground with 125 sites, and nearby are group camps and primitive camping areas. A trading post with a display of pioneer artifacts has basic groceries and camping supplies. Other facilities are a laundry, a recreational building, carpet golf, a playground, and picnic areas. York Lake is S of SC 216 and the main campground.

Of historical significance is the "Living Farm," a replica of an 1846 South Carolina frontier farm. The "Homeplace," constructed of pine and chestnut, is a two-story log farmhouse with a crafts demonstration and other household activities. The farm also includes a barn, a smokehouse, a blacksmith/carpenter shop, a sorghum mill and cooker, a corn crib, a cotton gin, small outbuildings, an herb garden, livestock and chickens, and a pioneer vegetable garden. I found Park Superintendent Lew Cato in the vegetable garden with a roto-tiller on a hot summer day. "With only eight of us in a park this size," he said, "we have to be able to do everything." Each September the park has a two-day festival of pioneer games, country cooking, arts and crafts, and authentic folk music.

The park maintains 10.2 miles of the 15-mile Kings Mountain Hiking Trail, a joint project with Kings Mountain National Military Park.

Access: From the jct of SC 161 and SR 216 near the North Carolina state line, turn W on SC 216 to the park entrance. From the W turn E on SC 216 at I-85.

Gold Nugget Trail

Length: 2.3 mi rt ct (3.7 km); **easy**; USGS Map: Kings Mountain; trailhead: campground.

I started this trail at campsite #71 at the trail sign, but I soon learned that campers had added numerous side trails. I hiked them all, counting the mileage for backtracking. For example, the trail can be entered at campsite #50 or downstream at the jct with the Kings Mountain Hiking Trail. Some of the trees and shrubs along the trail are loblolly and Virginia pine, oaks, dogwood, maple, birch, elm, mountain laurel, fetterbush, and blueberry bush. When I followed the downstream route, I returned by taking a L at the Kings Mountain Hiking Trail back through the parking area.

Kings Mountain Hiking Trail

Length: 15 mi rt (24 km); **moderate**; USGS Maps: Filbert, Kings Mountain, Kings Creek, Grover; trailhead: campground main parking area.

Designated a national recreational trail in June 1981, the Kings Mountain Hiking Trail traverses low foothill country in Kings Mountain State Park and Kings Mountain National Military Park. It is an extension of a trail formerly called Clark's Creek Trail. Although entrance to the trail is at a number of crossroads and at the Visitor Center of the military park, I will describe it from the state-park campground so the trailhead is at a full-service campsite.

Ray Matthews and I began the trail from the group picnic area with shelters at the parking area; we descended for 0.2 mi to cross a tributary of Clark Fork and jct with the Gold Nugget Trail. We ascended gradually on a wide trailway with white blazes and crossed the primitive campground road at 0.4 mi. At 1.1 mi we reached the national-park boundary, and at 1.2 mi we passed a stream on the R. Around us were mountain laurel, yellow root, rattlesnake orchids, club moss, wild ginger, fetterbush, and wood betony. We approached another stream on the L at 1.3 mi, followed it upstream to a stretch of false downy foxglove. At 1.7 mi we crossed a larger stream of the Long Branch tributaries, heading upstream on an even grade. After crossing the stream again at 2 mi, we ascended gradually to the summit of a hill at 2.3 mi. Sticky foxglove bordered the trail in a young oak forest. At 2.4 mi we reached a trail jct. To the L it was 0.2 mi to the Visitor Center of the national park. We heard the firing of a musket in that direction: The park was having a 1780 demonstration of cooking a pot of beef stew. "It's kinda in honor of the overmountain men who had beef for a meal here at the battle," said Steve Marlowe, a park staff member.

Because we had already hiked the Battlefield Trail and seen the Visitor Center, Ray and I continued on the main trail to descend steeply and reach a small stream at 2.5 mi.

This stream flows out of the battlefield summit where the patriots bathed their wounded on Oct. 7 and 8, 1780. We ascended to an old fire road, which is the Overmountain Victory Trail route, and went 0.1 mi, turning L at 2.9 mi. (The gated fire road and the Overmountain Victory Trail continued straight.) After climbing a gentle grade, we crossed SC 216 at 3.2 mi. We continued ahead on an exceptionally well-maintained trail in an open oak forest. We soon descended in a rocky section to cross Stonehouse Branch on an old bridge at 3.6 mi. Although pine beetles have destroyed most of the pine forests in the area, we saw a few living pines in this section. Ferns, fetterbush, yellow root, and wild azaleas were prominent before we began to ascend at 4.5 mi. At 4.7 mi we reached a ridge crest, which led to the jct of the firetower spur trail. We hiked the 0.5-mile spur over a hill, down to a saddle, and up to the firetower on Browns Mountain (1,045 ft) where the view was the best we would see anywhere on the trail. Returning to the main trail, we descended through a beautiful open forest with occasional slate formations. At 5.4 mi we reached Garner Branch and a park service–designated campsite. We ascended to the boundary line between the parks and crossed over an open space into the state park at 5.9 mi. (It is 0.5 mi L on the open boundary line to Piedmont Road.)

We passed through a lumbered area, entered a mature hardwood forest with undulating trailway, and reached a stream at 6.4 mi. Growing here were wild azaleas, switchcane, and ferns. At 6.6 mi we reached the Piedmont Road, SR 731, a graveled extension from SC 55. (It is 1.6 mi L to SC 216.) At this jct Sammy Gooding picked up Ray, and Bob Brueckner took his place. Mountain laurel, borders of galax, wild ginger, Christmas fern, royal fern, black cohosh, strawberry bush, fetterbush, and yellow root grew near the clear stream. We went downstream and ascended over a ridge and down to another stream with more mountain laurel at 7.3 mi. The trail curved up and around a ravine for 0.2 mi before descending back to the stream. We ascended over a ridge into a spacious deciduous forest at 7.8 mi. At 8 mi we noticed damage to the trail by horseback riders, a damage that continued sporadically for the next 5 mi. At an old logging-road crossing at 8.2 mi, we saw a magnificent display of monarch, pipevine, swallowtail, and fritillary butterflies at a bank of goldenrod and rose pink. A grist of honeybees and yellow jackets were in the area. We reentered the woods, downstream. This section of the trail, at 8.7 mi, could be a good campsite. Huge poplar, beech, gum, oak, hickory, and ironwood on the hillsides and bottomland gave a fine shady location. Fragrant spicebush and crested dwarf iris were along the trail.

At 9.3 mi we crossed a service road and entered a bottomland. Here was a stand of walnut, the most we had seen in the park. Poplar and mulberry were scattered over dense woodland sunflowers, thistle, and ironweed (*Vernonia noveborarensis*). We crossed a wood footbridge over a tributary of Long Branch at 9.7 mi, turned L on a park service road, and followed it for 0.1 mi before turning R, into the forest. Abruptly we entered an old field with piles of quartz rock, reindeer moss, purple blooming liatris, scrubby pines, and dead pines. I expected to see a copperhead, but only a small black snake showed up. We crossed another service road at 10.5 mi and reached a tributary of Long Branch at 10.7 mi. Here is another good campsite with ferns and cascades above a pool. At 11.2 mi we turned R, on a logging road. After 0.2 mi we turned R, off the road into the woods. At the confluence of the tributary with Long Branch, we turned L upstream and followed the branch banks, sometimes up on the slopes. At 11.7 mi the branch had cascades. The horse trail crossed the hikers trail at 12.3 mi and again at 12.5 mi. Although the horse trail was marked with a horseshoe label, hooves had churned the hiking trail to a thick porridge. This spot has space for camping near cascades. "It is a good place to cool your feet," said Bob, as we looked at a perfect rock bench in the middle of the stream. We rock-hopped across the stream and saw a patch of crane-fly orchids. Leafless in summer, the stalk and flowers of the orchids are almost the color of the brown forest duff. After crossing two more small streams we passed under a power line at 12.8 mi and reached Apple Road at 13.3 mi. (From here, L, it is .25 mi to SC 216.) Across Apple Road was a grove of cedars and an old cemetery at 13.6 mi. From here to the SC 216 crossing, the trail undulated through an open deciduous forest. We crossed SC 216 at 14.6 mi and entered a young pine grove, which changed to hardwood on a slope. Quartz glistened. We descended to the stream and completed our loop. We turned R and reached the campground parking area at 15 mi. (If you include the hiking distance to the firetower, 1 mi, and the hike to and from the Visitor Center, 0.4 mi, it would be 16.4 mi.)

If you plan to camp out on the trail, and I hope that you will, be sure to register and camp only at Garner Branch in the Kings Mountain National Military Park. (See Chapter II, Section 1.) Also, if you camp in the state park, let the park hq know who you are and where you will be camping.

Information: Contact Superintendent, Kings Mountain State Park, Route 3, Box 532, Blacksburg, SC 29702; (803) 222-3209/9363.

Lake Hartwell State Park (Oconee County)

Lake Hartwell State Park has 680 acres with a large family campground, laundry equipment, a trading post–tackle shop, and a community rec building, as well as picnic areas, a nature trail, and playground equipment. Fishing for bass, crappie, walleye, catfish, and bream is the major sports activity, but there are additional water sports: boating, sailing, windsurfing, and skiing.

Access: On I-85, on the E side of the Hartwell Lake, take exit 1 to SC 11, 0.5 mi N to the park entrance, L.

Beech Ridge Trail

Length: 1.4 mi rt (2.2 km); **easy**; USGS Map: Flint Hill; trailhead: trading-post parking area.

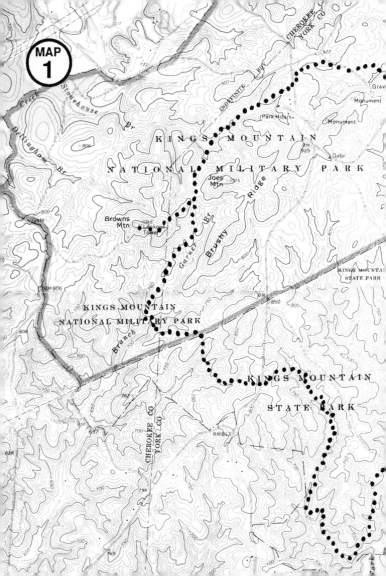

MAP
2

KINGS MOUNTAIN
ONAL MILITARY PARK

K I N G S   M O U N T A I N
S T A T E   P A R K

Campground

Lake
Crawford

Long

Branch

Cem

Branch

Clark

Lake
York

Lake
York
566

Jenkins

K I N G S   M O U N T A I N   S T A T E   P A R K

Long

Branch

Clark

Fk

N

Kings Mountain Hiking Trail

On a route of low hills and lake edges, we followed the interpretive markers between the trading post and the entrance to the campground. Along the trail we saw regenerating loblolly pine, beech, dogwood, oak, holly, maple, and ferns. We also saw evidence of former clear-cutting and former pastures and farmland.

Information: Contact Superintendent, Lake Hartwell State Park, Route 1, Box 192, Fair Play, SC 29643; (803) 972-3352/3561.

Landsford Canal State Park (Chester County)

Landsford Canal began in 1820 when the Board of Public Works contracted with Robert Leckie to build a dam, canal bed, guard lock, four lifting locks, the necessary bridges and culverts, and a lock keeper's house. It was to be constructed on land given by William Richardson Davie, a patriot who would benefit from the connection of the canal with his mill at the construction site. The basic units of measurement for determining the individual features were the perch, which has 24 cubic feet, and the chain, which was 66 feet. Apparently the initial calculations were incorrect, because Leckie petitioned the state legislature for additional funds in 1823. Abram Blanding was authorized to make a second measurement.

The canal was the northernmost one of four built to circumnavigate the shoals and falls of the Catawba and Wateree rivers. Constructed on the western bank of the Catawba, the Landsford Canal dropped 32 feet in 9,600 feet (a 33 percent slope). Hornblende and siente found on the site were used, but the granite in the locks may have come from the York District or from a quarry near Great Falls.

Of the many canals built in the state before the 1840s, only the Landsford remains without substantial alterations. It is uncertain how long it operated because of the continuous problems with flooding and dry seasons. When Duke Power Company donated 200 acres of this area to the state in 1970, both archaeological and environmental study began.

At present the recreational facilities are limited to a picnic area, a community meeting house, and hiking trails for nature study.

Access: From Rowell at jct of US 21 and SR 327, go 1.6 mi on SR 327 to SR 690, turn L on SR 690 and go 0.5 mi to the parking area. (Another access is from Landsford on SR 330 for 2.2 mi to another parking area.)

Landsford Canal and Nature Trail

Length: 3 mi rt (4.8 km); **easy**; USGS Maps: Catawba, Van Wyck; trailhead: parking area.

When Steve Harris and I arrived at the parking area, Walt Schrader, a veteran hiker, was there waiting for us. "This is one of my favorite parks and trails," he said, elaborating on the historic value of the park before going off to a Sierra Club engagement.

From the parking area Steve and I went 0.1 mi in a cleared picnic area to the trailhead. We chose to walk the west bank of the old canal. We were in a climax forest, where for 140 years nature had been unhindered. Tall oaks, elm, beech, poplar, sweetgum, hickory, sycamore, river birch, and walnut competed for the sunlight. Underneath were columbine, wild geranium, mandrake, atamasco lily, and Japanese honeysuckle. Redbud, holly, dogwood, cedar, ironwood, and buckeye were scattered to form pockets of subcanopy. At 0.7 we passed the Nature Trail sign on the L, and at 1.1 mi we reached a canal lock. At 1.4 mi we passed another lock; a few yards ahead was the southern parking area.

On our return we took the Nature Trail, which meandered along the bank of the river rapids. Here we saw spiderwort, elderberry, ferns, wild onion, switchcane, muscadine, and horsetail. We saw only one deer, but other mammals in the park are raccoon, squirrel, fox, skunk, bobcat, opossum, rabbit, and mink. The avian population consists of more than 45 species with large populations of robin, junco, sparrow, nuthatch, and warbler. The Southern bald eagle has been snakes, the copperhead and timber rattler. (The only snakes we saw were garter and ringneck.) We heard plenty of amphibians, of which the tree frog and the cricket frog were the most vociferous. At 3 mi we returned to the parking area.

Support Facilities: For the nearest campground see Andrew Jackson State Park.

Information: Contact Superintendent, Landsford Canal State Park, Route 1, Box 423, Catawba, SC 29704; (803) 789–5800.

Oconee State Park (Oconee County)

Oconee State Park is scenic, peaceful, and characteristic of everything inviting about the Appalachians. Centered among mountain ranges, lakes, rivers, waterfalls, and historic places, the 1,165-acre park was donated to the state by Oconee County in 1935. Surrounded by wilderness regions of the Andrew Pickens District of the Sumter National Forest, the park is only 10 miles from the Chattooga River, a National Wild and Scenic River. To the north is the Ellicott Rock Wilderness Area; the Upper and Lower Whitewater Falls, among the highest in eastern America; Walhalla Fish Hatchery, one of the largest trout hatcheries in the world; and the Jocassee Lake, probably the state's most beautiful. South of the park is the Stumphouse Mountain Tunnel and the legendary Issaqueena Falls, and Tugaloo Lake. To the east is Oconee Station, an old Indian fort and the oldest building (1760) in the county.

In the park is the southern terminus of the Foothills Trail, the state's longest trail. Clogging and square dancing are part of the weekly folklife program; a museum portraying the pioneer life of the mountain people, biological study projects, and a restaurant serving the best of mountain cooking are part of the activities and facilities. With such an ideal sylvan environment for rusticating, it is no surprise that Bob Cothran has been the park superintendent for twenty years.

164

"I've always loved the mountains, particularly in the springtime," he says. "I guess I'll retire here . . . it is home." The peace and satisfaction on Bob's face were a reflection of Gibran's philosophy that "he who lives a single Springtime (with nature) is like one who lives for ages."

The park offers 140 campsites, 19 cabins, a primitive campground, a park store, a camper's recreation building and community recreation building, picnic areas, a seasonal restaurant, a 20-acre lake for fishing, swimming, and pedal boating, a playground, carpet golf, and hiking trails.

Access: From Walhalla on SC 28 go 1 mi N to jct of SC 28 and SC 107. Follow SC 107 for 2 mi to the park entrance. From Cashiers in North Carolina, follow SC 107 S.

Wormy Chestnut Trail

Length: 2.2 mi rt (3.5 km); **easy;** USGS Maps: Tamassee, Walhalla; trailhead: near bathhouse.

Steve Harris and I started on this nature trail late on a spring afternoon. Leaving the bathhouse area, we followed the trail along the lake through a stand of white pines, crossed a grassy meadow and picnic area, and entered the woods again where mountain laurel, pinxter, yellow violets, and ferns were abundant. At 0.4 mi we turned L at a "Nature Trail" sign and followed a ridge, then a slope, and reached a paved road at 0.7 mi. We crossed the road at a parking area and ascended on a well-maintained trail. Patches of huckleberries were on the side of the trail, and gold stars bloomed under our feet. Descending, we saw wild orchids, ostrich and cinnamon ferns, Indian cucumber root, devil's bit, and fetterbush. At 0.9 mi we passed an old spring and campground area; remains of a rock dam were nearby. At 1 mi we were back at the paved road, but we chose to take a L on the road rather than backtrack on the trail. This route led us for 0.4 mi on the road to cabin #4 and the lake. Here we went across a boardwalk and on a scenic trail around the lake. Alder, yellow root, ferns, wood betony, false indigo, galax, and trailing arbutus grew in the area. At

2 mi we reached the lake's dam and spillway, where we turned R and walked back to the trading post and campground.

Oconee Trail

Length: 3.2 mi rt (5.1 km); **moderate**; USGS Maps: Tamassee, Walhalla; trailhead: amphitheater parking lot.

Steve Harris and I started out early, hoping to photograph wildlife. We were rewarded with meeting deer, raccoons, wood ducks, box turtles, squirrels, and fence lizards, but no bear (campground rumor held that bear were in the area). The trail terrain was rugged and wild in sections after we passed the Oconee Lake.

From the parking lot behind the trading post we followed a trail marked "OT." Ranger James Bynum said this was done by a troop of Boy Scouts from Summerville. At the lake we turned R, wound through the woods, and crossed the dam at 0.7 mi. We went up a narrow ravine through a mountain-laurel thicket. A number of crosstrails, if taken to the L, led back to the campground. We continued straight ahead following the "OT" signs and descended to a stream lined with fetterbush, ferns, and Canada violets at 1.3 mi. At 1.5 mi a sign at an old woods road indicated we had finished Section #1. A turn L would take us to the cabins (we did not investigate where a R would have gone). To enter Section #2 we went straight ahead, descending and ascending in ravines on an ungraded trail. Steve and I agreed that the Boy Scouts who designed this trail into the chasms had more energy than we had. At 2.4 mi we crossed an old trail and again descended into a hollow. We emerged from the forest at the Foothills Trail on the R and the paved road to the cabins on the L at 2.7 mi. We walked to the R on the paved road for an additional 0.5 mi to return to the campground.

Foothills Trail (Park Section)

Length: 1.2 mi (1.9 km); **easy;** USGS Maps: Tamassee, Walhalla; trailhead: Foothills Trail sign.

To reach this trailhead go 0.5 mi E on the paved road from the trading post and campground to the Foothills Trail sign on the SE cabin-area road. Parking space is limited. From this point you can go 0.4 mi within the park boundary to a jct on the R with the Tamassee Trail or to the L on the Foothills Trail. If you take the latter, you can hike to the Long Mountain Lookout Tower for a round trip of 4.4 mi. If you hike the Tamassee Knob Trail for a round trip, it is 5 mi. (See section on the Andrew Pickens Ranger District, Sumter National Forest, for descriptions of these trails.)

Information: Contact Park Superintendent, Oconee State Park, Star Route, Walhalla, SC 29691; (803) 638–5353/5296.

Paris Mountain State Park (Greenville County)

In 1935 the state acquired 1,275 acres of forest from the city of Greenville to create the Paris Mountain State Park. The acreage included mountaintop ridges of Virginia pine, rugged slopes with dense stands of rosebay rhododendron, and clear cascading streams. One of these streams was impounded in 1898 as a reservoir for the Greenville Water Works. It served the city until the early 1930s, when the Table Rock and North Saluda reservoirs took its place. The CCC developed the area in the mid-1930s, and the park opened in June 1937. Some of the CCC stone and wooden buildings, such as the bathhouse, remain in use.

Paris Mountain got its name from Capt. Richard Pearis (Paris), the first white settler in the Greenville area, ca. 1766. He held a trust of 10 square miles (present-day Greenville), which had been given to him by George II of England.

Facilities in the park are a 50-site campground, a primitive campground, an amphitheater, picnic areas, a bathhouse, a lake for swimming and fishing, a campground for organized youth camping, playground equipment, hiking trails, and nature-study areas. "We hope to extend our hiking trails," Park Ranger David Blackwell said, "so that hikers can go from Sulphur Springs to Buckhorn Lake." He showed me around the park and stopped by the state's largest Virginia pine near the Sulphur Springs Picnic Area.

The park has more than 75 species of trees and shrubs, more than 80 species of wildflowers, and more than 30 species of birds. Finches and wrens are seen frequently.

Paris Mountain Trail

Length: 6.6 mi rt (10.6 km); strenuous; USGS Map: Greenville NW, NE; trailhead: Sulphur Springs Picnic Area.

Dick Hunt and I began this unmarked trail at the Sulphur Springs Picnic Area parking lot. After 100 yards we crossed a footbridge over a creek. To our L was the state's largest Virginia pine, more than 8 ft in cir. (The park also has the state's largest Table Mountain pine, near the top of Paris Mountain.) Continuing upstream, we passed under large oaks, pines, and poplars. Hugging the creek banks and on the steep slopes were alder, yellow root, mountain laurel, and rosebay rhododendron. Ferns, partridge berry, and mosses covered the level spots. We crossed the creek again at 0.3 mi near a large gazebo, and at 0.5 mi we noticed an unmarked jct with a spur trail to the L. (This unmaintained and unmarked spur trail crossed the creek below the Mountain Lake stone reservoir, ascended steeply to the ridge crest, then descended to a ravine at 0.1 mi. The trail ascended steeply again to another ridge at 0.4 mi and turned L on an old woods road to the Sulphur Springs Picnic Area parking lot at 0.7 mi—a total of 1.3 mi for the loop.)

After exploring the spur trail we continued upstream and climbed the bank at the reservoir. New Jersey tea, sensitive briar, goat's pea, and Indian plantain grew on the red-clay banks among rocks and exposed tree roots. At 0.6 mi we rock-hopped the creek in a grove of fetterbush and low-hanging rhododendron. Ahead of us was a poplar with warty knobs, centered in a fork in the trail at 0.8 mi. We took the trail to the R across the creek, climbed the stone steps, and rock-hopped the stream again. At 1 mi we reached an ideal campsite. (The area is designated as a primitive campground, and permits from the superintendent's office are required.) Nearby were wild hydrangea, crested dwarf iris, pussy toes, wild ginger, sweet pepperbush, and rosebay rhododendron. We ascended on a steep grade where the stream cascaded on our R, and rock-hopped again at 1.3 mi where the creek splashed over a tier of rocks.

We began a steep climb through a stand of chestnut oak and rocky terrain. After a small dip over the ridge came the final ascent along a slope to the mountaintop. At 1.7 mi we reached an old roadbed, once used to reach a former firetower. Across the road were the foundations of the firetower, rock and brick chimneys of a former forester's home, and artifacts of other outbuildings. At this point a number of trails extended through the forest, but the correct route was to take the old road to the R. Along the way was a mixed forest with plenty of sourwood and mountain laurel. We followed a gradual grade on a generally smooth surface for 1.6 mi to the paved park road for a total of 3.3 mi. From here we could have hiked the paved road to the R down the mountain for 1 mi to the Sulphur Springs Picnic Area. But we did not know at that time it was 1 mi; so, we hiked back up the mountain on the old road and down the rough terrain to be sure we got back to where we started.

Lake Placid Trail

Length: 0.7 mi (1.1 km); **easy**; USGS Map: Greenville NE; trailhead: bathhouse.

I started this trail at the bathhouse, aware that bathers close to the trail would wonder what I was doing pushing a measuring wheel. I had gone about 50 yards when Jamie Rodgers, a 9-year-old boy with freckles, rode up beside me on his Mongoose bike. "Can I go with you?" he asked. His bike bumped over the little footbridge at the lake headwaters. He had ridden the trail so many times he knew each tree at each interpretive post—beech, sycamore, black locust, poplar, hickory, and dogwood. "I live just down the road from the park, I come up here every day," he said. At 0.4 mi I walked down to the base of the dam, but Jamie chose the nearby road to avoid the rocks and the creek. We continued on the trail by a picnic shelter and crossed a wood viaduct with five stone pillars built by the CCC. At 0.7 mi we returned by the swimming area. "Would you like to go around again?" Jamie asked, poised on his Mongoose as if to race with "Clicker," the measuring wheel.

Information: Contact Superintendent, Paris Mountain State Park, Route 12, Box 221, Greenville, SC 29609; (803) 244–5565.

Rose Hill State Park (Union County)

Between 1828 and 1832, a federal-style three-story house of red brick and split-shingle roof was constructed on a rolling hill south of Union in Union County. It had a front-door fanlight, a graceful spiral stairway in the center of the main hall, a ballroom, and, on the third floor, a classroom for the owner's 13 children. In the 1850s it was remodeled with stucco over the bricks and two-story porches.

It was "Rose Hill," the home of William H. Gist (1807-1874), who was elected to the South Carolina House of Representatives in 1840 and to the Senate in 1844. Four years later he was elected lieutenant governor and ten years later, governor. He is often referred to as the state's "Secession Governor." But he was more than a political figure; he was also manager of his cotton plantation at "Rose Hill." In 1960 the mansion and 44 acres were purchased for a state park.

Visitors today will see a completely remodeled structure with a rebuilt outhouse kitchen and a number of other outbuildings. One exhibit building has a display of plantation life and cotton culture; another has two carriages. "I hope

171

we can get the carriages restored," Chris Hightower, park superintendent, said as he showed me the plantation grounds.

Access: From jct of US 176 and SC 215 in Union go 8 mi S on SR 16 to park entrance.

Rose Hill Nature Trail

Length: 0.6 mi (1 km); easy; USGS Map: Whitmire N; trailhead: behind the group picnic shelter.

I entered the forest from the open field behind the group picnic shelter and followed the trail signs. The forest was mainly oaks and pines. Honeysuckle formed a forest ground cover and a number of wildflowers, such as rattlesnake orchids, were noticeable. At 0.4 mi I turned sharply L and ascended to the rose gardens. Adjoining them is the formal garden in the shape of the Confederate flag.

Information: Contact Park Superintendent, Rose Hill State Park, Sardis Road, Route 2, Union, SC 29379; (803) 427–5966.

Sadlers Creek State Park (Anderson County)

Sadlers Creek State Park is 395 acres of hardwood and pine forest on the north side of Hartwell Lake. It was leased from the U.S. Army Corps of Engineers in 1966. The park offers fishing, boating, water skiing, and camping. In addition to the 100 campsites on the peninsula, it has a primitive campground, recreation building, picnic area, playground, and community activities building.

Although the Cherokee Indians once lived in the area, only a few artifacts have been found. A few English settlers' house foundations have also been found; an old brick foundation was located near the park superintendent's residence. "My uncle, Gordon Smith, once lived there," Park Ranger Herbert Jones said.

How red was the clay on the shoreline with a red sunset up the lake! Silhouetted ducks came up the clay banks for food. By dark the screech owls were giving their eerie sounds over the din of the cicadas.

Access: From the jct of SC 24 and 187, take SC 187 for 7 mi to the park road on the R and go 1.2 mi to the park entrance.

Pine Grove Trail

Length: 0.6 mi (1 km); **easy;** USGS Map: Hartwell NE; trailhead: pavilion parking area.

From the parking area at the pavilion, I went R, near the restroom, and followed the trail sign. On a well-graded and well-maintained trail I passed through a mixed forest by the lake. I saw oaks, hickory, pines, maple, honey locust, dogwood, wild cherry, sumac, deerberry, redbud, and honeysuckle. Chunks of quartz added beauty to the winding path. At 0.2 mi I crossed a paved road with a cul-de-sac to the L, made a curve around a bench (designed as a love seat), crossed the road again, and returned to the point of origin at 0.6 mi.

Information: Contact Superintendent, Sadlers Creek State Park, Route 4, Box 375, Anderson, SC 29624; (803) 226–8950/7156.

Table Rock State Park (Pickens County)

No one seems to know his name, but many know the legend of a prodigious Cherokee chieftain god who used the "Sah-ka-na-ga," Great Blue Hills of God, as he wished. To dine he sat on a 2,700-foot mountain, and for his table he used a 1.3 billion-year-old granite mountain, now called Table Rock. It is 3,157 feet high and composed of feldspar, biotite, quartz, and amphibole. It has patches of vegetation on the summit already mixed like a garden salad for the chieftain. This colossal table of volcanic origin is part of the 3,069-acre Table Rock State Park.

Development of the base area by settlers began in the early nineteenth century, and by 1840 a hotel was constructed for a vacation resort. In 1935 the state acquired the park area as a gift from the city of Greenville and Pickens County. Five years later the park opened to the public after development by the CCC.

Park facilities include Pinnacle Lake, a 36-acre swimming, boating, and fishing area; a picnic area; a carpet golf course; a nature center; two campgrounds with a total of 100 units; a country store; a community recreation center; a meeting house; 15 cabins; a bathhouse; a lodge and restaurant (closed Dec. 23 through Jan. 31), and three exciting trails for hiking.

Access: Turn off SC 11 at the park signs, 4.4 mi E of the jct with US 178 and 4.7 mi W of the jct with SC 8.

Table Rock Trail

Length: 6.8 mi rt (10.9 km); **strenuous**; USGS Map: Table Rock; trailhead: Nature Center.

I started on the Table Rock Trail, a National Recreation Trail, early one morning with a group of friends. After 0.1 mi we left the asphalt trail near a waterfall on Carrick Creek, crossed the creek on a wooden bridge, and at 0.2 mi turned R, on the red-blazed trail. (The green-blazed Carrick Creek Trail also follows this route for the first 0.5 mi.) A warning sign reminded us not to underestimate our time and be caught on the trails after dark. We walked through a ground cover of partridge berry in a basic oak-hickory forest with scattered pines and hemlock. After crossing Green Creek for the last time, the Carrick Creek Trail veered L at 0.5 mi and the Table Rock Trail ascended steeply in an open forest. Gigantic boulders appeared poised to roll down the steep mountain side, smashing the Cherokee Chieftain's toes. At 1.6 mi we reached a rain shelter built by the CCC in 1938. At 1.9 mi we climbed to the jct with Pinnacle Trail at Panther Gap. Signs estimated it would take 1 1/2 hours to hike to the Governor's Rock at 2.5 mi. The rock steps here were carved out of the granite by a battery-powered air hammer. At 2.7 mi there was a spring (but it is recommended that you do not drink from it).

We reached the forest-covered summit at 3 mi, then descended for another 0.4 mi to a sweeping view of Table

Rock Lake, Caesar's Head, and the smaller foothills. Hans Freytag of Greenville was sitting at this scenic place with his teenage twins, Annette and Michael. A textile engineer who was born in Germany, he told us: "We hiked in Bavaria, we love nature."

Sitting nearby were Taylor Watts, Kevin Clarey, and Les Parks, three first-class Boy Scouts of Troop 26 in Easley. "We tried to run up the mountain," said Les, the youngest, still short of breath. They were camping at the park's primitive campsite.

As I left the Chieftain's dining table, I thought about what Mike Hendrix, park superintendent, had said to me the day before: "Everything about this park I like: the lake, the streams, Table Rock; it's like a magnet—once you are on it, it's hard to get off."

Pinnacle Trail

Length: 7.2 mi rt ct (11.5 km); **exceptionally strenuous**; USGS Maps: Table Rock, Eastatoe Gap; trailhead: Nature Center.

I followed the same route for this trail (called a connector on the state's application for the status of a National Recreation Trail) as for the Table Rock Trail to Panther Gap at 1.9 mi. Here I turned L on the ridge, following the yellow blaze. The trail climbed to the first peak, but skirted the S slope of the second peak to Hemlock Gap at 2.6 mi. (At this point an 0.8-mi connector trail, L, descends to rejoin the Pinnacle Trail without climbing the Pinnacle.) Continuing ahead on a steep ascent, I reached the summit (3,425 ft) of the Pinnacle at 3.6 mi, the highest point in the park.

I was disappointed that there was no view. Instead, a sign warned me that I would "be prosecuted to the full limit of the law" if I trespassed on the watershed of the City of Greenville a few yards N. A former climber, Chet, had written on the sign, "I did it for Jan." There was solace in seeing a garden of wildflowers—horsemint, meadow rue, yellow flowering bear's foot, New York fern, and more Carolina pink (a scarlet gentian-shaped flower with five yellow corolla lobes) than I have seen anywhere. Although *Lilium canadense*, Canada lily, grows nowhere else in the state but in this area, I found what I think is a rare red *Lilium grayi*, the orange bell lily.

I descended 0.2 mi to join the Foothills Trail for a descent to the Nature Center. At 4.2 mi was a magnificent view of the farms and forest S of the Pinnacle. Wild quinine and blackberries grew on damp spots of the rock face. The trail descended steeply on slippery rocks and roots and narrow sections along Carrick Creek. At 6.4 mi I rejoined the green-blazed Carrick Creek Trail and exited at the Nature Center for a round trip of 7.2 mi.

Carrick Creek Trail

Length: 1.8 mi (2.9 km); **easy to moderate;** USGS Map: Table Rock; trailhead: Nature Center.

From the Nature Center I followed the same route as for the Table Rock Trail, but after 0.5 mi turned L on the green-blazed Carrick Creek Trail. In a mixed hardwood forest were dogwoods, sourwood, and mountain laurel. I crossed a small stream at 0.9 mi and reached a jct with the Pinnacle Trail and Foothills Trail at 1 mi. I turned L, descended, and crossed Carrick Creek a number of times. Sheets of water seemed to slide through the flumes, lightly from rocky lips, and cascade over one another at rugged strips of rocks. (Please obey the signs and do not swim or slide down the rock slopes.)

Information: Contact Park Superintendent, Table Rock State Park, Route 3, Pickens, SC 29671; (803) 878–9813/6641.

Wildcat Wayside State Park (Greenville County)

Wildcat Wayside is a 63-acre state park limited to picnicking and nature study. It was transferred to the state-park system in 1971 from the state highway department.

Access: From the jct of US 276 and SC 11 at Cleveland go W for 5 mi to the Wayside on the R. From the US 276 and SC 11 jct W, go E 0.7 mi to park on L.

Wildcat Nature Trail

Length: **0.8** mi rt (1.3 km); **easy**; USGS Map: Cleveland; trailhead: parking area.

From the parking area we climbed the steps of the bank, crossed a bridge over a cascade and entered an old picnic ground. We crossed another bridge at 0.1 mi and followed a pleasant trail under large hemlocks by Wildcat Branch. At 0.4 mi we reached the base of a high slab of a granite slide, over which the branch flows. Mountain laurel, rhododendron, and wildflowers grew along the trail.

Information: Contact Program Section, Director of State Park, Dept. of PRT, 1205 Pendleton St., Columbia, SC 29201; (803) 758–3622.

Aiken State Park (Aiken County)

Purchased in 1934, the Aiken State Park opened two years later with 1,067 acres. Its location on the Aiken Plateau includes four spring-fed lakes and the winding South Edisto River. Millions of years ago the area was a beach for an ancient ocean. Facilities in the park include 25 campsites (under an exceptionally beautiful canopy of longleaf pines), a youth camp for Boy Scouts, picnic areas, a lake for swimming, fishing (for bream, bass, and crappie), pedal boating, and hiking trails.

Access: From the jct of SC 4 and SR 53 in Windsor, take SR 53 5 mi N to park entrance.

Jungle Trail

Length: 2.4 mi (3.8 km); easy; USGS Map: Seivern; trailhead: parking area at swimming lake.

I started at dawn from the parking area of the picnic and swimming lake and soon noticed that the trail was being relocated to raise it from a boggy level. Water in this area comes from the clear spring water that feeds the lakes. At 0.1 mi I took the L fork. Bays, wax myrtle, ostrich ferns, sweet pepperbushes, and switchcane were thick on the trail borders. At 0.3 mi I went L again where bracken, sensitive ferns, and blueberries were frequent. At 0.8 mi I took the L at an intersection to the Fishlake picnic area. I turned R on the paved road to the Riverside picnic area where a strong artesian well provided cold drinking water. Reentering the woods, I faced the intersection again and took the L toward Cypress Stump picnic area. Along the way I stopped to feast on the ripe blueberries; a deer saw me, watched a few seconds, then bolted into deeper woods. At 1.5 mi I saw where turpentine had been extracted from the longleaf pine. After 0.2 mi I crossed the paved road and a stream to the Cypress Swamp picnic area. Immediately I curved R to cross the road again and enter the forest. At 1.9 mi I crossed a boardwalk and heard considerable noise from the forest. I saw cardinals, warblers, and towhees busy with the morning chores. The loop was now complete at 2.3 mi, where I turned L to return to the parking area for a total of 2.4 mi.

Information: Contact Superintendent, Aiken State Park, Route 1, Box 24, Windsor, SC 29856; (803) 649–2857.

Barnwell State Park (Barnwell County)
Barnwell State Park, with 307 acres, was donated to the state by Barnwell County in 1937; the park opened in 1939. Historians say that the first American-made steam locomotive, built for the South Carolina Railroad Company, made its maiden run out of Charleston to this area in 1833. The nearby town of Blackville was named after Alexander Black, who secured funding for the railroad. Park facilities include 25 campsites, five vacation cabins, picnic areas, a community recreational building, lake swimming and fishing, a playground, and hiking trails.

Barnwell Lake Trail and Discovery Trail
Length: **1.7 mi** ct (2.7 km); **easy**; USGS Map: Blackville; trailhead: family campground.

Every time I have been to this trail, it has rained. On the rainy morning that I measured the trail, I left from campsite 11, followed the trail to the dam at 0.1 mi, crossed a boardwalk, and skirted R of the camp cottages. (On the L between cabins 2 and 3 is the trailhead for the Discovery Trail, a 0.2-mi loop trail for the physically handicapped. It leads through a fine section of tall hardwoods and pine with yellow jessamine and wild orchids decorating the ground. Entrance to three cabins is 0.6 mi R from the park entrance.) After examining the Discovery Trail I continued ahead through the forest of poplar, holly, and bays near a marsh. I followed the edge of the second lake by a swimming area and the community center at 0.6 mi. Large oaks and pines were here. I descended to the spillway on a service road where other large trees make the understory sparse. When

I reached the paved road bridge at 0.7 mi, I turned R over the bridge and made a sharp R to streamside. Following upstream over boardwalks, I reached the dam at 0.8 mi, turned L, and entered the woods to reach a picnic shelter area at 1.1 mi. To the R was an unusually attractive fishing pier and observation deck. I completed the loop at 1.4 mi and turned L to my point of origin at 1.5 mi (1.7 mi including Discovery Trail). (A 0.2-mile fisherman's trail continues along the upper lake to an old spring in a bog.)

Information: Contact Superintendent, Barnwell State Park, Route 2, Box 147, Blackville, SC 29817; (803) 284–2212.

Cheraw State Park (Chesterfield County)

Cheraw State Park, established on March 22, 1934, is the state's oldest, and the second largest, with 7,361 acres. (The Sandhill State Forest adjoins it on the southwest.) Named from the Indian word Cheraw, meaning "Fire Town," the park was made possible by local citizens and businesses of the town of Cheraw and Chesterfield County who gave the state 704 acres. After acquiring the additional property, the state created the 3-mile, 300-acre Lake Juniper (also called Eureka Lake), constructed 25 campsites by the lake, eight cabins, a community center, sheltered picnic facilities, a swimming area, trails, and an archery range. Other facilities allow for fishing boats and pedal boats. Two large organized group camps—Camp Forest and Camp Juniper—are on the south side of the lake to provide privacy. A separate gated entrance to the group camps is on US 52, 0.3 mi southeast from the park entrance.

Located in the Sandhills, this park has sections of white sand that look like snow patches. Pine forests, the chief timber source, are under timber management because of a 1955 fire that damaged 50 percent of the park. Wildflowers, songbirds, and migratory wildfowl are prominent. One cold January night a hiking companion, Buster White, and I were camped in the park. Snow had been forecast; the campground was deserted. Daylight changed all that. Five recreation vehicles arrived from Ohio and the sun burned through the mist. "I bring my family here every winter to see the Canada geese," explained a naturalist, Breck Poplowski, from Columbus. "I brought some other families this year . . . without the snow it's like Florida to us." Breck told me about a rare plant in the park (*Hudsonia ericoides*), a low spreading evergreen flowering shrub.

Access: From jct of US 1/52 and SC 9 in Cheraw, go S on US 1/52 for 2.4 mi to fork. Entrance on US 52 L is 0.8 mi on R; entrance from US 1 R is ahead for 1.6 mi on L.

Dogwood Lake Nature Trail and Wilderness Trail

Length: 2.1 mi ct (4.3 km); easy; USGS Map: Cheraw; trailhead: Dogwood Picnic Area.

From the Dogwood Picnic Area and shelter we went R, descending to the lake. Across the dam and spillway, we went R around the lake to an unusual boulder at 0.5 mi. Across a boardwalk at headwaters were 13 interpretive markers. Vegetation included longleaf pine, mountain laurel, cedar, juniper, switchcane, holly, dogwood, yellow jessamine, trumpet plant, and asters. Both red-cockaded woodpeckers and blue birds have been seen. We completed the loop at 0.9 mi and returned to the parking area.

Another trail, the 0.6 mi **Wilderness Trail** begins at the swimming area bathhouse and office. After walking through a forest of oaks, bays, longleaf pines and holly, we crossed a footbridge at 0.4 mi. The trail dead-ended at the spillway; we backtracked for a total of 1.2 mi.

Other things to see and do in the area include the Cheraw National Fish Hatchery (unless the federal government has closed it by the time you read this book), 1 mi S on US 1 from the park; the Carolina Sandhills National Wildlife Refuge and the Sandhill State Forest, farther S on US 1; and Old St. David's Episcopal Church (1768) in Cheraw, 2 mi N of the park.

Information: Contact Superintendent, Cheraw State Park, Route 2, Box 888, Cheraw, SC 29520; (803) 537–2215/2291.

Dreher Island State Park (Newberry County)

The 340-acre Dreher Island State Park has multiple peninsulas in the 50,000-acre Lake Murray northwest from Columbia. When it was leased from the S.C. Electric and Gas Company in 1970, there was some controversy about its safety. It had been a WWII bombing range, and, in 1958, the Air Force uncovered and destroyed approximately 2,200 duds on the premises. In 1972, Mike Stevens, historic research coordinator of PRT in Columbia, recommended that the park honor the B-52 bomber of WWII, its pilots (one of whom was Gen. Jimmy Doolittle), and its missions over Japan, by naming the park, a "World War II Interpretive Park."

Most of the early settlers in this area were Scotch-Irish and German. One German community was called "Dutch Fork," the site of George Drehr's Mill (note old spelling). William (Billy) H. Dreher, for whom the park is named, was a descendant of the "Dutch Fork" Germans.

Facilities in the park include 111 campsites, a camp recreation building, a primitive campground, a trading post, a tackle shop, a community recreation building, a number of picnic areas, a playground, fishing, a boat ramp, a swimming area, and a youth camp.

Robert Parrish, park superintendent, told me about an unmarked and generally unknown trail made by Boy Scouts. I explored it from across the road at the Youth Camp entrance. After 0.2 mi under the power line, I saw a sign, "Eagle Project by Gerald Meetze, 1981." The trail turned L at the sign in an open mixed forest with an understory of cedar, maple, dogwood, sourwood, and mountain laurel. After 0.1 mi the guide points required a compass. Following the guide points I returned to the park road after 1 mi.

Access: From US 76 in Little Mountain take SR 271 for 2.8 mi to SR 20. Follow SR 20 for 3.5 mi to jct with SR 26. Turn L on SR 26, and follow SR 26 to SR 571 and then to the park for 4 mi. If from US 76 in Prosperity, follow SR 26 all the way to SR 571.

Billy Dreher Nature Trail

Length: 0.2 mi (0.3 km); **easy;** USGS Map: Lake Murray W; trailhead: behind the community rec bldg at parking area.

I noticed a sign that read, "Billy Dreher Nature Trail, an Eagle project by David Haskell, Troop 95, 1981." I walked under tall oaks, pines, walnut, mulberry, and gums, many of which were dressed in English ivy. After 0.1 mi I saw the foundation and fallen chimney of Billy's ancestral homeplace. The trail circled back to the parking area.

Who was Billy Dreher? Research in the PRT office and in the Lexington and Newberry counties register of deeds offices, led me to Harriette Chapman Epting (Mrs. James H. Epting). She told me that Billy was born June 13, 1857; died April 8, 1938; and was buried in the Prosperity cemetery. He was a farmer, and he "loved his spirits in earthenware jugs," she said. "He also loved the women, but he never married."

She said she was not related to Billy, but Billy's niece, Lillian, was the half-sister of her grandfather, John Jacob Chapman. Billy had three sisters: Almenia (mother of Lillian), Martha (who married a Dennis), and Louisa (who married a Price). Lillian, who never married, moved in with her uncle Billy at the homeplace to take care of him, but in 1929 they moved off the island because Lake Murray was being impounded between 1927 and 1930. They moved to Prosperity to live with Billy's sisters. Lillian survived them all, but needed someone to take care of her in her old age. That person was Harriette, who at the death of Lillian was willed the Dreher property.

"I have Billy's metal driver's license in my purse," Harriette said. "I've carried them since Aunt Lillian gave them to me. Do you think I could use Billy's license to have a permanent pass to the park?" she said, smiling. "Why don't we ask?" I replied.

Information: Contact Superintendent, Dreher Island State Park, Route 1, Box 351, Prosperity, SC 29127; (803) 364–3530/4152.

Lake Wateree State Park (Fairfield County)

Lake Wateree State Park takes its name from the Wateree River that was dammed to make the lake. It is a beautiful 238-acre park between I-77 and Lake Wateree, near Great Falls. It is open all year and has outdoor recreation areas for family camping with full service, picnicking, sailing, boating, and fishing for white and largemouth bass, stripers, catfish, bream, and crappie. It has a commissary-tackle shop, boat ramps, and in-boat fueling station.

Access: From I-77 E of Winnsboro, take SC 41 E to US 21. Turn L and go N 2.1 mi to jct with SC 101, River Rd, and turn R. Follow SC 101 4 mi to the park entrance, L, for a total of 8.8 mi from I-77.

Desportes Island Nature Trail

Length: 0.7 mi (1.1 km); **easy**; USGS Map: Flint Hill; trailhead: entrance road.

The trail is a partial loop at the E end, and it begins on the entrance road across the jct with the campground entrance. Another entrance is at the edge of the parking lot at the tackle shop. The trail can be used by the physically handicapped. Along the way we saw wildflowers, ferns, loblolly pines, oaks, and sparkleberry. In all seasons there are wild turkey, deer, ducks, and other waterfowl.

Information: Contact Superintendent, Lake Wateree State Park, Route 4, Box 282-E-5, Winnsboro, SC 29180; (803) 482–3123.

Lee State Park (Lee County)

Lee State Park, opened to the public in 1941, contains 2,839 acres of natural pristine forest, snowy white sandhills, sequestered swamps, and outstanding recreational facilities for swimming, camping, fishing, picnicking, and community-center activities. The area is a delight for birders, hikers,

and equestrians. For those interested in nature study, there is the usually languid Lynches River, the Sandhill Natural Area, and hidden oxbow lakes. A 4.5-mile loop road and self-guiding auto trail, which can also be hiked, provides a dozen stops at historic, scenic, and unique points of interst. One unique point is on Mulberry Island, where two artesian wells bubble in cairns, and another is an elevated privy near a picnic area. A horse show ring is used by local horse clubs. "We have nearly 30 miles of horse trails," said the superintendent, Mike Mathis. Campground facilities include 50 sites, and there is a special campground on the loop road for Boy Scouts.

Access: From I-20 at jct of SR 22 go NW 1 mi on SR 22 to park entrance. (From US 15 and SC 34, 3.4 mi N of Bishopville, take SR 22 R and go 3.6 mi on SR 22 to park entrance on R.)

Artesian Nature Trail

Length: 1 mi (1.6 km); **easy**; USGS Map: Bishopville E; trailhead: picnic and parking area.

From the park entrance I drove 1 mi and turned L to the picnic area and community building at the parking area. After parking, I hiked across the dam, the site of an old grist mill. Spanish moss hung from oaks. At 0.1 mi I turned R, followed the banks of three small former fish-hatchery lakes and entered a forest with a swamp on the L. Vegetation was loblolly, oak, hickory, holly, and dogwood. Exceptionally large sweet gums and tulip poplar towered on the L. I crossed on the entrance road in a sand barren at 0.5 mi and a small stream at 0.7 mi. I continued around the edge of the forest by beds of partridge berry and spots of pipsissewa, and to two gurgling artesian wells feeding the lake at 0.8 mi. The trail returns to the dam and the parking area at 1 mi.

Sandhill Nature Trail

Length: 0.6 mi (0.9 km); **easy;** USGS Map: Bishopville E; trailhead: park campground.

I entered by the sign from across the road at the campground. After 0.1 mi was the loop-trail fork: either direction led through loblolly, longleaf pine, scrub oak, holly, and a variety of *vaccinium* specimens. An example of nature's art was the lime-green reindeer moss intertwined with yellow jessamine over patterns of xeric white sand. After the loop, I returned to the campground.

Information: Contact Superintendent, Lee State Park, Bishopville, SC 29010; (803) 428-3833.

Little Pee Dee State Park (Dillon County)

On my first visit to this park Stanley Looper, park superintendent, hiked with me on a 0.7-mi temporary loop nature trail, but since then another superintendent, Mike Spivey, has completed a new loop.

In the park I have identified more than 80 trees and flowering plants—from orange milkwort to elephant's foot—and at least seven species of oaks. A wide range of songbirds kept my attention through the afternoon, and I went to sleep that night listening to a cacophony—but sometimes a harmonious choir—of frogs: tree chirpers, clackers, leopards, and young bulls.

Across the lake, over the spillway and left on an old road is a 1.2-mile round-trip hike. The park also has a number of fire lanes you can hike, but check with the ranger first. Park facilities include 50 campsites, picnic areas, fishing, hiking, swimming and nature study.

Named after the Pedee Indians who once owned the area, the location has also been called "The Devil's Woodyard." Composer Stephen Foster originally wrote Pedee in his "Old Folks at Home," but in the second version changed it to Swanee.

Access: Take SC 57 SE out of Dillon for 11 mi to SR 22, turn L and go 2 mi to the park entrance. It is 1.1 mi to the campground and parking area.

Information: Contact Superintendent, Little Pee Dee State Park, Route 2, Box 250, Dillon, SC 29530; (803) 774–8874.

Beaver Pond Nature Trail

Length: 1.3 mi rt (2.1 km); easy; USGS Map: Fork; trailhead: near campground parking lot.

The trail begins, L, on the entrance road just before the campground. I followed it through an area of planted pines, near the edge of the bay. After 0.6 mi I reached a beaver pond. Here were beavers, a beaver hut, and ducks. The trail continued in a loop through a forest of mixed pine and hardwoods.

Information: Contact Park Superintendent, Little Pee Dee State Park, Route 2, Box 250, Dillon, SC 29530; (803) 774–8872.

Lynches River State Park (Florence County)

The 668-acre Lynches River State Park was purchased in 1971. Since then it has progressed through two development stages and entered its third for recreational facilities. It has a community recreation center, a picnic area, playground equipment, a boat dock, a ball field, nature trails, and a swimming pool, which opened in 1982.

Access: From Florence go S on US 52 for 10 mi to SR 147 on the R, and go 1.8 mi on SR 147 to the park entrance on the R.

Swamp Fox Trail and Stagecoach Trail

Length: 1.7 mi rt ct (2.7 km); easy; USGS Map: Florence W; trailhead: parking area by the river.

From the parking area we followed the trail sign through a large grove of wild azaleas, where oaks and hickory were draped with Spanish moss. At 0.1 mi we reached a fork; we went L to join the Swamp Fox Trail L and the Stagecoach Trail R at 0.2 mi. We first hiked the Stagecoach Trail among thick stands of sparkleberry, mosses, and wild orchids. At 0.3 mi we veered L at a fork, and at 0.4 mi we crossed a stream and noticed holly, dogwood, river birch, and fetterbush before entering a pine forest at 0.5 mi. We turned R on an old stagecoach roadbed, and at 0.9 mi we left the road R and followed a narrow trail back to the parking area at 1.1 mi. After lunch we returned to complete the Swamp Fox Trail. At 0.2 mi we turned L, descended on steps into a floodplain (in the winter and early spring, this area may be totally under water), crossed a boardwalk section, and meandered between the cypress knees and tall trees. On our L we saw (for my first time in the state) the showy white spider lily. We soon reached the river, explored downstream for a short distance, and returned upstream through ferns, *justicia*, pickerelweed, and lizard's tail. When we neared the end of the loop we met a fisherman with six children, all eagerly participating in a fishing trip. We asked what he was catching. "A headache," he replied. "Have you ever taken six kids fishing and the darn fish ain't biting?" We returned to the parking lot after 0.6 mi on the Swamp Fox Trail for a combined trail length of 1.7 mi.

Information: Contact Superintendent, Lynches River State Park, Route 1, Box 223, Coward, SC 29530; (803) 389–2785.

Poinsett State Park (Sumter County)

Poinsett State Park is a 1,000-acre hilly and unique park on an otherwise-flat area near the Wateree Swamp on the W side of Manchester State Forest. Donated to the state in 1934 by Sumter County, the park facilities consist of 50 campsites, four vacation cabins, primitive and group campgrounds, a recreation building, a picnic area, a lake for swimming and fishing, playground equipment, pedal boats, and some unusual natural features. One of the features is Fuller's Earth, a sedimentary formation that is high in silica. Its name comes from an early use by cloth processors—fullers—to absorb or remove greases from wool. Coquina is another unusual feature here. You will notice this rock, made of naturally cemented shell fragments, probably 50 million years old, used in construction of the bathhouse and other structures. The presence of coquina indicates that at one time this area was covered by the ocean.

The park is named in honor of Charlestonian Joel Roberts Poinsett (1779-1851), a distinguished Latin American diplomat and naturalist whom one historian has called the "most versatile and cosmopolitan American of his time." In 1828 when Poinsett was U.S. minister to Mexico he brought home a wild plant (*Euphorbia pulcherrima*) that his fellow scientists named "poinsettia" in his honor.

More than 50 species of birds have been seen in the park, and more than 65 species of trees and shrubs have been classified.

Access: From the jct of US 76, 378, and SC 601 (1.7 mi W of Shaw Air Force Base), go S on SC 601 for 9.9 mi to SR 63 and turn R. Go 1.7 mi farther to park entrance. From downtown Sumter go 10.5 mi W on SC 763 to SC 261 and turn L on SC 261 to the park entrance.

Coquina Nature Trail and Hilltop Trail

Length: 2.4 mi ct (3.8 km); **easy;** USGS Map: Poinsett State Park; trailhead: parking area.

From the parking area near the bathhouse, I followed the trail signs across the lower area of the lake to the spillway and ascended in a surprisingly sylvan environment. Here were galax, mountain laurel, and trailing arbutus in contrast with coastal plain Spanish moss farther up the hillside. After passing a rain shelter, I reached a jct with Hilltop Trail at 0.8 mi. Coquina Nature Trail veered L while Hilltop Trail continued R. I chose the Hilltop Trail, hiking on a ridge. Because it was wintertime, all the oaks were gray and bleak, and the Spanish moss blended in with them. A strong wind swayed the moss mournfully, and the afternoon sun made eerie shadows. It was a choreographic *montrer* of Black Mingo dancing skeletons. At 1.2 mi I descended to the jct with the Laurel Group spur trail on the R. (From here the spur trail was 0.2 mi.) I followed the trail L and rejoined the Coquina Trail along Shank's Creek. At 1.9 mi I crossed a boardwalk in a swamp area of bays, fetterbush, and birch. More swaying banners of Spanish moss welcomed me back to the parking area.

Lookout Trail

Length: 2.5 mi rt (4 km); **easy;** USGS Map: Poinsett State Park; trailhead: parking area.

A ranger was my guide on this unofficial trail route. We left the parking lot, went N on an old road, and climbed steeply up a hill to a picnic area, called the Lookout, at 0.4 mi. We descended on a service road, crossed the paved campground road at 0.6 mi, and walked under a power line. A sign along the way said "Nature Trail." At 1.1 mi we turned R, into a forest of pines and oaks with sphagnum moss as thick as a sponge. The trail was faint, but the ranger knew the route and we reached the park entrance road at 1.2 mi. He had to return to the park office, but I reentered the trail across the road and rejoined the Coquina Trail for a return to the ranger office and parking lot at 2.5 mi.

Information: Contact Superintendent, Poinsett State Park, Route 1, Box 38, Wedgefield, SC 29168; (803) 494–8177/8192.

Redcliffe State Park (Aiken County)

Donated to the state in 1973 by John Shaw Billings, a descendant of the Hammond family, this 350-acre estate, Redcliffe, is a showpiece of Greek Revival architecture, Southern antiques, art collections, and landscaping. It was first the home of former governor James Henry Hammond (1806-1864), who had it constructed in 1858 on an airy slope of red-clay cliffs near the Savannah River. Hundreds of fruit trees for the orchards and grapevines for the vineyards were planted, including the impressive avenue of magnolias, which decorates the entrance to the mansion. The park has a picnic area, but no campground. When Superintendent Eugene Cobb showed me the mansion's interior he said that, in addition to visitors, the house is used for weddings, receptions, and meetings.

Access: From US 278, 1.5 mi E of Beech Island, take SR 580 and go 0.2 mi to park entrance on R.

Redcliffe Trail

Length: 1.7 mi (2.7 km); **easy;** USGS Map: Hollow Creek; trailhead: parking area.

I left the mansion, crossed a portion of the spacious lawn, and entered the woods near a park residence. The trail was on an eroded road, which descended deeply into a forest. It began to rain, first as a trickle in the gully of red clay, then a deluge. The road became a red river as I wobbled, balancing myself awkwardly with a camera, notebook, and measuring wheel under my raingear. At 0.6 mi was the lake, green as malachite. Surrounding me was the allure of a tropical rain forest with tall oaks, poplars, pines, and the largest crepe myrtles I have ever seen. Cedar and dogwood were being enveloped by an intertwining of wet wisteria, ivy, honeysuckle, and Spanish moss. A lone pinkroot bloomed by the trail. I crossed the head of the lake at 0.7 mi and turned R into a tunnel of cane. From here I ascended on an improving roadbed to a more even contour at 1 mi where I turned R at a road jct. I left a forest of hickory, oaks, pines, and sassafras at 1.3 mi for a beautiful view of farm fields and the mansion. After another 0.4 mi on the edge of the field and entrance road, I was back at the parking area. "Have you seen our state champions?" the superintendent asked. I had not, but I told him I would see them on a less rainy day. Redcliffe has four known "big trees": the littlehip hawthorn (*Crataegus spathulata*) with nearly 3 ft; the white mulberry (*Morus alba*) with over 9 ft; the sand post oak (*Quercus Stellata*) with over 9 ft; and the orange trifoliate (*Poncirus trifoliata*) with 4 ft and 5 in in cir.

Information: Contact Superintendent, Redcliffe State Park 181 Redcliffe Rd, Beech Island, SC 29841; (803) 827–1473.

Rivers' Bridge State Park (Bamberg County)

This historic area is the state's only state park commemorating the Confederacy. After you enter the park from SC 641 on SR 8 (7.5 mi E of Sycamore, or 7 mi W of Ehrhardt off SC 64), go 0.6 mi to the site of the Battle of Rivers' Bridge on the left. Plaques on the breastworks explain how Gen. William T. Sherman's army advanced north toward the Salkehatchie Swamp in early February 1865. Protecting the 16 bridges through the swamp were Confederate infantry, artillery, and cavalry forces of 1,200 men. Musket fire protected the bridges, but the Federal forces felled trees to make a crossing 6 miles upstream, safe from the breastworks. The result was that the Confederate Gen. Lafayette McLaws withdrew his troops. Although the delay did not prevent Sherman's forces from marching to burn McPhersonville and Columbia, the delay may well have saved other cities north of Columbia as the war was drawing to a close.

Of the 390 park acres, the first 90 (which encompassed the battle sites) were given to the Confederate Memorial Association in 1938 by John D. Jenny. Adjoining land was subsequently purchased, and in 1945 the state acquired the area for recreation and historic emphasis. Park facilities provide a swimming pool, a recreation building, a picnic area, a 25-site campground, a playground, fishing in the Salkehatchie River, primitive camping, and a nature trail.

Lupine Nature Trail

Length: 0.4 mi (0.6 km); **easy**; USGS Map: Olar; trailhead: campsite #8.

I entered the park recreational area and followed a sign to the family campground. From campsite #8 I began the hike through a young forest of holly, pines, oaks, and other hardwoods. There was a wide display of yellow jessamine and reindeer moss in the open areas. Scattered Spanish moss hung from some of the oaks. Although this was a short, quiet trail, it was excellent for nature study. The roseate lupine here was probably *Lupinus villosus*, similar to another species generally found in the sandhills range.

Information: Contact Superintendent, Rivers Bridge State Park, Ehrhardt, SC 29081; (803) 267-3675.

Santee State Resort Park (Orangeburg County)

The 2,364-acre Santee State Resort Park has nearly 1.5 million visitors annually, ranking second among the state parks. The explanation for this heavy traffic to an inland park is that Santee is the gateway to nationally famous Santee-Cooper Country, a sportsman's paradise covering three counties. In this paradise are 171,000 acres in Lakes Marion and Moultrie with 450 miles of shoreline, a national wildlife refuge, a golf course, beach resorts, historic sites, and the crossroad arteries of I-95 and I-26. The Santee Cooper Commission reports that the area is rated in the nation's top five fishing spots and "one of America's top 10 vacation spots." The area is the home of the freshwater king of fighting fish, the striped bass, but white and black bass, crappie, and bream are more general near the park area. The park occupies the south shore of Lake Marion, between the village of Santee east and Poplar Creek west.

"Eighty percent of our visitors come to fish," said Mike Davidson, park superintendent. "They also dominate the use of our cabins and our campground." The best fishing months, he said, are usually March through May.

I met Wilber and Margie Redd from Williston, who were fishing on the park pier. "We've been coming here for 15 years," Wilber said. "Who catches the most fish?" I asked. They agreed it was an even score. "But I kinda think Margie holds a record," he said, explaining how one windy morning he had lost a rod and reel in the lake. That afternoon Margie thought she had a big one, but much to her surprise and his pleasure she had hooked the eye of the lost rod and reel.

Park facilities include 30 of the popular rondette cabins and 150 campsites, a restaurant, picnic areas, a tennis court, a conference room, a swimming area, a primitive campground, a recreation building, an interpretive center, a playground, a fishing pier, and hiking and bicycle trails.

Access: From I-95 or US 301 jct in Santee go W on SC 6 for 1 mi to the park sign, and follow park directional signs.

Lakeshore Nature Trail

Length: 1.5 mi rt (2.4 km); **easy**; USGS Maps: Summerton, Vance; trailhead: end of East Park campground road.

This trail was formerly a loop created by the SC-NCHA Fall Campout in 1972, but now hikers must backtrack. From the cable gate I entered a mixed forest scattered with an understory of hawthorn (its folk medicinal value is for heart strain due to old age), dogwood, and sassafras. Views of the lake flickered through the large live oaks and wild grapevines. I descended to the beach at 0.7 mi and backtracked. (The road continued to wind around the cove. This made an excellent extension deeper into the forest where at 1 mi there were chinquapins and papaw only a few yards apart. Wildflowers bloomed on the road banks. At 2 mi I ascended a knoll and descended. After 2.9 mi I reached SC 6, less than 0.4 mi from the park entrance. A shuttle is a good idea here; otherwise the hike would be nearly 6 mi.)

Limestone Nature Trail

Length: 1 mi (1.6 km); **easy**; USGS Maps: Summerton, Vance; trailhead: parking area near pavilion and swimming area.

I followed the signs along the bank of a cove where wax myrtle leaned as if to embrace me with its fragrance. Interpretive signs were along the path. I crossed a boardwalk to a trail fork. (L went 0.2 mi to East Park Road.) I turned R and crossed a moist ground area with buckeye and papaw, then continued back through a mixed forest to signpost #6 and backtracked to the swimming area. This trail is excellent for a trip with the park naturalist who is usually on duty from June through August.

Oakpinolly Nature Trail

Length: 0.9 mi (1.5 km); **easy**; USGS Maps: Summerton, Vance; trailhead: Interpretive Center on West Park Road.

Access to this loop trail is from the Interpretive Center, the tennis court, or the "Village Round" in the cabin area. You will be on a generally open forest trail padded with pine needles and adventuresome grapevines. One spot halfway through the forest has switchcanes, ostrich ferns, and wild azaleas.

Support Facilites: The park cabins are competely furnished, including even the silverware, and accommodate a maximum of six persons. Reservations must be made well in advance. Each cabin has two bedrooms. If you are not staying in the cabins or campground and prefer an outside facility, a nearby KOA is off exit 102 on I-95, 0.4 mi on SR 400. Open all year, the campground has 200 sites, full svc, excellent rec fac. Address: KOA Santee-Lake Marion, Route 2, Box 84, Summerton, SC 29148; (803) 478–2262.

Other things to see and do nearby are the Santee Wildlife Refuge and Fort Watson Battle Site, 4 mi N on US 15-301, and Eutaw Springs Battlefield Site, 12 mi SE off SC 6.

Information: For the general area contact Santee Cooper Country, P.O.Box 40, Santee, SC 29142; (803) 854–2131. For the park contact Superintendent, Santee State Resort Park, Route 1, Box 79, Santee, SC 29142; (803) 854–2408/2546.

Sesquicentennial State Park (Richland County)

The 1,445-acre Sesquicentennial State Park was opened to the public in 1940; it had been donated to the state by the Columbia Sesqui-Centennial Commission in 1937, the city's 150th anniversary. Generally referred to as "Sesqui," it is a park of outstanding facilities, natural beauty with nature-study potential, and historic value. Among the facilities are group camping areas, an 87-site family camping area, picnic and swimming areas, trails, and sport fields. Lake fishing and pedal boating are also provided.

Unique to the park is the Train Exhibit Building, which houses a replica of America's first passenger train, "The Best Friend of Charleston," with other train exhibits. A 1756 Log House has been relocated from the county for display in the park near the main road soccer-tennis field. A State Forestry firetower is inside the park entrance gate; a climb provides a scenic view of the park's woodlands and the capital city skyline.

Access: From I-20, exit 74, at US 1 NE of Columbia go 3 mi NE on US 1 to park entrance on R.

Sandhill Nature Trail

Length: 2 mi (3.2 km); **easy;** USGS Map: Fort Jackson N; trailhead: parking area near the bathhouse.

From the parking area I went L of the bathhouse, following the trail clockwise through loblolly pines around the 30-acre lake. I crossed a small stream at 0.5 mi among oaks, dogwood, bays, poplar, bracken, and sassafras and crossed a boardwalk and a footbridge over an active brook at 0.6 mi. After another 0.1 mi a spur trail R led to an angler's tranquil pier. I continued R of the trail jct at 0.9 mi and R of the park road at 1.5 mi. The lake border had a number of wildflowers, including the *Drosera capillaris* sundew, a low plant with a pink corolla and sticky insect-catching leaves. (In contrast, the *Drosera intermedia*, which grows in the adjoining county of Lexington, has leaves that sparkle away from the rosette, and its corolla is usually white.) Other plants were ditch stonecrop, alumroot, honewort, pitcher plants, and prickly pear cactus. I passed through the picnic area to a footbridge and reached the jct with the Wild Plum Nature Trail at 1.9 mi. (A loop on the 0.2-mile Wild Plum Trail led across the branch below the dam.) I continued along the rim of the lake to complete the loop at the bathhouse and parking area.

Sesqui Physical Fitness Trail

Length: 3.5 mi (5.6 km); **easy**; USGS Map: Fort Jackson N; trailhead: road jct near the Log House.

This exercise and jogging trail (and hiking trail) began on the sand and gravel road and continued clockwise to form a loop from the Log House and soccer-tennis area. I passed a white cedar (*Chamaecyparis thyoides*) bog on the R. At 0.4 mi on the road, a "Foot Trail Only" sign is on the R for fitness stations. At 1 mi was a jct with a road on the L, but I continued R and passed a jct with the Sandhill Nature Trail at 1.4 mi. I passed the picnic area and kept R at the next jct at 1.8 mi. At 2 mi there was a jogging trail sign. Keeping R at other jcts, I returned to the Log House at 3.5 mi. Forests along the road were mainly pine, scrub oak, and a 200-acre one of planted pines. Another 100 acres in the bottomlands had primarily hardwoods.

Information: Contact Superintendent, Sesquicentennial State Park, 9564-D Two Notch Rd, Columbia, SC 29223; (803) 788–2706/0437.

Woods Bay State Park (Clarendon, Florence, and Sumter Counties)

There are hundreds of shallow, elliptical depressions known as bays in the state's coastal plains. The bays are also found in southeast North Carolina and northeast Georgia. Some of the depressions are dry; others are swamp, and a few others are beautiful lakes. They range in diameter from a few hundred feet to 5 miles. Attempts to explain this natural phenomenon include the meteorite theory, the ancient-ocean-springs theory, and the ancient-ocean-lagoons theory.

Woods Bay State Park has 1,541 acres, most of which are an open savannah near the pointed east end of the egg-shaped bay, and dense cypress swamp elsewhere. At the edge of the bay are sandy flats with loblolly pines and turkey oaks, and on the north side adjacent to the bay is the mill point pond. The park was named after Andre Woods, who once owned a gristmill at the pond. Wildlife is prominent, including numerous species of wading, perching, and preying birds. The land was purchased in 1973, and the facilities are limited to nature study and hiking, picnicking, and fishing.

Access: From I-95 (exit 141) and SC 53, take SC 53 NE for 1.3 mi. Turn R on SR 597, and go 1.6 mi. Turn L on SR 48, and go 2 mi to park entrance on R.

Mill Pond Nature Trail

Length: 0.9 mi (1.4 km); **easy**; USGS Map: Lake City; trailhead: picnic area.

Bill Sweet, park superintendent, and I were talking about how peaceful was the park. Only the sounds of the little blue herons, egrets, wood ducks, or water turkey (also called anhinga) were heard. "The anhinga has no oil glands," Bill said. "They get wet easily; that is why you see them spreading their wings to dry out." The park has bobcats, barred owls, and ospreys, he said, and "we try to make it an environmental and educational center for the public, particularly to students of nature."

The trail began at the picnic area near the parking lot and circled the mill pond. As we followed the dikes, we saw Spanish moss hanging from the cypress, gums, and pines. Growing near the edge of the pond were Virginia willow, sweet pepperbush, sweetbays, ferns, and lizard's tail. In parts of the pond area were water lilies. At 0.5 mi we reached a boardwalk that reached out into the bay and a nearby canoe trail. We walked out on the boardwalk for 0.1 mi. "We have approximately 100 alligators in here," Bill said. "Some are 12 feet long." He told me that at night the bay is full of sounds from the frogs—tree chirpers, bull, and leopards. Leaving the boardwalk, we saw white bells, yellow sundew, and bladderwort. On the way back to the parking lot, a chameleon ran in front of me and up a sapling.

Information: Contact Superintendent, Woods Bay State Park, Route 1, Box 208, Olanta, SC 29114; (803) 659–4445/4722.

SECTION 3. COASTAL REGION

Charles Towne Landing (Charleston County)

Charles Towne Landing, site of the state's first permanent English settlement in 1670, has such a wide range of attractions that hikers can "accumulate three miles before they realize it," a park public information specialist said. Other visitors may prefer a bicycle trail or to take an easy route on a tram tour. But everyone halts to look and listen on the Animal Forest Trail, an unforgettable delight for the entire family.

This natural preserve and historic site, which bills itself as "America's most unique state park," has 664 acres of untouched forests, landscaped pavilions, marshland, fragrant gardens, and special educational features. First visit the Visitor Service Complex for information. From there you may hike, rent a bike or a piroque, or take a tram out to the dock from the Transportation Center. More than 200 picnic tables are in the park, but camping is not allowed. Park facilities may be reserved for group picnics, banquets, and conventions. Feature-length movies are shown daily in the theater. Park hours are daily from 9:00 A.M. to 5:00 P.M. (9:00 A.M. to 6:00 P.M. in the summer), and admission is nominal.

Access: Entrance is off SC 171 in Charleston on the W side of the Ashley River, 0.6 mi SW from the jct of SC 7 and SC 171.

Charles Towne Garden Trails and Animal Forest Trail

Length: 3.2 mi ct (5.1 km); **easy**; USGS Map: Charleston; trailhead: Transportation Center.

From the Transportation Center, I entered a network of trails through 80 acres of many varieties of azaleas and camellias among 75 other species of flowers, trees, and shrubs. Unmarked avenues pass in between, or circle, the three lakes in the Gardens and reach the original settlement area at 0.5

mi. I turned R, to the wharf, where a full-scale replica of the 53-foot seventeenth-century trading vessel *Adventure* is docked. On the way back I veered R at the Fortified Area and entered the 1670 Experimental Crops Garden where rice, indigo, cotton, and sugar cane are grown in season. I continued to the Settlers' Life Area on the R, a reconstructed period village at 1 mi. To the L was an Interpretive Center, an audio-visual display of the settlement's first 100 years. I continued for 0.1 mi into the Animal Forest, a 20-acre natural-habitat zoo. Watching me as I watched them were red foxes; raccoons; skunks; deer wolves; elk; "Annie" the otter; pumas named "Caroline" and "Dordan"; bison; bobcats; bears named "Pete," "Pat," and "Penny"; owls; alligators, and other native animals along an 0.8-mile section of the forest. "My favorite animal is the timber wolf," a park aide said. "They are so beautiful . . . so full of mystery." From the exit of the forest, the 10,000-square-foot Geodesic Dome was on the R; the building is available for dinners, dances, trade shows, and educational programs. Returning to the Transportation Center, I completed a hike of 2.5 mi; for another 0.7 mi I could have taken the paths within the azalea and camellia gardens.

Support Facilities: One of the nearest commercial campgrounds is Oak Plantation Camps on US 17, S 9 mi from jct of US 17 and I-26. Full svc, rec fac. Open all year. Address is Route 2, Box 559, John's Island, SC 29455; (803) 766–5936.

Information: Contact Park Manager, Charles Towne Landing State Park, 1500 Old Town Rd., Charleston, SC 29407; (803) 556–4450/766–6455.

Colleton State Park (Colleton County)

Colleton State Park, the state's smallest, with only 35 acres, is nestled between the Edisto River and Canadys Steam Electric Generating Plant. Used by the U.S. Government as a CCC camp in the 1930s, the area was donated to the state in 1944. Facilities include a 25-site campground, picnicking, a playground, and fishing in the Edisto. Noise pollution is from the nearby traffic and from the sound of loudspeakers paging employees at the steam plant. You can fish in the Edisto for bass, bream, and crappie.

Access: At the jct of US 15, 10 mi N of Walterboro, and SC 61, go 0.5 mi N on US 15 to the park entrance on L.

Colleton State Park Nature Trail

Length: 0.4 mi (0.6 km); **easy;** USGS Map: St. George; trailhead: campsite #19.

I entered a mixed mature forest with scattered sections of Spanish moss and an understory of sweet pepperbush, buckeye, and sassafras. After reaching the park road, I turned L to return to the campground. The area was clean and well-maintained.

Information: Contact Superintendent, Colleton State Park, Canadys, SC 29433; (803) 538–8206.

Edisto Beach State Park (Charleston County)

Edisto Island, named for the peaceful Edisto Indians, is between the North Edisto and South Edisto rivers and faces the Atlantic Ocean. A 1,225-acre section of this enchanting island has been set apart from commercial development to form the semitropical Edisto Beach State Park. It is a jewel of diverse natural areas for botanists, archaeologists, and ornithologists. Beachcombers find plenty of shells—cockle, calico, scallop, whelk, olive—particularly after storms; sometimes they find petrified and fossilized fragments of ancient animal and plant life. Dense live oaks draped with Spanish moss, tall pines, and palmettos provide a canopy for haunting trails leading to vast open salt marshes. Facilities in the park include 75 family campsites, five vacation cabins, a picnic area, primitive camping, a camp store, an amphitheater, carpet golf, and oceanfront swimming and fishing.

Access: From the jct of US 17 and SC 174 at Osborn (7 mi E of Jacksonboro), go 22 mi on SC 174 to park entrance on L.

During my first visit to this peaceful island, I met an unofficial sentry, Johnny Metfield, relaxing at the park gate where I was waiting to see a ranger. I told Johnny I was going to hike the Indian Mound Trail. "The Indian Mounds?" he said, no longer appearing relaxed. "I don't think you wanta go there; them mounds are full of spirits . . . it's spooky back in them swamps . . . and there are moccasins, too." My interest was only enhanced.

Indian Mound Trail

Length: 3.6 mi rt (5.7 km); **easy**; USGS Maps: Edisto Beach, Edisto Island; trailhead: On R of road to cabins.

From the first state park sign on SR 174, turn R on road to cabins, and go 0.2 mi to a sign on the R. Prepare yourself: there are biting insects, poison ivy, and poisonous snakes in the area. In hot weather a repellent is essential.

I began on the old road, which has a heavy canopy of live oaks, but turned L on an unmarked trail at 0.1 mi. Red cedar, palmetto, loblolly pine, sassafras, yaupon, and wax myrtle formed thick boundaries among sections of the oaks. I saw many woodpeckers and squirrels and heard numerous animal sounds of unknown origin. At 0.4 mi the trail forked. (To the R was a short hike back to the park, handy for those who change their minds.) I continued L to a salt marsh and crossed on a boardwalk at 0.9 mi. Here the marsh provided food and shelter for waterfowl, marine life, and shellfish. Nearly halfway across the marsh, I heard the call of a marsh hen. Below me were thousands of busy periwinkles.

When I reentered the depths of the forest, a slight breeze moved the vegetation. I expected a Fizzgig of the *Dark Crystal* to leap at me with a shriek from a vine-covered stump. After 1 mi I turned L at a fork in the old road and reached the Indian Shell Mound near Scott Creek at 1.8 mi. This mound, like others in the park, may have been formed from Indian ceremonies, or it may have been simply a large pile of shell refuse. Some of the mounds may be 4,000 years old.

(Please do not disturb the mounds.) I backtracked on the old road, careful not to get lost as I explored the mysteries of the spur roads into the world of the Gelflings.

Information: Contact Superintendent, Edisto Beach State Park, 8377 State Cabin Road, Edisto Island, SC 29438; (803) 869–2156/3396.

Givhans Ferry State Park (Colleton and Dorchester Counties)

The outstanding feature of the 1,235-acre Givhans Ferry State Park is the Edisto River, on whose scenic high bluffs visitors can picnic, rent cottages, camp, hike, or use carpet-soft lawns for ballgames. Away from commercial noise, the park provides a tranquil 25-site campground and a community center. In the river are red-breast bream, bass, jackfish, crappie, and (much to my surprise on one fishing trip) flounder. Some of the regular visitors say they have seen alligators in the river.

Capt. Philip Givhan, a Revolutionary War officer and road commissioner, and his descendants maintained a ferry at this site. It was the primary crossing of the Edisto between Charleston and the upper western part of the state before the coming of railroads and highways. Mrs. W. F. Kinard of the Givhan community said that a popular local story is that the name Givhan came from the ferryman shouting for assistance with the cables: "Give me a hand." The Givhan home, over a bluff by the river, was burned by General Sherman's army in November 1864, after the destruction of the Colleton courthouse in Walterboro. (The gravestone on the bluff, near the park's community center, for an infant, Mary E. Ford, is thought to be from a family passing through the area in 1818.)

In the twentieth century the City of Charleston bought the property for its 24 mi Edisto-Goose Creek Tunnel water supply from the Edisto River. In 1934 the property was donated to the state with the provisions that the water intake and tunnel area would be protected.

I came off the nature trail on a sultry summer afternoon and met Roy Limehouse, a tall, dedicated ranger, who was picking up garbage cans in the campground. He said that as a teenager he'd spent more time in the park than anywhere else. "Campers are like my family," he said. At that moment some children riding bicycles waved and called him by name. "This job is the best thing that ever happened to me," he said with a broad smile. "Well . . . almost, my baby girl has to be the best."

On another visit I discussed the park with Superintendent Glenn Farr. Describing his familiarity with alligators at a former beach park assignment, he said when you want them to surface, "just clap your hands and swish the water. Some of my friends on a local garbage run told me alligators like marshmallows. 'No!' I said to them, 'you are just pulling my leg,' but one day, out of their sight, I tried it, and lo and behold, they were right."

Access: Enter the park on SR 30 near the jct with SC 61, 3 mi E of the community of Givhans.

Canal Nature Trail

Length: 1.3 mi rt (2 km); **easy**; USGS Maps: Maple Cone Swamp, Ridgeville; trailhead: picnic parking area.

From the most western picnic area, I began by the trail sign and descended slightly by the Charleston water intake on the L. Trees included magnolia, beech, pines, holly, and oaks. After 0.1 mi I came to a deep ravine, L, and a number of spur trails made by exploring hikers. At 0.5 mi a footbridge crossed what is locally called the canal. I followed an old road bordered with sweet pepperbushes, yellow jessamine, sensitive and ostrich ferns, and downy false foxgloves. Partridge berry patches were frequent. I reached a ball field at 0.9 mi and turned R again in a few yards into the forest. At campsite #9 I continued into the forest to the picnic area to complete the circuit.

Although not listed as a trail, there is a 5-mile service road across the road from the park entrance, which, like a crescent, goes into the forest and returns 0.7 mi from the park entrance on SR 30. When hiking this road, use caution about rattlesnakes in the area.

Information: Contact Superintendent, Givhans Ferry State Park, Route 3, Box 327, Ridgeville, SC 29472; (803) 873–0692/875–1457.

Hunting Island State Park (Beaufort County)

With 5,000 acres of forest, marsh, lagoon, and beach, the semitropical Hunting Island State Park should be on your must list of parks to visit. It is one of the state's most-visited parks; more than one and one-quarter million visitors register annually. A wide range of recreational facilities includes 200 sites for camping and 14 vacation cabins under the palmettos and pines. There are 3 miles of beach for tanning, swimming, surfing, and shell collecting. Robert Browning must have had such a beach in mind when he wrote of a large yellow half-moon and a "sea scented beach" in his "Meeting at Night."

This barrier island acquired its name from hunting of abundant wildlife. When the state acquired the property from Beaufort County in 1938, it redeveloped the island with protective measures for the wildlife, marshes, and the thick forests of palmetto and slash pine. This park is a place to observe South Carolina state trees in all their splendor. And if you wish to imagine islands made famous by Robert Louis Stevenson (or Spanish navigator Juan Fernandez), then search no longer; I think Stevenson had a park like this in mind when he wrote in his *Walking Tours*, where "thoughts take colors from what you see."

A climb of 181 steps in the Hunting Island Lighthouse (which is on the National Register of Historic Places) provides a magnificent view of the island and its estuaries. The first lighthouse was built in 1859, but beach erosion required the construction of another in 1875. By 1889 the sea had again threatened the light, and it was relocated to its current site. Using incandescent oil vapor, its candlepower was 100,000 and could be seen 18 miles away. In 1933 the lighthouse operation was discontinued.

Other facilities on the island are a park store, a nature center, a recreation building, a children's playground, picnic areas, and carpet golf. Fishing is best for whiting, spot, trout, bass, and drum in the summer and autumn. For hiking, birding, and nature study, the opportunities are constant and challenging. And on your way to or from the island, you could walk some of the historic streets in Beaufort, the state's oldest town.

Access: From the city of Beaufort at the bridge over the Beaufort River, go 16 miles on US 21 to Hunting Island across Johnston Creek. The campground entrance is on the L, SR 348; and another 0.7 mi on US 21 is the main park entrance on the L.

Lighthouse Nature Trail
Length: 0.9 mi (1.4 km); **easy**; USGS Map: St. Helena Sound; trailhead: parking area by the lighthouse.

From the lighthouse I crossed the paved area to the carpet-golf locality. Following the sign through a parking area, I took a wide trail road into a forest of palmettos and oaks, and a dense understory of yaupon for 0.4 mi to the beach. Instead of backtracking, I made a loop by taking the beach route to the parking area at the lighthouse.

Marsh Boardwalk Trail
Length: 0.5 mi (0.8 km); **easy**; USGS Map: Fripps Inlet; trailhead: Fripps Inland Road on SR 406.

From the park entrance on US 21, we went 1.8 mi farther on US 21, which became SR 406, to the parking area on the R. It was a day when the marsh grass was green, the tide was up, and the herons, gulls, and egrets fought the wind. A walk on this National Recreation Trail, a boardwalk with creosoted pilings, took us across the salt marsh to several small islands with white sand, pines, live oaks, and palmetto. Interpretive displays at two kiosks adjacent to the boardwalk provided information on the plants and animals species living in the marsh. In the summer a park naturalist provides guided walks for visitors, and sometimes crabbers and fishermen use the trail for access to a salt-marsh creek at the end of the trail. As we returned we heard the water lapping the pilings and saw the marsh grass wave in the wind—acres and acres of it as far as we could see. They were lustrous and stately, but what Dickey wrote in "The Salt Marsh" was right: they were "fields without promise of harvest." On our next visit we would see the marsh grass dead and gray, stalks scattered on the boardwalk by another wind and another tide.

Information: Contact Superintendent, Route 4, Box 668, Frogmore, SC 29920; (803) 838–2011/4602.

Huntington Beach State Park (Georgetown County)

Named in honor of Archer M. and Anna Hyatt Huntington of New York City, who owned the property from 1930 to 1960, this 2,500-acre scenic beach area is on the south end of South Carolina's "Grand Strand." The park has retained the Huntingtons' former summer home and studio, the 36-room "Atalaya" (meaning watchtower), modeled on a royal court from the Spanish Province of Granada. After Mr. Huntington's death in 1955, the furnishings of Atalaya were moved to New York City, and the studio sculpture equipment was transferred to their Brookgreen Gardens (across US 17 from the park entrance.)

Facilities in the park include a campground with 127 campsites (usually filled early in the day during the summer), ocean swimming, surf fishing, summer organized nature programs (one of which is to study the 255 species of birds that inhabit the park), picnicking, and hiking. Several viewing stands are scattered throughtout the park.

Access: Across the highway, US 17, from the Brookgreen Gardens (18 mi S of Myrtle Beach and 18 mi N of Georgetown), turn onto the park road, and go 1 mi to the park entrance gate.

Sea Oats Nature Trail

Length: 1 mi (1.6 km); **easy;** USGS Map: Brookgreen; trailhead: South Campground.

The first time I hiked this trail was with my wife, Flora. (She was an avid collector of shells, preferred beach trails to all others, and hiked most of the trails with me on the beaches from Maine to Key West.) We entered the forest near a trail sign through pines, live oak, yaupon, wax myrtle, and cedar, and at 0.2 mi we walked over a carpet of peltated marsh pennywort. At 0.6 mi we were on open sandy dunes among scattered patches of sea oats. Returning to the forest edge, we exited between campsites 125 and 127. At 1 mi we completed the loop and returned to the parking area.

Marsh Boardwalk Trail

Length: 0.3 mi (0.5 km); **easy;** USGS Map: Brookgreen; trailhead: left on North Beach Road.

From the Boardwalk parking area we walked on a bridge over a salt marsh to observation decks. We saw waterfowl such as marsh hawk, common egret, great blue heron, marsh hen, and coot. During one visit at low tide we saw fiddle crabs, blue crabs, mussels, oysters, and periwinkles.

Information: Contact Park Superintendent, Murrells Inlet, SC 29576; (803) 237-4440/9255.

Myrtle Beach State Park (Horry County)

As I entered the park after dark, the headlights of my van revealed an adult raccoon exploring a small stream by the roadside. I slowed to a stop. Two young raccoons peered at me curiously from a sapling. Those nocturnal mammals, and more like them, live on the 312-acre Myrtle Beach State Park, a preserve only 3 mi S of downtown Myrtle Beach. A state park since 1934, it has more than two million visitors annually, more than any of the other state parks. Its name comes from the fragrant coastal shrub, the wax myrtle, known for its use in bayberry candles, dye, medicine, and spices.

The noise from the Myrtle Beach Air Force Base across US 17 and the adjacent commercial district appear to have little effect on the tranquility of the animal life or camping in a park that is part of the "campground capital of the world." Its 300 campsites are usually filled from Memorial Day through Labor Day, serving nearly 190,000 campers annually. No reservations for camping are accepted, but reservations (which are assigned by a public drawing each Feb. 1) are required for cabin rentals. Other facilities and activities are surf and pier fishing, swimming in the ocean or in the park swimming pool, picnicking, and hiking. A store with groceries and fishing and camping supplies, as well as an activities center and refreshment stands, are also in the park.

Access: From the intersection of US 17, Ocean Blvd and entrance to the Myrtle Beach AFB, go S on US 17 0.1 mi to park entrance on L.

Sculptured Oak Nature Trail

Length: 1 mi (1.6 km); easy; USGS Map: Myrtle Beach; trailhead: near park fee station.

After entering the park from the park fee station, I passed a picnic area on the L (where you can park) and entered the trail opposite the road. (I parked at the pier parking area and walked back 0.2 mi to the entrance.) The trail went under tall loblolly pine, poplar, elm, hickory, holly, and live oak. The magnolia trees were exceptionally tall. Wild ginger and partridge berry grew in the duff. I crossed a stream at 0.1 mi and a boardwalk at 0.7 mi. This came out on the sand dunes, and I crossed a small estuary at the beach at 0.8 mi to the parking area at the pier. (If it is high tide you may prefer to backtrack.) Other hiking in the park is primarily on the beach.

Support Facilities: If the campground is filled, you have more than 12,000 campsites to choose from at commercial campgrounds in the Myrtle Beach area. But they also fill up quickly; it is wise to make reservations during the summer.

Three campgrounds that are near the park are: Pebble Beach Family Campground, 3000 S Ocean Blvd., (803) 238–2830; Pirateland Family Campground, Hwy Bus US 17, (803) 238–5151 or toll free 1 (800) 828–9280; Ocean Lakes Family Campground, Hwy Bus US 17, S, (803) 238–5636 or toll free 1 (800) 828–9280. Fall and winter months have reduced rates.

Information: Contact Superintendent, Myrtle Beach State Park, US 17, S, Myrtle Beach, SC 29577; (803) 238–5325/8710.

Old Dorchester State Park (Dorchester County)

In 1969 the West Virginia Pulp and Paper Company (WESTVACO) deeded to the state 97 acres that encompassed the colonial village and fort of Dorchester "for preservation as an historical site . . . and the enjoyment of the state." Extensive archaeological study immediately followed, and today visitors can return to the past by examining the tabby walls of the fort made of burned oyster shells (for limestone) and sand matrix, which had a cemented quality. The fort's architectural design, a Scottish "flanked redoubt," is the only one of its kind built in America. Also, visitors can see remnants of the tower of St. George, built in 1752, and study the displays at the exhibition building.

The village's colonial history began in 1696 when a group of Congregationalists from Dorchester, Massachusetts Bay, settled here for frontier advancement. They established lots and streets for the building of homes, a millsite, and a thriving market place near the Ashley River. By 1719 there were 113 English families and 1,300 slaves. Within the next four years they built a bridge across the river, a public bridge maintained by "all the males from sixteen to sixty." The bridge was rebuilt many times, but the only sign today of the bridge location is the road embankment. "We hope someday to build a footbridge across the river," Charles Cumbee, park superintendent, said while we sat at the old fort and talked about the past. "The river is affected by the tides, and I have seen alligators on the banks," he said.

During the Revolutionary War Dorchester was a strategic point, and British troops occupied the town in April 1780. In December of 1781 Col. Wade Hampton drove the British out. Before the British retreated to Charles Towne they destroyed the "40 houses and a church." (A majority of the Congregationalists had left in the 1750s for a "healthier climate" in Georgia.)

Access: From Summerville take SC 165, S for 3 mi to jct with SC 642. Turn L, go 2 mi, and turn R on SR 373. From SC 61 at Cooks Crossroad take SC 165 N for 1.4 mi to SC 642, turn R, and go 2 mi to SR 373.

Boosho Creek Nature Trail

Length: 0.7 mi (1.1 km); **easy**; USGS Map: Stallsville; trailhead: picnic area.

I entered a mature hardwood forest at the sign near the picnic area and parking area. Across the park road, I turned L at an unmarked trail jct at 0.2 mi and completed the circle at 0.7 mi through a forest of oaks, hickory, elm, ironwood, magnolia, gum, and dogwood. Honeysuckle and scattered ferns provided large sections of ground cover.

Information: Contact Superintendent, Old Dorchester State Park, 30 State Park Rd., Summerville, SC 29483; (803) 873–1740.

Old Santee Canal State Park (Berkeley County)

The 200-acre Old Santee Canal State Park is among the state's newest parks. A day-use park, its key feature is the historic Santee Canal that connected the Santee River with the Cooper River. In addition to a land trail through the park, there is a 1-mi canoe trail.

Access: At Moncks Corner take the US 52 Bypass. Halfway from its jct with US 52, turn off on a street going SE to the park entrance.

Old Santee Canal Trail

Length: 3.0 mi rt (4.8 km); **easy**; USGS Map: Cordesville; trailhead: parking area.

The main trail is a loop of some earthen pathways, and nearly 1.5 mi of boardwalks. The 3-ft- and 6-ft-wide boardwalks meander through scenic swamp sections of bottomland hardwoods of live oak, sycamore, black gum, and hickory. Spanish moss and reeds are among the large cypress areas. Wildlife includes osprey, wading birds, and other waterfowl. (The boardwalk is designed to accommodate the physically handicapped.)

Information: South Carolina State Parks, 1205 Pendleton St., Columbia, SC 29201; (803) 734–0156.

SECTION 4. OTHER STATE PROPERTIES

Sand Hills State Forest (Chesterfield and Darlington Counties)

In 1939 the South Carolina State Commission of Forestry received 92,000 acres for the U.S. Department of Agriculture's Resettlement Administration program. Under this program, infertile land was restored to timber harvesting, wildlife and fish management research and recreation. Since the late 1930s nearly 30 million pine seedlings of slash, longleaf, or loblolly have been planted. Timber management avoids soil damage and uncontrolled fires. Revenue from timber sales has made the forest self-sustaining, and one-fourth of its income is paid to the local counties in lieu of taxes.

Increasing the wildlife population is another intensive operation. Thirteen ponds have been stocked with bream, catfish, and bass. Numerous patches of lespedeza, rye, peas, and millet have been planted for deer, dove, squirrel, and quail. Both fishing and hunting are open to the public, but state licenses and a forest permit are required.

There are short nature trails at the Sugar Loaf Mountain area, and many of the 200-plus miles of truck trails are suitable for hiking. I have hiked some of the roads in the wintertime to study wildlife and in June to pick blueberries. Camping is allowed in the forest in specific areas with a permit.

Sugar Loaf Recreation Area

This area has facilities for fishing, picnicking, birding, nature study, and hiking.

Access: At the jct of US 1 and SR 29 (12.9 mi S of Cheraw State Park and 1.1 mi S of Sand Hills State Forest Headquarters), take SR 29, Ruby Road, NW for 3 mi, and turn R at SR 63, Scotch Road. After 0.3 mi turn R at the gate, and follow road 0.7 mi to the lake and another 0.8 mi to Sugar Loaf Mountain.

Sugar Loaf Mountain Trail

Length: 0.6 mi (1 km); **easy;** USGS Maps: Middendorf, Patrick; trailhead: parking area.

Thoreau contended that some areas where one walks are sacred. I felt that way about this area when Scott Smith and I walked the prescribed trail at Sugar Loaf Mountain and Horseshoe Mountain. We first climbed the steps on Sugar Loaf, a 160-foot dome-shaped mound of ferrous sandstone. A monadnock (a rocky mass that has resisted erosion), Sugar Loaf has lost much of its protective cap over millions of years. Thoreau observed in his many hikes that the finest stone cutters were not of copper or steel, but "air and water working at their leisure with a liberal allowance of time." So it is at Sugar Loaf.

What surprised us most was that plants of both exeric and mesic environments were growing near each other. Dr. Doug Raynor, of the S.C. Wildlife and Marine Resources Dept., explained that impervious rock layers hold the rainfall in some areas, while in other places seepage dominates. We saw tree huckleberry, staggerbush, mountain laurel, trailing arbutus, ferns, titi, leucothoe, leopard's bane, jessamine, aster, and something I had not seen anywhere else—the tiny Wells pyxie-moss (*Pyxidanthera barbulata var. brevefolia*), a nationally endangered species. (I later learned that the tiny Bradley fern, *Asplenium bradleyi*, is so rare that it may be endemic only to Sugar Loaf.) After Sugar Loaf we hiked Horseshoe, a nearly 55-foot-tall mound shaped like its name. Here as at Sugar Loaf the sandstone had a variety of colors, and the chief trees were longleaf pine and turkey oak.

Information: Contact Forest Director, Sand Hills State Forest, Box 128, Patrick, SC 29584; (803) 498–6478.

Santee Coastal Reserve (Charleston County)

Before the arrival of the French Huguenots in the late 1600s (Arnaud Bruno de Charbusiers may have been the first settler in 1691), this coastal sanctuary was inhabited by the Santee Indians. Afterwards, in the eighteenth and first half of the nineteenth centuries, the area prospered on rice and sea island cotton. Joseph Blake, at the zenith of his plantation power and before the Civil War, had 900 slaves on a preserve of 1,252 acres known as "Washo." But what slave labor had created, the Civil War, powerful hurricanes, and the ricebirds destroyed by the end of the century.

In 1898 the Santee Club was founded and organized by Capt. Hugh R. Garden for sports hunting. In addition to the purchase of Blake's Plantation, Ormond Hall, and Little Murphy Island, the club leased a number of other islands and "reserves" of old rice fields. The Club adhered to a strict system of conservation and never exceeded more than 30 members. One of the early members was President Grover Cleveland. Game wardens assisted in protecting what was considered to be the "largest wading bird rookery in the east." Poaching has always been a problem. In its efforts to protect the waterfowl, the club maintained and repaired more than 100 dikes.

The Santee Club was dissolved in 1974, and the property, with 23,024 acres, was given to the Nature Conservancy, a national nonprofit organization committed to preserving natural diversity. It has been said that it was the "most valuable gift in private conservation's history." The property included 3,600 acres of mainland longleaf pine, excluding Blake's Plantation. Except for the Blake Reserve, the Conservancy deeded most of the sanctuary to the state through the Heritage Trust Program; the state's Wildlife and Marine Resources Department took over the management. With the dissolution of the Santee Club, a new club, the Collins Creek Club, was organized. It pays annual fees to receive hunting rights for 25 years.

The reserve adjoins the Francis Marion National Forest on the southwest, the Cape Romain National Wildlife Refuge on the south, and the North Santee River on the north. On the east and southeast are maritime forest, sand dunes, and the Atlantic beach. Most of the refuge is marsh, but sections in the southwest are upland with some bald cypress ponds, swamp, and Carolina bays. The Intracoastal Waterway splits through the center, and the South Santee River forms part of the delta on the north side. Approximately 8,000 acres are on Murphy Island and 5,000 acres on Cedar Island.

There are 14 Carolina bays, oval or elliptical depressions, in the reserve. The easternmost bays have cypress, poplar, maple, red and sweet bays, but the other bays are more savannahlike, and herbaceous species are favored. Twelve species of orchids are here and at least five species of lilies. Two rare plants, yellow fringeless orchid (*Habenarla integra*) and blue Burmannia (*Burmannia biflora*) are found in the area.

Probably every Atlantic species of shorebirds is found in the 11 miles of beaches. A former property manager, Billy Cody, said the reserve had "sheltered as many as 120,000 to 170,000 ducks at one time." He remembers when the sky would be darkened with flocks of pintail, teal, widgeon, and mallard. Other birds are quail, crows, owls, hawks, swallowtail kites, and numerous species of songbirds. The mammal population includes deer, fox, raccoon, bobcat, opossum, and "wild" boar. Among the reptilian species are the rat snake and garter snake. Alligators and loggerhead sea turtles are also on the refuge. Marine and estuarine fish include flounder, sheepshead, largemouth bass, spot, whiting, striped bass, mullet, and lady fish.

The Santee Coastal Reserve and the Washo Reserve are open to the public from 8:00 A.M. to 5:00 P.M., Monday-Friday. They are closed from Nov. 1 to March 1, except by permission from the S.C. Coastal Wildlife and Marine Resources Commission. Vehicular traffic is limited to designated routes. Hunting and fishing are restricted by state, federal, and reserve laws. Dogs, cats, and other pets are not permitted. Although some restricted areas are planned for camping, visitors should first check with the reserve hq.

Access: From US 17/701, N bound (1.6 mi N of Moores Corner), take SR 857 R at the Santee Coastal sign. Go 2.7 mi, and turn R at a community center onto a sandy road

to the reserve. (S bound, take SR 857 L after 1 mi from
the S Santee River bridge, and go 1.5 mi to the community
center.)

Santee Coastal Reserve Nature Trails

Length: 6.2 mi rt ct (9.9 km); **easy;** USGS Maps: Cape
Roman, Minim Island; trailhead: parking area.

After we turned onto the sandy road from the community
center at SR 857, Scott Smith and I drove 1.8 mi to a nature trail on the left. We hiked this old roadbed in an area
of pines for 0.6 mi and returned to the main road after a
1.2-mi round trip. Ahead, on the main road we drove another
0.9 mi to a nature trail sign on the R in an open grassy
field. From here we hiked another 0.7 mi, 1.4 mi round trip,
through an avenue of live oaks, swaying Spanish moss, and
pines. Large anthills were en route. Ahead was the reserve
parking area and the office to the L, where a huge live oak
spread 150 ft and had a circumference of 24 ft.

From the parking area we walked across a dike on an
old vehicle road and followed the trail signs. At 0.9 mi we
passed an observation deck on the R. We watched the back-
water lap against the lacustrine trees and shrubs before continuing through the forest. Along the route we saw places
where "wild" boar had been routing in the soft mud, particularly under oaks. At 1.8 mi we reached a wildlife observation blind and boardwalk to the L. We were leaving the
titi, wax myrtle, and sea oxeye for borders of sedge, rush,
and cordgrass. As far as we could see, there were acres of
water lilies, fragrant as laurustine, and beyond them were
more marshes and hummocks to Murphy Island. Waterfowl
were abundant. We observed this magnificent area for a long
time and wondered what it's like at night. "Probably full of
sounds and mystery," I said. "Drayton Mayrant has said that
'sea islands have jungle gods, regnant here while all the
mainland sleeps.' "

Support Facilities: Buck Hall Campground, Francis Marion National Forest. From jct of US 17/701 and SC 45 at Mc-Clellanville, go S on US 17/701 for 7.4 mi to FR 242 on L. (From Awendaw on US 17/701, it is 2.3 mi N to entrance sign R on FR 242.) Facilities are for camping, fishing, and picnicking near the Intracoastal Waterway.

Information: Contact Manager, Santee Coastal Reserve, South Carolina Wildlife and Marine Resources Department, Box 37, McClellanville, SC 29458; (803) 546–8665.

Whitten Center (Laurens County)

Whitten Center, named in honor of its founder, Dr. Benjamin O. Whitten, opened in September 1920. It is a 1,808-acre community in Clinton with more than 1,000 clients and is one of four similar state facilities for the handicapped. On the wall in a hallway is an embroidered sign, the Beatitudes for the Retarded Child, by C. Parsley. In part it stated ". . . Blessed are they who can softly say 'try harder, you'll do better on another day.' Blessed are they who understand my limited mind. . . ."

In addition to the center's programs in health, development, and service support, it has a camping and nature program. Jeff Stackhouse, director of the program, told me that the network of trails at the center were designated for the clients, but that visitors with permission were welcome. "Our experimental outdoor program for the clients," he said, "provides day camping, overnight camping, horseback riding, fishing, hiking, pedal boat riding, archery, picnicking, bird-watching, and other educational outings."

Access: From Clinton go SE 2 mi on US 76 to entrance on the L.

Creek Trail and Explorer Trail

Length: 4.3 mi rt ct (6.9 km); **easy** to **moderate**; USGS Map: Joanna; trailhead: parking area at Unit 24.

Dick Hunt and I went to the Camping and Nature Center past Unit 31 and followed the service road to the Creek Trail for 0.5 mi. At the labeled C jct, we followed the signs across the Sands Creek footbridge to the Explorer Trail. Here we turned R and hiked 0.8 mi in an open grassy area with elderberry, milkwort, peppergrass, ironweed, and rose pink. We rock-hopped across Sands Creek and curved R to a jct with the Creek Trail. It was another 0.5 mi back to the C jct. This time we followed the other section of the Explorer Trail for 1.7 mi around Pond #2 to make another loop L at G jct, K jct and E jct. At D jct we made a R and hiked 0.5 mi back to C jct on the Creek Trail. (Although we explored some of the side trails, we did not count their distance in our combined mileage.) From C jct we ascended the service road to the Camping and Nature Center for a total of 4.3 mi.

Information: Contact Director, Whitten Center Camping and Nature Programs, Box 239, Clinton, SC 29325; (803) 833-2733.

Wildlife Management Areas

Through the South Carolina Wildlife and Marine Resources Department (SCWMRD), the Wildlife Management Area (WMA) Program initiated in the early 1950s has 1,276,770 acres (607,225 owned by NFS and 669,545 with corporate and private owners) open to the public, both sportsmen and nonhunters. The many campgrounds and scenic areas offer year-round recreation and enjoyment, but hiking or camping are allowed on the corporate and private properties only with permission. Although hiking is allowed anywhere in the national forests, camping may be restricted and permits necessary. Nonhunting hikers are cautioned by the WMA to know the hunting seasons of these properties and to wear the international orange caps and jackets.

To clarify the boundaries of these areas, the WMA cautions all users to remember that only properties displaying signs with the diamond-shaped yellow and black SCWMRD logo are open to the public. In 1980 the department launched the RESPECT Campaign, a project to encourage all outdoorsmen to protect the state's natural resources and its outdoor sports by adhering to ethical rules of conduct in the field: respect for nature, respect for the game pursued, respect for the landowner, respect for fellow sportsmen, and respect for the law.

The SCWMRD has listed the corporate and private individuals who have generously contributed their holdings for the public's enjoyment and have provided their land through cooperative agreements with the department. Without these lands, public use as now provided in the state would be impossible. One of the agreements between the state and the landowner is that if the landowner feels sportsmen are being destructive, inconsiderate, or disrespectful of this privilege, the area will be unavailable for public use. The following landowners have contributed land to the department's WMA Program:

U.S. Forest Service	607,225
Catawba Timber Company	169,401
Champion International Corporation	160,890
Crescent Land and Timber	106,890
Brunswick Pulp Land Company	37,270
John Hancock Life Insurance Company	34,429
Federal Paper Board Company	17,997
International Paper Company	16,683
S.C. Public Service Authority	14,714
Westvaco	12,899
Clemson University	8,447
Corps of Engineers (Thurmond Lake)	8,168
Boise Cascade Corporation	7,709
S.C. Electric and Gas Company	6,380
Timberlands, Inc.	5,000
T. C. Coxe, Jr.	5,000
J. F. McLeod & J. F. McLeod Farm Realty	4,595
Canal Industries (Chester)	4,438
Union Camp Corporation	4,394
Corps of Engineers (Santee)	4,266

Canal Industries (Conway) 3,959
Georgia Power Company 3,336
S.C. National Bank 3,252
S.C. Public Service Authority
    (Witherbee and Pee Dee Tracts) 2,869
United Methodist Church 1,830
Springland, Inc. 1,499
Belk-Simpson Company 958
Estelle W. Dunbar 850
Helen W. Hendricks Trust 693
James Devers, Jr. 684
Lavinia B. George 569
Alderman-Shaw Company 408
H. J. Smith 286
City of Clinton 276
Gary Wood 240
S.C. State Ports Authority 233
Dorothy Beaty 209
Lanny R. Gregory 150
James M. and Jack L. Brown 135
William and Joab Lesesne 92

There are four major WMAs—Mountain, Western Piedmont, Central Piedmont, and Francis Marion—and 18 secondary WMA lands. All of these are shown in detail on maps
by the SCWMRD. You may contact the department for the
free maps and two helpful booklets, *Wildlife Management Areas*
and Fishing and Hunting Rules and Regulations. Designated trails
in the WMA outside of the NFS are rare, but the potential
for seeing the state's wildlife and natural environment is
there.

Organized in 1952 at the regular session of the legislature, the department is charged by law to provide the public
with the management, protection, research, conservation, and
preservation of the state's vital wildlife, marine, and natural
resources.

Information: The department is located downtown at the capital complex in the Rembert C. Dennis Building, and the address is South Carolina Wildlife and Marine Resources Department, P.O. Box 167, Columbia, SC 29202; (803) 734–3888.

Webb Wildlife Center (Hampton County)

Near Garnett and adjoining the Savannah River is the Webb Wildlife Center and Management Area, a research and demonstration facility that provides multi-use wildlife and timber-management service. The center offers year-round outdoor recreation—fishing, hunting, hiking, canoeing, birding, and nature study. (Fishing is not allowed on Sundays, and hunting is restricted to specific seasons.) In addition, the center offers educational programs in wildlife and forest management for organized groups and school groups of any age.

In 1941 the state's Game and Fish Department purchased 5,741 acres, which include the historic property that was owned by John Tison, Sr., in 1737. Approximately 75 percent is upland stands of longleaf, slash, loblolly, shortleaf, and pond pine. A hardwood forest of oaks—live, willow, laurel, water, and overcup—elm, ash, and maple is on the upper floodplains; and on the river swamp floodplains are stands of old-growth bald cypress and water tupelo. Animal life includes wild turkey, deer, quail, raccoon, bobcat, rabbit, gray and fox squirrel, dove, osprey, hawks, wading and migratory birds, alligator, and the rare bird-voiced tree frog. A scientific and educational–use permit is required. To avoid conflict with other groups, a request for permission must be made in advance by telephone or letter. No camping is allowed, except by prior arrangements and for educational purposes. The center is planning an Upland Nature Trail.

The center is named after James W. Webb, the former executive director of the state's Wildlife and Marine Resources Department. He is remembered for 37 years (including 27 as the state's first wildlife biologist) of some of the best conservation programs in the nation.

Access: In Garnett at jct of US 321 and SR 20 go W on SR 20 for 2.8 mi to the Webb Wildlife Center entrance on L. Drive on a straight road lined with live oaks and Spanish moss. After 1.4 mi on entrance road, reach the center's hq.

Savannah River Swamp Trail

Length: 3.6 mi rt (5.7 km); **easy;** USGS Map: Brighton; trailhead: Bluff Lake parking area.

From the center's office, we drove for 2 mi on a dirt road to the trailhead at Bluff Lake. It had rained, and some of the sloughs had water, but it was not deep enough to keep us from hiking all the way to the Savannah River and back. Parts of the trail were grassy and almost dry, though it was wet elsewhere. Among the list of oaks were overcup, laurel, willow, and water. The wildlife biologist at the center mentioned that we should watch out where we walked because a cottonmouth moccasin could be on the trail. Bald cypress, water tupelo, and elm were more prominent in the lower sections of the river swamp. The cypress is best described by William Gilmore Simms (1806-1870) in "The Edge of the Swamp":

> Cypresses, Each a great ghastly giant, eld and gray,
> Stride o'er the dusk, dank tract—with buttresses
> Spread round, apart, not seeming to sustain,
> Yet link'd by secret twines, that underneath,
> Blend with each arching trunk. . . .

Support Facilities: Access to Americamps-Point South campground is from I-95 jct (exit 33) with US 17. Go 0.1 mi N on US 17, then 0.5 mi N on road behind Best Western Motel. Full svc, rec fac. Open all year. Address: Americamps, Point South, Yemassee, SC 29945; (803) 726–5728.

Information: Contact Manager, Webb Wildlife Center, Garnett, SC 29922; (803) 625–3569.

CHAPTER IV

County and Municipal Trails

SECTION 1. COUNTIES

Palmetto Islands County Park (Charleston County)

Palmetto Islands County Park is a 943-acre family-oriented natural park, whose attributes include semitropical forests, marshes, lakes, tidal wetlands, meadows, and a series of 16 islands. The park is designed to bring its visitors close to the low country's largest natural land asset, the marsh. Natural trails wind throughout the park, and boardwalks cross marsh areas, allowing visitors to view plant and animal life found in a typical marsh environment.

In addition to foot trails, the park also offers a 1.5-mi bicycle trail, a unique 350,000-gallon natural swimming hole, picnic areas and shelters, a 50-ft observation tower, fishing and canoeing in Boone Hall Creek, pedal-boat rentals, nature study, and a Big Toy Playground for children of all ages. The park is for day use only, usually opening at 10:00 A.M. and closing between 5:00 and 7:00 P.M. depending on the season. This park (and other park facilities at Folly Beach County Park and Beachwalker Park) is owned and operated by the Charleston County Park and Recreation Commission.

Access: Northeast of Charleston on US 17, 7 mi from the Cooper River bridge, take the Long Point Rd L, SR 97. (For southbound traffic it is 1.2 mi S on US 17 from the jct of US 17 and SC 41.) Go 1.1 mi to the park entrance on Neddlerush Parkway, R, that dead-ends at the park gate.

Osprey Trail, Nature Island Trail, and Marsh Trail

Length: 1.6 mi ct (2.6 km); **easy**; USGS Maps: Fort Moultrie, Charleston; trailhead: park center.

We followed the 0.2-mi Osprey Trail from the park center to a marsh, where a boardwalk offered an excellent view of large osprey nests high on top of power lines. From here we followed the bicycle trail W to the trailhead of the longest and most unique trail in the park, the 0.8-mi Nature Island Trail. After crossing a boardwalk to an island, we found an extensive self-guided nature trail. (An accompanying brochure assisted us in learning about its unique characteristics through identifying various plants and land features.) The plants we saw along this trail included live oak, water oak, fresh-water gum, yaupon, palmetto, yellow jessamine, red cedar, and pine. Because the 0.6-mi Marsh Trail is at the E end of the park, we could have driven to the most eastern parking area, or walked the bicycle trail for about 0.5 mi to the connection. Vegetation includes spartina grass, black needlerush, sea oxeye, groundsel tree, wax myrtle, and Cherokee bean. This trail also has boardwalks.

Information: Contact Park Manager, Palmetto Islands County Park, 444 Needlerush Parkway, Mt. Pleasant, SC 29464; (803) 884–0832.

Pocotaligo Swamp Park (Clarendon County)

The Pocotaligo River has headwaters in Sumter County: streams such as Green Swamp, Pocalla Creek, Nasty Branch, Brunson Swamp, Long Branch, and Hatchet Camp Branch. It flows across Clarendon County to join the Black River, flowing into Williamsburg County. Pocotaligo moves through miles of concealed silent swamps, wild and shrouded in secrets since the days of the Indians, its wildlife sequestered. A glimpse into its murky magnificence is from a boardwalk trail at a small park on the north edge of Manning.

Access: From downtown Manning go N on US 301 for 1.6 mi to entrance on L, S of the river's bridge.

Pocotaligo Swamp Trail

Length: 0.5 mi rt (0.8 km); easy; USGS Map: Manning; trailhead: parking area.

From the parking and picnic area we followed the signs to the boardwalk. Ghostly Spanish moss hung from the black gum, bald cypress, bay, willow oak, water tupelo, and red maple along an interpretive trail. From an observation deck we watched a group of turtles crowd each other off a log. All too soon we were at the end of the boardwalk, where the faster-moving river seemed to say it was taking its secrets to the sea.

Information: Contact Director, Manning Dept. of Parks and Rec., 411 N. Brooks St., Manning, SC 29102; (803) 435–8424/8477.

Pleasant Ridge County Park (Greenville County)

Pleasant Ridge, formerly known as Pleasantburg, is a 300-acre county park that was first donated by Greenville County to the state system in 1950, but transferred back to the county in 1988. During the 1930s a CCC campground was here. Facilities include a 25-site campground with hook-ups, hot showers, and two cabins (completely furnished), a picnic area, a lake for swimming and fishing, and a playground.

Access: On SC 11, 2.5 mi E from jct of US 276 at Cleveland and 2 mi W from jct of SC 11 and US 25.

Pleasant Ridge Nature Trail

Length: 0.7 mi (1.1 km); easy; USGS Map: Tigerville; trailhead: picnic area.

From the picnic area I followed the trail sign and crossed a footbridge to an old wagon road bordered by yellow root, hemlock, rhododendron, and mountain laurel. On a ridge were the remnants of a log cabin, probably from a CCC campground. At 0.2 mi I left the old road and went L into an oak-hickory forest. The understory is of holly, mountain laurel, and dogwood. Across a stream at 0.4 mi was the site of an old whiskey still; I turned L. At 0.5 mi a spur trail led off to the R to the lake area. I crossed another stream and descended on an old, wet, rocky road. Cascading on the L was a stream with a heavy bank of fetterbush. Completing the loop I returned to the trail origin.

Information: Contact Superintendent, Pleasant Ridge County Park, Route 2, Cleveland, SC 29635; (803) 836–6589.

Greenwood County Park (Greenwood County)

In 1938 Greenwood County donated 914 acres to the state for a Civilian Conservation Corps campground. From this transfer came the development of Greenwood State Park. Although a few graveyards have been located within the boundary, the greater historical significance is its location near Ninety Six, once a trading village on the Keowee Path, and Star Fort, a British outpost in the Revolutionary War. The old Island Ford Road, begun in 1776, went through this area, which was part of "The Treat Survey" mentioned in early documents. In 1988 the state arranged to transfer the park back to the county.

Situated on the south side of Lake Greenwood, the park has 125 campsites in two campgrounds, a primitive camp, a trading post and tackle shop, a campground recreational building, a picnic area, a lake swimming area, a playground, carpet golf, and a boat ramp.

Access: From Ninety Six go 3.4 mi E on SC 34 to SR 41. Turn L on SR 41 and go 1.5 mi to park entrance across SC 702.

Greenwood Lake Nature Trail

Length: 0.8 mi (1.3 km); easy; USGS Map: Dyson; trailhead: behind the Recreation Building.

I entered the unmarked but well-maintained loop trail behind the Recreation Building in a pine forest with an understory of gum, dogwood, mulberry, and wild cherry. The first L fork led into a more mixed forest that included an oak and elm as part of the top canopy. Honeysuckle covered the ground. At 0.4 mi I passed the lake on the L and returned to the point of origin.

Information: Contact Superintendent, Greenwood County Park, Route 3, Box 108, Ninety Six, SC 29666; (803) 543–3535.

Laurens County Park (Laurens County)

Access: The park is 3.1 mi E from Laurens on US 76. Take the L on SR 274 and go 1.3 mi to park entrance on the R. The park has a sheltered picnic area, a children's playground, tennis and basketball courts, a baseball field, and a fishing lake.

Laurens County Park Nature Trail

Length: 0.8 mi (1.3 km); **easy**; USGS Map: Laurens S; trailhead: picnic area.

The nature trail begins in the picnic area under hardwoods at a sign. After crossing the dam at 0.1 mi we entered the hardwood forest to make a loop around the lake. Vegetation was mainly young oaks, pines, beech, ironwood, hickory, and dogwood. Wildflowers we saw included downy false and sticky foxglove, false flax, and asters. Ferns grew near the two streams. At 0.5 mi we crossed the lake's headwaters and returned through a mixed forest to the point of origin.

Information: Contact Recreation Coordinator, Laurens YMCA Recreation Service, P.O. Box 794, Laurens, SC 29360; (803) 984–2621.

Chau Ram Park (Oconee County)

Chau Ram Park is one of three recreational facilities provided by the Oconee County Parks and Recreation Commission. The other two are High Falls Park and South Cove Park on Lake Keowee, but only Chau Ram has a trail. Facilities at Chau Ram include campsites with water and electric hook-up, a picnic area, a playground, a recreational building for special events and group activities, fishing and swimming at the Chauga River, and carpet golf.

Access: From Westminster take US 76 W for 2.5 mi to entrance on the L.

Chauga Nature Trail

Length: 0.5 mi (0.8 km); **easy**; USGS Map: Holly Springs; trailhead: campground.

In the campground I entered the trail at campsite #22 and followed on a slope where goat's pea, huckleberry, bracken, galax, and trailing arbutus grew. Trees and shrubs included hawthorn, pink rhododendron, mountain laurel, dogwood, pines, and oaks. The trail descended on switchbacks in a rocky and steep area to scenic views of the roaring Chauga cascades at 0.2 mi. Huge boulders and flat rocks made this an unusually picturesque locale. Moss and ferns graced the hillside. I crossed a small stream at the picnic area and ascended the hillside to the point of origin at 0.5 mi.

Information: Contact Director, Oconee County Parks and Recreation Commission, P.O. Box 188, Walhalla, SC 29691; (803) 638–4212.

Campobello-Gramling School Outdoor Laboratory (Spartanburg County)

This unique outdoor laboratory was the result of cooperative efforts of the school, the Spartanburg Conservation District, and the South Carolina Land Resources Commission.

Access: From the jct of US 176 and SC 11 in Campobello, go S on US 176 for 1.6 mi to Campobello-Gramling Elementary School on the R.

Campobello-Gramling Trail

Length: 0.8 mi (1.3 km); **easy;** USGS Map: Inman; trailhead: SW corner of the school.

From the parking area I went to the SW corner of the school, near the tennis courts, and followed the trail laboratory sign. A number of the botanical specimens were labeled; some of the additional ones were strawberry bush, mock strawberry, pipsissewa, partridge berry, penstemon, and Christmas fern. Trees were mostly young pines, oaks, sourwood, poplar, maple, hickory, and sweet gum. I crossed a footbridge at 0.3 mi and backtracked after reaching Motlow Creek.

Information: Contact Principal, Campobello-Gramling Elementary School, Campobello, SC 29322; (803) 472–6495.

Museum of York County (York County)

In October 1982, the Rock Hill *Evening Herald* ran a 12-page supplement on the Museum of York County. It was about a dream come true; a dream in the 1950s by the Junior Welfare League of Rock Hill and by leaders such as Maurice Stans and J. Lee Settlemyre. There are myriad attractions in this museum: a planetarium, an environmental theater, and two art galleries—the Grant Art gallery (named in honor of Vernon Grant, Rock Hill's nationally known artist) and an alternative gallery with local accents. The museum also boasts the Hall of Western Hemisphere and the Hall of the Carolinas—but the most spectacular is the Maurice Stans African Hall, dioramas with the world's largest collection of species of African hooved mammals.

A curator of natural history told me that the museum "docent program," volunteer teachers, was of great assistance. "I enjoy the students who come to learn. . . . When they appreciate what you are doing, it makes it all worthwhile," she said. It was closing time; she locked up, and as we were leaving I realized that one of my students, Steve Harris, was so engrossed in the exhibit that he was locked inside the museum. "Somebody would have found him," she assured me, as she reopened the door.

Another special feature at the museum is the nature trail, which has a wood carving of the state's Carolina wren and yellow jessamine at the trailhead. Picnicking is allowed. The museum is open daily, 9:00 A.M. to 5:00 P.M. (1:00 to 5:00 P.M. on Saturday and Sunday).

Access: From downtown Rock Hill at jct of US 21, Cherry Road, and SR 195, Mt. Gallant Road, take SR 195 W for 6.5 mi to museum entrance on L.

York County Nature Trail

Length: 0.5 mi (0.8 km); **easy**; USGS Map: Rock Hill; trailhead: behind the museum.

Steve and I took with us a map of the carefully planned trail within a 10-acre garden of plant selections from the coastal, piedmont, and mountain areas. We counted more than 50 species. At 0.3 mi we could see Big Dutchman's Creek from an observation deck. After completing the loop we returned to the amphitheater, picnic area, and trail entrance.

Information: Contact Director, Museum of York County, 4621 Mount Gallant Road, Rock Hill, SC 29730; (803) 366–4116.

Aiken (Aiken County)

Founded in 1834, Aiken is a fashionable year-round resort and a popular sports center for thoroughbred training, fox hunts, drag hunts, and golf in the winter months. Some of the nation's top horses are trained here, and the Racing Hall of Fame, established by the local Jaycees, is at Hopeland Gardens. The annual Triple Crown—harness racing, trials, and steeplejack—is held each March. The city's chief industry is textiles, and among its more significant buildings is the Aiken County Museum on Chesterfield Street; it houses an exhibition of the area's early history. Here also is the famous Hitchcock Woods, a 1,200-acre forest preserve. Maintaining the area park system is the Aiken Recreation Department, which has two parks with trails: Hopeland Gardens and Virginia Acres Park.

Hopeland Gardens

The 14-acre Hopeland Gardens is a tranquil area with a network of paved walkways, a lake, floral gardens, an outdoor stage for plays and concerts, and a special trail for the handicapped.

Access: From jct of US 78, SC 302, and SC 19, downtown, go S on SC 19 for 1 mi to the corner of Whiskey Road and Dupree Place. Turn on Dupree Place to the parking entrance on L.

Hopeland Gardens Trail

Length: 0.3 mi (0.5 km); easy; USGS Map: Aiken; trailhead: in front of the Thoroughbred Hall of Fame.

From the parking area I took an avenue of ivy and tall oaks to the Thoroughbred Hall of Fame building. I followed the signs on a paved trail where 28 permanent labels in print and Braille described the plants, which included some that are fragrant. (The trail is also constructed to accommodate wheelchairs.) Other trails in the park interconnected or looped back to the point of origin.

Virginia Acres Park

With a diversity of sports facilities, the Virginia Acres Park also houses the Odell Weeks Recreation Center and city park headquarters. There are eight lighted tennis courts, two shuffleboard courts, four outdoor and one indoor basketball court, four racketball courts, one soccer field, picnic shelters, and a trail for jogging or walking.

Access: The park is on SC 19, Whiskey Road, E of the city, between SC 302, Pine Log Road, and Price Avenue.

Virginia Acres Trail

Length: 1 mi (1.6 km); **easy;** USGS Map: Aiken; trailhead: parking lot.

From the parking lot of the Odell Weeks Recreation Center, I went N near Whiskey Road to a jogging trail sign. The trail also connected with spur routes to other park activities; it returned to the parking lot.

Support Facilities: The closest camping is Pine Acres Campground. From jct of I-20 and US 1 (exit 22), go S on US 1 for 4 mi. Open all year, full svc, no rec fac; (803) 648–5715.

Information: Contact Director, Aiken Recreation Dept., P.O. Box 1177, Aiken, SC 29801; (803) 648–0151.

Camden (Kershaw County)

Historic Camden celebrated its 250th anniversary in the spring of 1983 as the state's oldest inland city. First named Fredericksburg (by the Wateree River), it changed its name 10 years later to Pine Tree Hill when the settlers moved to higher ground. In 1768 it was appropriately named in honor of British champion of colonial rights Charles Pratt, Lord Camden.

Camden is a city of tradition, of charm and style, of restored homes and public buildings, and of culture and a high quality of life. And it is a shrine for horse racing. Some observers credit its health and beauty to Haiglar, King of the Catawbas and friend of the early settlers, whose image is on the tower of the former City Hall as a weather vane. He, if no one else can, informs the city which way the wind blows. When I asked Linda King, Chamber of Commerce administrative assistant, about the downtown trees, she said, "They are Bradford pears and you can purchase them from Springdale Nursery here in Camden"—an able promotion of local business.

The Camden area has nearly 275 miles of equestrian trails. Famous as one of America's finest thoroughbred race-horse centers for 150 years, Camden is the host each fall to the Colonial Cup International Steeplechase and to the Carolina Cup in the spring.

Historic Camden Visitor Center

Camden's Revolutionary period has been restored by the Camden District Heritage Foundation, which began the work in 1970. Archaeological research identified the sites of buildings in the original settlement near the 1200 block of Broad Street. There are four restored buildings—the Craven and Cunningham frame cottages and the Bradley and Drakeford log cabins—now filled with museum exhibits and dioramas. The Joseph Kershaw House, headquarters for Lord Cornwallis, is also being restored. In addition, the center has a children's animal farm and crafts and exhibits in the Exchange office.

Access: From I-20 at the US 521 jct N is 1.4 mi on the R. If from downtown, turn S on US 251 at jct with US 521/1/601 for 0.9 mi.

Historic Camden Trail

Length: 0.7 mi rt ct (1.1 km); **easy;** USGS Map: Camden S; trailhead: parking area.

From the Exchange we walked on a dirt road to the magazine area of earthworks, turning R to the forest of tall oaks and a wide path. Yellow jessamine was fragrant. At 0.2 mi we passed under a power line near Big Pine Tree Creek. The trail turned R, and we passed a pond, then

237

returned to the parking area E of the maintenance building at 0.4 mi. After reentering the dirt road, we followed it to the Joseph Kershaw mansion and returned at 0.3 mi.

Pine Tree Hill Trail

Length: 9.8 mi rt (15.7 km); **easy**; USGS Maps: Camden S, Camden; trailhead: Visitor Center parking area.

Access to the Pine Tree Hill Trail is at the Historic Camden Visitor Center parking area. It has 63 historic sites, most of which are private homes.

I chose a Sunday morning to hike this trail to avoid traffic. From the parking area I crossed Broad Street and walked on Meeting Street to the Presbyterian meeting house and cemetery, then to the Quaker Burying Ground site 3. On Sept. 6, 1759, Samuel Wyly leased this area to the Quakers for a cemetery and meeting house under "the terms of 999 years at a yearly rental of one peppercorn, if lawfully demanded." The Quakers later leased the property to the town of Camden for 99 years at a rental of $1.00 a year. The cemetery has the graves of three Kershaw County heroes: Richard H. Hilton and John C. Villepique, recipients of the WWI Congressional Medal of Honor, and Richard Kirkland, the compassionate Confederate soldier who risked his life for dying Union soldiers at the Battle of Fredericksburg. (See site 62.)

At 0.2 mi I returned to Broad Street and turned L to site 4, where Baron De Kalb, hero of the Battle of Camden, was buried by the British with full military honors in August 1780. In 1825 his remains were moved to a site on De Kalb Street. (See site 63.) At 0.5 mi I arrived at the jct of Bull and Broad streets, once the center of town. President George Washington, on his first Southern tour, did not sleep here but he did address a gathering of local citizens on May 27, 1791. On the 600 block of Bull Street is site 6, the burial enclosure of Col. Joseph Kershaw, founding father of Camden, for whom the county is named.

Back on Broad Street, I turned L and reached the 600 block for site 8 at 0.7 mi. Erected in 1826, the original Mills Court House was designed by Robert Mills, a native South Carolinian who designed the Washington Monument in the nation's capital. The structure was rebuilt three times and used until 1906. It is now the Masonic Lodge. At site 9, across the street from the lodge, is the Revolutionary gaol (jail) built in 1771. This is the jail where 14-year-old Andrew Jackson was imprisoned briefly (see Andrew Jackson State Park). Legend has it that young Andrew watched the Battle of Hobkirk Hill from a hole he had cut in the second-story wall.

At the jct of Broad and York streets, I turned R and went to the Fine Arts center on Fair Street where the Bonds Conway house, site 11, has been moved from 411 York St. The story of Bonds is significant because, in 1793 at the age of 30, he was the first black citizen in Camden to buy his own freedom.

I returned on York Street to Market Street and turned R at 1.4 mi. I was puzzled about site 13 on Market Street until I read my guidebook. Instead of a mausoleum it was a Civil War storage for arms and ammunition. I continued on Meeting Street to Arthur Lane, turned L, and went back to Broad Street to site 15 at the corner of Broad Street and Rutledge. Here at the top of the tower is a 5-foot iron effigy (ca. 1820) of Catawba Indian King Haiglar, "the Patron Saint of Camden."

Site 17 on the 1100 block of Broad Street is the site of Lafayette Hall, once the home of John Carter. It burned in 1903, but a cedar tree planted in 1825 still stands. The new Court House is here now. At 2.1 mi I passed site 18, followed by sites 19 to 22, which were private architectural landmarks.

At site 23 I reached Broad and Laurens streets at Monument Square. The area has large oaks and pines and mounds of azaleas in a parklike area honoring the Confederate dead.

One monument honors Lt. Col. James Polk Dickinson (1816-1847) who died in the Mexican War. An inscription reads:

> How beautiful in death,
> The warrior's cause appears,
> Embalmed by fond affection's breath
> And bathed in woman's tears.

On the SE section of the square is the Camden Archives, a repository for historic documents and objects such as the original tower clockworks. After passing historic private homes at sites 24 to 30 along Broad Street from the 1400 block to the 2000 block, I arrived at Hobkirk Hill at 3.8 mi. Site 31 marks the area on the ridge overlooking Camden where Gen. Nathanael Greene's troops were defeated after a brief battle with Lord Rawdon's British forces just before dawn on April 25, 1781, at the battle of Hobkirk Hill.

The next 18 sites (33 to 50) are elegant private homes. I admired them as I passed by in the following order: Kirkwood Lane from Broad Street to Ancrum Road; followed Ancrum Road to Union Road and turned R, turned R at Lakeview Avenue, turned L at Brevard Place; turned R on Mill Street; turned L on Greene Street; turned L on Fair Street to sites 39 and 40, and returned to Greene Street. At the jct of Greene Street and Lyttleton Street, I turned L on Lyttleton (missing sites 43 to 44) and continued on Lyttleton Street to site 51, Rectory Square, at Lyttleton Street and Chestnut Street. I had walked 7 mi; I sat down at the square's pantheon to rest and eat a snack from my day pack. Around me were six columns, each memorializing Camden's Confederate War generals—James Cantey, James Chestnut, Zach Deas, John D. Kennedy, Joseph B. Kershaw, and John B. Villepique. The pantheon was erected in

1911 from funds raised by the schoolchildren of Camden. A marker read:

> The silent pillar, gold and gray,
> Claimed kindred with their sacred clay;
> Their spirits wrap the dusty mountain;
> Their memory sparkles o'er the fountain.

I left the Square under the shade of large oaks and by gardens of azaleas and crepe myrtle. I continued S on Lyttleton Street to Laurens Street, turned L for 2 blocks to see site 54, and returned to go W on Laurens Street to see sites 56 and 57. Backtracking to Lyttleton I turned R and followed Lyttleton Street to Haile Street. Here I turned L on Haile Street for 2 blocks to see site 60, to my R on Mill Street. I backtracked to Lyttleton Street, turned L and reached Hampton Park at 8.3 mi.

Hampton Park was named for Gen. Wade Hampton, Confederate officer and later governor of the state. A monument here honors Sgt. Richard Kirkland, who at the Battle of Fredericksburg, Dec. 13, 1862, carried water again and again in the line of fire to the suffering and dying Union soldiers. Named the "Angel of Mary's Heights" by the troops, he died nine months later in the Battle of Chickamauga, at age 20. Of the 71,000 South Carolinians who served in the Civil War, he was one of the 12,922 who died. The monument was erected as a tribute from the schoolchildren of Camden in 1910.

From Hampton Park I turned R on De Kalb Street to the monument where Maj. Gen. Baron De Kalb, Revolutionary War hero, was re-interred in 1825. Behind the monument the Bethesda Presbyterian Church worship service was over, and most of the parishoners had gone home to Sunday dinner. I left my day pack and measuring wheel near the entrance and went in to sit quietly, admire this 1822 architectural masterpiece by Robert Mills, and to think about the five porches of Bethesda in John 5:2.

I walked back to my car for a total of 9.8 mi. (I could have taken a shorter route if I had not backtracked to view the sites in numerical order.) Hikers may wish to purchase the 20-page *Historic Site Directory*, 5th edition, from any of the agencies listed below or from the Visitor Center. Boy Scouts may earn the Pine Tree Hill medal and patch by hiking this trail and taking a written test. The Visitor Center is open 10:00 A.M. to 5:00 P.M., Tuesday through Saturday, and 1:00 to 5:00 P.M., Sunday.

Information: Contact any of the following in Camden, SC 29020. Camden District Heritage Foundation, P.O. Box 710, (803) 432–9841; Kershaw County Historical Society, P.O. Box 501, (803) 432–9841; Greater Kershaw County Chamber of Commerce, 700 W. De Kalb St., (803) 432–2525; or Camden Archives, 1314 Broad St., (803) 432–3242. Or contact Boy Scouts of America, P.O. Box 144, Columbia, SC 29202; (803) 765–9070.

Charleston (Charleston County)

Charleston is often referred to as "America's most historic city." In 1670 "Charles Towne" was established in the Carolinas by Anthony Ashley Cooper, Earl of Shaftesbury. His establishment of American nobility titles for the owners of large plantations laid the foundations and opened a gateway for much of the city's elegance and refinement.

The state's second largest city, it was once the state capital. Today, its charm, its beauty, and its heritage are carefully preserved. "We are proud of our heritage," said Mayor Joseph P. Riley, Jr. "It is a city for everyone . . .any time of year." Others have described it as a "city of romance," "a city of cultivated manners," "the Carolinas' Williamsburg," "the best example of civility," "a living history book," "the Carolina city of old-world charm," and "a proud survivor of every calamity." Dickey described the city as "full of walled gardens, which I love more than any other construction of man."

Charleston has nine major museums, including Patriots Point, which is the world's largest naval and maritime museum, and the Charleston Museum (1713), which is the oldest in America. Architectural rehabilitation and stabilization of dozens of historic buildings have been the principal concern of the Historic Charleston Foundation, founded in 1947. Visitors can tour the 789-acre historic district on foot or by horse-drawn carriage.

There are more than 12 historic churches. The city parks and gardens and recreational facilities are numerous, and the Spoleto Festival U.S.A. attracts an international audience each spring. Tour boats leave daily from the Municipal Yacht Basin heading to Fort Sumter. (See Fort Sumter National Historical Monument in Chapter II.)

The Charleston Trident Chamber of Commerce provides a visitor's guide/map of the city with a numbered list of 46 points of historic interest. Another guide is an 18-page booklet with a map, titled *The Complete Walking Tour of Historic Charleston*. It is written by Nita Swann and illustrated with the artwork of Nicki Williams, Betty Schwark, and Jim Gensmer. The guide lists 65 historic sites (and 23 alternate sites) and is available from the visitor center. The "Old Walled City" dates from 1703, and the lines of former fortifications can be traced in the area. It is recommended that you first go to the Information Center, 85 Calhoun St., for directional maps. From there you should park your car at the Cumberland Street parking garage.

Old Walled City Trail

Length: 2.3 mi (3.7 km); **easy**; USGS Map: Charleston; trailhead: 23 Cumberland St.

From the Old Powder Magazine (1703) at 23 Cumberland St. we began a walk of the "Old Walled City." At the corner of Cumberland and Meeting was the Carteret Bastion, the NW corner of the old wall. We turned L on Meeting Street; on the R was Gibbes Art Gallery. On the L was the Circular Congregational Church, organized in 1681, but the current building was constructed in 1891. Continuing on Meeting Street across from Chalmers Street is Hibernian Hall (1799). At 100 Meeting St. is America's first fireproof building, erected in 1822.

In the corner areas of Meeting and Broad are a number of historic firsts: City Hall (1801), County Court House (1792), United States Post Office and Federal Court (1896), and St. Michael's Protestant Episcopal Church, the oldest church edifice in the city (1751). Its bells were imported from England in 1764. Near here on Broad Street are the Confederate Home and the Citizens and Southern National Bank Building (1797); and at the corner of Broad Street and Church Street is "Cabbage Row." This spot inspired the setting for the *Porgy and Bess* operetta.

From here we continued R on Church Street to the Heyward Washington House (1770), home of Thomas Heyward, signer of the Declaration of Independence. At Tradd Street we turned R to Meeting Street and turned L to the First (Scots) Presbyterian Church, organized in 1731 but built in 1841. At 51 Meeting St. we visited the Nathaniel Russell House (1809), and at 16 Meeting St., the Calhoun Mansion (1876).

After 0.8 mi we reached South Battery Street and turned R to make a curve of 0.4 mi around the White Point Gardens to Murray Boulevard and "The Battery" area. The gardens are landscaped with shrubs and flowers, and monuments are placed in the area to represent the cycle of American wars in which Charleston has been involved.

At the corner of Murray Boulevard we turned L and followed East Battery Street to the Edmonston-Alston House, then to Missroon House at 44 East Battery. The Vanderhorst Row (1800) was at 76-80 East Bay St. At 83-107 East Bay St. we passed the Rainbow Row houses, named for the pastel colors of the historic buildings. To our R was the Old Exchange and Custom House (1767-71) at 122 Bay St. From here we turned L on Broad Street to the South Carolina National Bank (1817). At the corner of Broad and Church we turned R to Chalmers Street and saw the Pink House (1745), a three-story house with one room on each floor. Continuing on Church Street, we visited the Dock Street Museum (1809) and the French Huguenot Church (1844-45) at the corner of Church Street and Queen Street. At 146 Church St. was the St. Phillip's Protestant Episcopal Church (1838), the church that had the oldest original congregation (1670). The Market Street Area (1788-1804) is between Church Street and East Bay Street. After a visit there we walked back to the Cumberland Street parking area at 2.3 mi.

Information: Contact Visitor Information Center, 85 Calhoun St. (P.O. Box 975), Charleston Trident Chamber of Commerce, Charleston, SC 29402; (803) 722–8338.

Chester (Chester County)

Named by settlers from Pennsylvania in 1755, the town is the county seat and has a population of about 7,000. Located in the center of the county, it is also the hub of six rail routes of the Seaboard Coast Line, Carolina and Northwestern, Lancaster and Chester, and Southern railways. Eleven highways spread out like a fan from the center of town. Its recreation program is administered by a joint city/county commission. One of the parks is Wylie Park, which has seven tennis courts, a large swimming pool, a picnic area, a basketball court, and a nature area.

Access: From the jct of SC 72, US Bypass 321 and SC 9, and West End Street, go 0.6 mi on West End Street to the park and to the park hq.

Wylie Park Trail

Length: 0.3 mi (0.5 km); **easy;** USGS Map: Chester; trailhead: park road.

From the West End Street, I entered the gate at the picnic area and followed a recreation department staff member, Lydia Sorrow, to the trail entrance on the L. Although the trail was unmarked, it could be taken in a loop by returning to the paved road and the point of origin. In a mixed forest with pines, cedar, oaks, gum, and wild cherry, the honeysuckle and wisteria were cosy to them all. Ebony spleenwort in bunches of pink wood sorrel made bouquets; silverberry leaned over the trail to force fragrance in my face, and atamasco lilies were growing near the wet spots. A sign at the gate read: "Presented by Joseph Wylie to the city of Chester for their comfort, pleasure and innocent amusement, 1899."

Information: Contact Director, Chester County/City Park and Recreation Department, 100 West End St., Chester, SC 29706; (803) 385-2530.

Columbia (Lexington and Richlands Counties)

Columbia, the capital city in the center of the state, the focal point of state government since 1790, has been described by historians, politicians, and writers from many perspectives. Probably only one writer, James Dickey, has assessed its value meridionally. "But the best thing," he wrote in *The Starry Place Between the Antlers*, "is the way it balances Appalachia and the Atlantic."

Its wide boulevards—Assembly, Gervais, Senate, and Sumter—frame the capitol building, a masterpiece of Southern elegance and design. The imposing statehouse is built of native granite in Roman Corinthian style. It is more than the heart of state government; it is also a center for wholesale and retail trade, industry, finance, and education. Within a few blocks of the capitol building are the University of South Carolina (1801) and the Richland County Courthouse. In addition to USC, other institutes of higher education are Allen University (1870); Lutheran Theological Southern Seminary (1830); Columbia College (1854); Benedict College (1870), and Columbia Bible College (1923).

In 1790 the General Assembly met in the statehouse, and the following year George Washington visited the city during his Southern tour. South Carolina was the first state to secede from the union, and it was here that the Ordinance of Secession was drawn on Dec. 17, 1860, at Columbia's First Baptist Church on 1306 Hampton St. More than four years later on Feb. 17, 1865, Gen. William T. Sherman's army, marched north from Savannah and occupied Columbia. At least 1,386 buildings were burned within 84 blocks, as revenge, claim some historians.

Attractions in the city include the Town Theatre (since 1919), one of the nation's oldest little theaters, on Sumter Street; McKissick Museum and Columbia Museum of Art and Science; Robert Mills Historic House and Park (Mills was the designer of the Washington Monument in Washington, D.C.); South Carolina Archives Bldg.; Woodrow Wilson's boyhood home; and the 50-acre Riverbanks Zoological Park, one of the nation's finest. Fort Jackson, on the east boundary of the city, is one of the nation's largest U.S. Army training centers.

The Department of Parks and Recreation maintains 33 parks. Those with walking trails are described below. The parks range from open green areas and playgrounds to large community parks with gymnasiums to small neighborhood parks.

Earlwood Park

Earlwood Park Trail

Length: **0.5 mi** (0.8 km); **easy**; USGS Map: Columbia N; trailhead: parking area.

Access: 2 blocks S from the jct of SC 16 and SC 215 on SC 215, Main Street.

Although the walking area is not a designated trail system, I walked through oaks and pines and willows. A paved jogging trail near the entrance is at 0.2 mi. Other facilities are provided for picnicking and tennis.

Maxcy Gregg Park

Maxcy Gregg Park Trail

Length: **0.3 mi** (0.5 km); **easy**; USGS Map: Southwest Columbia; trailhead: parking area.

Access: This park is on 500 Pickens Street and at the Blossom Street jct. Serving as a youth center, this park provides swimming and a nature center. I walked for 0.3 mi one way along the banks of the stream among live oaks, magnolia, poplar, and cultivated gardens of azaleas, camellias, and seasonal floral displays.

Historic Columbia Canal and Riverfront Park

The park is located near the confluence of the Broad and the Saluda rivers, where they become the Congaree River. Interpretive markers explain the history and services of the Columbia Canal, the Pump House and old waterwork system, other historic structures, and the plant and animal life. Constructed by the state more than 150 years ago, the purpose of the canal was to bypass the dangerous shoals at the junction of the rivers. Although the canal's usefulness decreased after the railroads, it was rebuilt in the 1890s for the purpose of generating electricity. It has been in use ever since. The waterworks at the canal continues to serve the city also. Currently its filtering capacity exceeds 70 million gallons of water daily.

Columbia Canal Trail

Length: 5 mi rt (8.0 km); **easy**; USGS Map: Columbia N; trailhead: parking lot.

Access: Turn S from Elmwood St on Huger St to Laurel St, R; or N from Hampton St on William St (or Huger St) to Laurel St, L.

From the parking area we descended to a footbridge that is across the Columbia Canal to the levee and the Congaree River. At 0.2 mi was the historic waterworks. From here we turned upstream on the levee on a paved, scenic trail that is used for jogging, bicycling, and walking. The area is landscaped with white and pink crepe myrtle. Natural shrubs, wildflowers, sycamore, and sweet gum are prominent. A sign at 0.4 mi, near the picnic area, describes the river cooters. We walked under the I-26 bridge and RR at 0.7 mi. The paved area ended at 0.9 mi and gravel began. When the trail ended at 2.5 mi, at a conversion dam, we backtracked.

Congaree Bicentennial Park

Congaree River Trail

Length: 0.5 mi (0.8 km); **easy**; USGS Map: Southwest Columbia; trailhead: parking area.

Access: From US 1-US 378, Geddes Street, and Gist Street jct. Turn on Gist Street and turn on first R.

I passed the first boat ramp and parked in an area near the second boat ramp. The trail wound along the river bank downstream among large sweet gum, oaks, elm, ash, sycamore, and hornbeam, most of which had a heavy base of grapevines and honeysuckle. Fishermen move the crossties used for a border to find worms. Near a large fallen sycamore, I backtracked to the parking area on the loop.

Support Facilities: (See Sesquicentennial State Park.)

Information: Contact Director, Parks and Recreation Department, 1932 Calhoun St., Columbia, SC 29201; (803) 733–8331.

Darlington (Darlington County)

Darlington, the county seat, is best known for its leadership in tobacco marketing and the Darlington International Raceway. In addition it has the Joe Weatherly Stock Car Hall of Fame Museum with the largest collection of race cars in the world. It is also the largest automobile auction market in the nation. As for parks, the largest is beautiful Williams Park (approximately 400 acres). A small, unique park is the Frank and Mark Sue Wells Park at the corner of Avenue A and S. Main Street by the railroad track. This miniature park has a picnic table, a 100-yard designed trail (**Wells Park Trail**), shrubbery, and a few trees including cedar, pecan, and catalpa.

Williams Park Trail

Length: 1.8 mi ct (2.9 km); **easy;** USGS Map: Darlington; trailhead: parking area.

From downtown at the courthouse square take SC 34, Cashua Street NE, go 2 blocks to SR 446, Spring Street, and turn L. Go 0.2 mi to parking area on R between Park Drive and Swift Creek bridge.

From the parking area we followed the trail R through large elm, ash, poplar, gum, and mulberry. In some places wisteria was encroaching on the dogwood, mulberry, redbud, and azaleas, and at other locations it had intertwined itself in competition with the Spanish moss to high-hanging displays of green and purple and gray. Jewelweed, Scotch broom, ferns, and daylilies were not far from the tentacles of the wisteria. There was an abundance of songbirds. At 0.3 mi we reached a jct to N. Spain Street on the R. We passed an old well pump. To our L the trail looped back to the parking area, and to our R was Park Street at 0.4 mi. We first hiked a less-used trail ahead for 0.5 mi to an exit at Cashua Street near Bellyache Creek bridge. Backtracking, we completed the loop mentioned above. The trail passed two sheds, crossed three boardwalks in a swampy area over Swift Creek, and wove through tall birch, cypress, oak, and gum. Arrow arum and lizard's tail were prevalent, and benches in beds of ground ivy were along the trail. Returning to the parking area, we crossed three more boardwalks at Swift Creek. Across the street was the smallest chapel I have been in. It could accommodate only two or three people. A sign told us it was for meditation. (I have since learned from the Chamber of Commerce that it is maintained by Bill Brasington of 105 Evans Circle.)

Information: Contact Director, Recreation Dept., P.O. Box 94, Darlington, SC 29532; (803) 393–3626.

Florence (Florence County)

In 1846 Gen. William W. Harllee of Marion received a state charter to construct a railroad from Manchester to Wilmington. Construction began in 1853, and a station for the North Eastern Railroad was based at present-day Florence. The early settlers and developers needed a name for the station; the railroad construction superintendent suggested Florence, the name of General Harllee's oldest daughter. In 1871 the town was chartered, and in 1888 a county by the same name was established by the state legislature. Today Florence remains the hub of extensive railroad lines and is a major retail and wholesale distribution center. It is also a beautiful city with city parks, museums, and the Florence Beauty Trail with brilliant floral displays. The 12-mile motor trail is in the central and southwest area of the city around the parks and by a country club. The trail starts at Timrod Park on Coit Street at the corner of Cherokee Road. It is sponsored by the Rotary Club in association with the Greater Florence Chamber of Commerce. There are trail signs along the way. The brilliant floral display of trees, shrubs, and flowers is at its peak from late March to early April.

Jeffries Creek Park

Jeffries Creek Trail

Length: 0.8 mi ct (1.6 km); easy; USGS Map: Florence W; trailhead: parking area.

From the jct of US 52/301, S. Irby Street, and Second Loop Road in downtown Florence, drive 1.5 mi to Edisto Drive Extension and turn R. After 0.7 mi turn L on Wisteria Drive for 0.2 mi to park entrance or farther ahead to S. Deberry Boulevard entrance for 0.5 mi under tall ash, poplar, maple, oaks, elm, and sweet gum where Spanish moss hangs in clusters.

We turned L over a bridge. Bordering the well-graded trail were ferns, mandrake, elderberry, switch cane, and willow. At 0.3 mi we crossed a bridge to the picnic area and to the end of the island. We backtracked to follow the trail over more bridges and to another picnic area and children's playground. Exit L here goes to the street. We returned to W. Wisteria Street after 0.8 mi in the 55-acre park.

Lucas Park

Lucas Park Trail

Length: 0.6 mi rt (9 km); **easy;** USGS Map: Florence W; trailhead: Azalea Lane.

Downtown at the jct of US 52/301 and Cherokee Road, turn W on Cherokee Road and go 2 blocks to Camellia Drive or 3 blocks to Park Avenue on the L. Go 2 blocks on Park Avenue to Azalea Lane and turn L.

The 12-acre park has a children's playground, tennis courts, gardens, and brick treadway. On the trail are oaks, poplar, pines, dogwood, and sweet gum. Azaleas, spirea, and other ornamental shrubs make this a park of springtime beauty.

Timrod Park

Timrod Park Trail

Length: 1 mi rt (1.6 km); **easy;** USGS Map: Florence W.; trailhead: S. Coit Street.

Downtown at the jct of Cherokee Road and US 52-301, take Cherokee W for 1 block to jct of S. Coit Street and turn R. We started our walk from S. Coit Street and followed upstream. The park has a children's playground, picnic area, and lighted tennis courts. Tall trees included poplar, sweet gum, magnolia, and oaks. Azaleas and dogwood were copious and colorful. We entered the tea-rose garden and visited the one-room schoolhouse of Henry Timrod (1828-1867), poet laureate of the Confederacy; he taught, among others, "Katie," who was later to become his wife. At 0.6 mi we reached the Florence Museum at Spruce Street and Graham Street. It is open without charge daily, 10:00 A.M. to 5:00 P.M., except the last two weeks in August. We backtracked to our point of origin.

Information: Contact Director, City of Florence Recreation Dept., P.O. Box 1476, Florence, SC 29503; (803) 665–3253.

Greenville (Greenville County)

Greenville, incorporated in 1907, was Pleasantburg until 1821. It is a city with a population of more than 60,000 and is the county seat of Greenville County. It has more than 400 manufacturing plants and has been called the "Textile Center of the World," but recently chemical, plastic, and machinery products have become prominent. Its major institutions of higher education are Bob Jones University (1927), Furman University (1826), and Greenville Technical College (1962). The Greenville County Museum of Art has the Andrew Wyeth Collection, the largest anywhere outside the holdings of the artist. The Art Museum at Bob Jones University has one of the nation's foremost collections of rare Biblical materials and sacred art. The city Parks and Recreational Services and the Greenville County Recreation Commission have established eight bicycle tours and loops comprising a total of more than 140 miles in the Greenville vicinity. One of these, the Reedy River Tour in the heart of the city, has a section in Cleveland Park that can be used as an excellent foot trail.

Reedy River Falls Historic Park and Greenway

The 24-acre Reedy River Falls Historic Park and Greenway was developed by the Carolina Foothills Garden Club on land given to the city by Furman University in 1969.

Access: In downtown Greenville at the jct of S. Church Street (US Bus 29) and University Ridge, take University Ridge around the County Square Complex to the jct of Howe and Hitt streets at the park entrance.

Reedy River Falls Trail

Length: 0.5 mi (0.8 km); **easy**; USGS Map: Greenville; trailhead: park driveway.

After reaching the access I parked by the driveway near the river. Among the azaleas was a sign installed by the Carolina Foothills Garden Club for an azalea planting. It read, "given to the glory of God and in loving memory of Sara Gossett Crigler and Betsy Highsmith Bruce by Frances Oates Beattie, 1972." From the sign I made a loop among the azaleas to the waterfalls. Large oak, sycamore, birch, elm, and ash spread a high canopy over the ornamental shrubs and wildflowers. The smell of ground ivy was prominent at the base of a huge sycamore with a 14.5-foot cir. Behind it the water of Reedy River poured over tiers of rock ledges, a natural downtown waterfall.

Cleveland Park Trail

Length: 3.3 mi rt (5.3 km); **easy**; USGS Maps: Greenville, Greenville SE; trailhead: Reedy River Falls Park.

As I was parked at Reedy River Falls Park, I walked to the cul-de-sac and entered the Cleveland Park Trail downstream on an 8-foot-wide asphalt walkway for bicycling, jogging, and hiking. It is a well-designed trail, priceless for an intercity natural space. It is on this trail that the 10-kilometer Reedy River Run is held each spring. At 0.1 mi I crossed a metal footbridge over the Reedy River. I passed by large birch, elm, and oak trees. Elderberry and trees of heaven were mixed with dogwood and redbud. At 0.3 mi I passed the Anderson Memorial and did a clover leaf loop at the McDaniel Avenue bridge. At 0.6 mi I crossed a small stream in a meadow where false dandelion, dayflower, sorrel, lady fingers, and jewelweed grew. At 0.9 mi I passed twin cement footbridges and saw that exercise stations began immediately beyond on the L. To my R was a large dogwood with a 3.5-foot cir. At 1.2 mi I crossed the Woodland Way bridge over Reedy River, went upstream to a picnic area, and crossed Richland Way. At this point I entered a magnificent hardwood forest where for 0.5 mi I had to imagine that I was in the city and to my L was the state white poplar champ, over 11 ft in cir. At 2 mi I turned L to visit the rose garden, which was at its height of blooming. I followed the trail to the recreation center, visited the city zoo, and returned to continue my hike by the French Friendship railroad car. To my R were six lighted tennis courts. At 2.4 mi I crossed the cement footbridge over the Reedy River to rejoin the trail and then crossed McDaniel Avenue. A lady wearing apple-green shoes was being pulled ahead by a black toy French poodle with red ribbons on its ears. "I'm the one on the leash," she said, when the poodle stopped to sniff the measuring wheel. "I can't turn him loose—he would run away. Once he got lost, and I found an empty 22 cartridge for a whistle. That is the only sound he will respond to," she said, breathing heavily. She said she walked on the trail every day.

When I returned to the cul-de-sac at 3.3 mi I met Dr. Richard Chivers, a romance languages teacher at Wren High School and runner in the State Grand Prix. I told him about the lady and the dog on the trail and that I'd forgotten to ask for their names. "Well, as for the dog, I would call him Beauregard," Richard suggested. "It is such a good Southern name."

Information: Contact Administrator, Greenville Park and Recreational Services, Box 2207, Greenville, SC 29602; (803) 240–4350.

Greer (Greenville County)

Greer is named for J. Manning Greer, an early farmer who donated land for a Southern Railroad track from Greenville to the community. First called Greer's Station and incorporated in 1875, the community changed its name to Greer Depot in 1893, but changed it again in 1901 to Greer. There is a legend that farmer Greer's benevolence was on condition that no whiskey ever be sold in town. Today Greer is Greenville County's second largest city, "the heart of the piedmont," and growth is based on industry, commerce, and agriculture. Its parks and recreation program has two recreation centers and six parks with lighted facilities. One of the parks is Tryon Park.

Tryon Park

Access: From the jct of US 29 and SC 14, go W to Tryon Street and turn L. Pass Tryon Street Elementary School to Oakland Street and turn L.

Tryon Park Trail

Length: 0.2 mi (0.3 km); **easy**; USGS Map: Greer NW; trailhead: parking area.

From the parking area on Oakland Street, I went past a picnic shelter and descended into the forest of oaks and pines. Two footbridges crossed a deep ravine. A spur trail led to the Tryon Street Elementary School, and I circled back to the origin of the walk. Facilities at the park include six lighted tennis courts, a children's playground, a mini golf course, a recreational building, and the woods area for nature study.

Information: Contact Director, Parks and Recreation, 226 Oakland Ave., Greer, SC 29651; (803) 877–9289.

Mauldin (Greenville County)

On the way into Mauldin on US 276, there is a sign that reads: "The City With a Future." It is an apt slogan because of the city's rapid commercial and industrial growth and development since 1956—rapid enough to be on what local citizens call the "Golden Strip." Formerly called Butler's Crossroad, it was organized in 1910 and subsequently was named in honor of Lt. Gov. W. L. Mauldin.

Mauldin City Park

One of two city parks, the 13-acre Mauldin City Park has a senior citizens center, a children's playground, two lighted baseball fields, lighted softball and soccer fields, and a picnic area.

Access: From the center of town on US 276, turn on E. Butler Avenue and go 1.6 mi to jct with Corn Street. Turn L to parking area on L.

Mauldin Park Trail

Length: 0.5 mi (0.8 km); **easy**; USGS Map: Greenville SE; trailhead: parking area.

From the parking area I walked on the paved 6-foot-wide trail in a loop around the recreational facilities. It is an excellent trail for walking or jogging.

Information: Contact Director, Parks and Recreation Department, P.O. Box 249, Mauldin, SC 29662; (803) 288–3354.

Orangeburg (Orangeburg County)

Historic Orangeburg, "where living is a pleasure," is the county seat of Orangeburg County. It was named for William, the Prince of Orange, after a settlement of Swiss, Dutch, and German immigrants was established by the General Assembly in 1735. A prosperous small city, it has successfully combined area farming and industries of wood, textiles, and chemicals with its downtown commercial life. Its major educational institutions are South Carolina State College, which has the I. P. Stanback Museum and Planetarium (1896), Claflin College (1869), and Orangeburg-Calhoun Technical College (1968). Known as a city of roses, it has the year-round Edisto Memorial Gardens at which the South Carolina Festival of Roses is held the first weekend in May. Among the city's parks and areas of recreation are Edisto Memorial Gardens and Summers Memorial Park.

Edisto Memorial Gardens

The 85-acre gardens are open all year and free to the public. Opened in 1927 the gardens are known for the magnificent display of more than 6,000 roses and 125 varieties, an attraction that operates in conjunction with the American Rose Society and the All American Rose Selection Committee. An additional 4,000 camellias, azaleas, and other flowering shrubs make this one of the state's most colorful and distinguished gardens. With daylilies, crepe myrtle, asters, and other summer flowers, there is a constant display of beauty. The park facilities include tennis courts, picnic areas, rest rooms, and hiking trails.

Access: From downtown jct of US 601 and 301, go W on John Calhoun Drive to gardens on R at Riverside Drive.

Edisto Gardens Trails

Length: 1.5 mi (2.4 km); **easy;** USGS Map: Orangeburg; trailhead: parking area.

Debbie Cooper and Richard Galway of the American Rose Society had been telling me about the roses in Edisto Gardens long before they brought me here. It was a late May afternoon when we sauntered through avenue after avenue of color—pink, orange, scarlet, lavender, purple, white, mauve, burgundy—and sweet fragrance. "This is a Tropicana," Debbie said as she gently moved a large bud toward me to smell. "A rose is sweeter in the bud than in full bloom," she said, smiling, and quoting John Lyly. Blue-black pipevine butterflies were visiting rose after rose.

After a walk over the bridges to the lakes and swamp, we skirted the quiet Edisto, "the longest blackwater river in the world." We switched from one path to another, enjoying the tranquil scenery. Cypress, oaks, sweet gum, and pine shaded the area. Spanish moss hung in streamers. We rested at the pavilion before crossing the street and returning through camellias and the daylily garden. (The following spring I returned to see the thousands of azaleas and camellias in full bloom.)

Summers Memorial Park

Access: From US 21, Boulevard Street NE, and jct with Carolina Street (Mental Health Center sign), go 0.3 mi on Carolina Street to Wilson Street and turn L. Go two blocks to Park Street, on R.

Webster Woods Trail

Length: **0.5 mi** (0.8 km); **easy**; USGS Map: Orangeburg; trailhead: street parking.

I walked by a small stream in a park of tall pines, elm, ash, and oak draped with Spanish moss. Holly and dogwoods grew underneath in a generally open area between Park, Webster, and Summers streets. On Summers Street a memorial park sign read: "Donated in 1929 to the city in memory of Thomas Raysor Summers, son of Abram West and Caroline Moss Summers, who lost his life in action in WWI, in Watau, Belgium."

Information: Contact Director, Orangeburg Parks and Recreation Dept., 620 Middleton St., Orangeburg, SC 29115; (803) 534–6211.

Rock Hill (York County)

The City of Rock Hill Parks, Recreation and Tourism Department administers and maintains 26 parks with more than 255 acres. Its program is divided into five divisions—activities (centers, marketing, arts, special events, and senior citizens); community services (Cherry Park, youth sports, concessions); facilities/safety (risk management, pools, playgrounds); therapeutics (special populations); and tourism.

The city has a population of over 40,000, and was founded in 1852, taking its name from a nearby rock mound. It is also known for Winthrop College (1886), its textile and other industries, and Glencairn Garden, a 7.6-acre preserve featuring azaleas, dogwoods, wisteria, a goldfish pond, and fountains. Located at 725 Crest St., Glencairn Garden was started by Dr. David A. Bigger in 1928, and his family deeded it to the city in 1958. Three of the city's parks have trails, which are described below.

Fewell Park

Fewell Park Trail

Length: **0.8 mi** (1.3 km); **easy**; USGS Map: Rock Hill; trailhead: parking area at center.

From downtown at US 21, Cherry Road jct with SC 274, take SC 274 0.2 mi W to fork with India Hook Road; in the center of the fork is Alexander Road. Take Alexander to corner of Glendale. The day I visited this park, I began the 0.8-mile 20-stop physical fitness trail in a pine forest from the park center. I enjoyed the forest of cedar, dogwood, oaks, wild cherry, elderberry, and pine, but equally enjoyed what I found back at the center. It was one of those occasions when a local social club had left a table of refreshments for "those men running the exercise course." The park also has two lighted tennis courts and a picnic area.

Boyd Hill Park

Boyd Hill Trail

Length: 0.4 mi (0.6 km); easy; USGS Map: Rock Hill; trailhead: parking area.

From downtown at US 21, Cherry Road, across the street from the Fairgrounds, take Constitution Blvd for 0.2 mi to parking area.

From the parking area I walked a loop across a small stream under laurel oaks, pine, poplar, and sweet gum. It was a refreshing short tour that made me wish the walk was longer.

Cherry Park

Cherry Park Trail

Length: 1.5 mi (2.4 km); easy; USGS Map: Rock Hill; trailhead: parking area.

From I-77, take Exit 82 B to Cherry Road, proceed S for 2 mi and take a L into the park. The park is located on a 68-acre site with five softball and five soccer fields. The central tower has meeting rooms and scorekeepers' news media areas. A multiple-use lighted trail for bicyclists, joggers, and walkers winds around the beautifully landscaped park. Shaded picnic and playground areas are also provided.

Information: Contact Director, Rock Hill Recreation and Park Department, 211 S. Cherry Rd., Rock Hill, SC 29730; (803) 327–1136.

Simpsonville (Greenville County)

Simpsonville City Park

Simpsonville Nature Trail

Length: 0.5 mi (0.8 km); **easy**; USGS Map: Williamston NE; trailhead: parking area.

From Main Street and SR 417, Curtis Street, in downtown Simpsonville turn on Curtis, pass City Hall, and turn L to the Simpsonville City Park. The 15-acre park has a children's playground, a picnic area, softball and baseball fields, lighted tennis courts, a basketball court, and community center for civic and social events.

On an asphalt trail, I circled the park among oaks, pines, and cedars. The town is named after the "first real settler" in the area, Peter Simpson, and is on US 276, "The Golden Strip," 10 mi SE from downtown Greenville.

Information: Contact Director, Simpsonville Parks and Recreation, P.O. Box 668, Simpsonville, SC 29681; (803) 963–5958.

Spartanburg (Spartanburg County)

Spartanburg was founded in 1785, and both the city and county were named for the Spartan Regiment of the South Carolina militia, which distinguished itself during the Revolutionary War at the Battle of Cowpens. An industrialized city, two of its major products are textiles and peaches. The latter is emphasized with a picture of a ripe juicy peach on each of the city's street signs. The city is also known for its two outstanding colleges, Wofford (1854) and Converse (1889). In addition, it has set an excellent example of how a city and county can use its resources for a diversity of recreational services to its citizens. A joint park and recreation department has established more than 25 major parks, playgrounds, exhibit areas, and sports complexes. Six community centers serve the city and country from Landrum near the state line to Pacolet on the SE side of the county.

Although it's not a park, there is a trail area near the Spartanburg High School. It is the 0.5-mi River Birch Trail, constructed in cooperation with the Junior League, School District Seven, and the city of Spartanburg. The trail has a variety of hardwoods, shrubs, and wildflowers on a trail of asphalt and wood chips. Access is from US 29 on Fernwood Drive to Beechwood St. Turn L and go to Sydnor Drive. It is behind the high school.

One of my favorite parks is Cleveland, located on the north edge of the city on US 176 and SC 56. The park has lighted tennis courts, ball fields, picnic areas, an exercise station, a children's playground, a miniature train ride, and a lake with paddleboats. But there is another special park in the city, Duncan Park, which has a trail and is described below.

Duncan Park

Duncan's Park baseball stadium is the home of the Spartanburg Spinners. It also has other lighted ball fields, tennis courts, a children's playground, a racketball/handball court and a well-designed hiking/jogging trail near the lake.

Access: Downtown, at the jct of US 221 and SC 56, corner of S. Church and Henry streets, take SC 56 on Henry and Union streets for 1.3 mi to the park on the R.

Duncan Park Trail

Length: 0.8 mi (1.3 km); **easy**; USGS Map: Spartanburg; trailhead: parking area.

From the parking area I followed the signs and completed the partial loop through a forest of oaks, dogwood, poplar, maple, hickory, and scatterd pines. Wildflowers grew near the footbridge and at the lakeside.

Support Facilities: The closest public campground is Croft State Park, 4.2 mi E on SC 56. Open all year with excellent rec fac and full svc. Contact Superintendent, Croft State Park, Route 4, Box 28-A, Spartanburg, SC 29302; (803) 585–1283. A private campground is KOA, 2 mi N of exit 69 on I-85, or 1 mi W of exit 17, on I-26. Open all year with exceptional rec fac and full svc. Contact KOA, Route 7, Box 354D, Spartanburg, SC 29303; (803) 576–0970.

Information: Contact Director, Spartanburg City/County Parks and Recreation Dept., 180 Daniel Morgan St., P.O. Box 5666, Spartanburg, SC 29304; (803) 596–3733.

Sumter (Sumter County)

The city, the county, the fort in Charleston harbor, and the national forest are all named for distinguished Revolutionary War leader and senator Thomas Sumter (1734-1832), the "Gamecock General of the American Revolution." Founded in 1788, the city has developed into an excellent example of an economically balanced commercial and agricultural area. Economic support from the nearby Shaw Air Force Base has also been a factor. More than 13 parks and playgrounds are a credit to the city's progressive system of education, culture, and business. One of these parks is the outstanding Swan Lake Gardens.

Swan Lake Gardens

Founded in 1927 and developed by H. C. Bland, this 100-acre park with 45 acres of lakes is known for its tranquillity and beauty and for its millions of Japanese Iris blossoms; there are more here than at any other place in the nation. Facilities include a playground, a picnic area, tennis, and nature trails. The annual Sumter Iris Festival is held here in late May, with the Fall Fiesta of Arts in late October. The Iris Festival had its beginning in 1940, and except for a few years when it was not held, it has been an annual event of social, cultural, and educational activities. It is open daily, 8:00 A.M. to sundown. Free.

Access: In downtown Sumter at the jct of US 15/76/378, follow W. Liberty Street (SC 763) for 2 mi W to the park.

Swan Lake Trails

Length: 1.6 mi ct (2.6 km); **easy**; USGS Map: Sumter E; trailhead: parking area.

We first visited this enchanting park when the azaleas, dogwood, jessamine, and camellias were in bloom, but when we returned to see the iris festival it was difficult to describe its unique beauty. We walked around the lake S of Liberty Street, where more than 25 varieties of the huge flowering Kaempferi Iris were growing in every color of the rainbow. There was the gleeful sound of children feeding the ducks and the geese. Swan Lake has six varieties of swans, including the graceful White English and Australian swans. Cypress were draped with Spanish moss, and lilies added more brilliance. At 0.4 mi we crossed the dam to loop back to the parking lot at 0.7 mi. From here we crossed Liberty Street and looped around the north section of the lake to Haynsworth Street and back for a total of 1.6 mi.

Information: Contact Director, Swan Lake Gardens, P.O. Box 1449, Sumter, SC 29151; (803) 773–3371.

Union (Union County)

The town of Union, first known as Unionville, is the county seat of Union County, founded in 1785; both names were from the "Union Church," which served the early Episcopalians, Presbyterians, and Quakers who had immigrated from Virginia and Pennsylvania.

Foster Park

"Foster Park Is Truly a Beautiful Site. Let's Keep It That Way," reads the sign near a parking area on Park Drive. It appears that this is exactly what the public is doing. Formerly Veteran's Park, the area has a picnic area and children's playground on the east side of the lake, a fitness trail and handball/tennis court on the west side. Careful landscaping and the planting of trees and shrubs add to the beauty of the park. On my visit to the park, a number of friendly ducks expected some bread crumbs, and an American egret stood watching for minnows.

Access: In Union go to the corner of North Boulevard and Lakeside Drive to the parking area.

Foster Park Trail

Length: 0.6 mi (1 km); easy; USGS Maps: Union W, E.; trailhead: parking area at handball/tennis court.

From the muraled handball/tennis court we went R, circling the lake on a wide and well-maintained trail used for walking, jogging, and, in one section, physical fitness. Vegetation along the trail included pines, dogwoods, domestic plants, and cattails at the upper edge of the lake.

Information: Contact Director, Union County Recreation Dept., (Union County Fairgrounds), P.O. Box 783, Union, SC 29379; (803) 429–1670.

Walhalla (Oconee County)

South Pine Street Trail

Length: 0.3 mi (0.5 km); easy; USGS Map: Walhalla; trailhead: behind South Pine Street Elementary School.

From the jct of Main Street and South Pine Street in downtown Walhalla, take South Pine to the Elementary School and park near the forest boundary. I followed the Outdoor Classroom signs by the amphitheater down to the bog, circling to the R on the return loop. Displays showed pacolet soils, rock and plant profiles. Among the flowering plants were climbing hydrangea, sericea, sticky foxglove, periwinkle, and woodland sunflowers. The trail is a model for other elementary schools to follow in constructing an outdoor natural-science laboratory.

Walterboro (Colleton County)

Walterboro is a historic city with a "proud tradition and a confident future." It was first named Hickory Valley in

1784 when owners of rice plantations chose the area for summer homes. Named later for two of those original settlers, Paul and Jacob Walters, the town became the county seat in 1817. More than 45 historic buildings provide an outstanding display of architectural charm and beauty. Three buildings are on the National Register of Historic Places—the Colleton County Court House (1822), Old Colleton County Jail (1855), and Walterboro Library Society Building (1820).

Walterboro-Colleton Recreation Center

The Walterboro-Colleton Recreation Commission administers the area recreation program. Among the parks is the 150-acre Walterboro-Colleton Recreation Center, which has three baseball fields, a sheltered picnic area, outdoor basketball and volleyball courts, a 17,000-square-foot community center, lighted tennis courts, and hiking trails.

Access: From downtown Walterboro go N on US 15 for 3.5 mi to SR 459 and turn R. Go 1.4 mi on SR 459 to SR 461 and turn R. Follow SR 461, Recold Road, for 1 mi and turn R to park entrance.

Colleton Trail

Length: 2.6 mi (4.2 km); **easy;** USGS Map: Walterboro; trailhead: parking lot at community center.

Eric Tang hiked this loop trail with me. We began at the R corner of the parking lot in front of the community center and passed the tennis courts on the R. It appeared that an old physical fitness course had once been near here. Following the trail markers, we crossed a small stream and reached a crosstrail at 0.6 mi. (To the R it is 0.1 mi to the high school grounds, and to the L it is 0.1 mi to the picnic shelters and gated service road.) We continued straight ahead through a mature forest of poplar, pines, and oaks. Ostrich and sensitive ferns, wild ginger, sweet pepperbush, and myrtle were part of the low vegetation. At 1 mi we turned R in a more dense forest, but soon entered a timbered area. Orange milkweed and sumac were prominent. At 1.1 mi we crossed

267

a paved road, entered a dense growth of berries, and came to a stream at 1.3 mi. We followed the trail downstream through a border of smilax and blackberry bushes. At 1.7 mi we recrossed the paved road and followed up another stream on a pleasant contour. We took the R fork at 1.9 mi. As the trail completed the loop, we saw false indigo, bristly locust, and sticky foxglove. After passing through a pine forest and then an oak forest, we returned to the picnic area and to the parking lot at 2.6 mi.

Support Facilities: Safari Green Acres Campground, jct of I-95 and SC 63 (exit 53). Open all year, full svc, rec fac. Walterboro, SC 29488; (803) 538–3450.

Information: Contact Director, Walterboro-Colleton County Recreation Commission, Box 173, Walterboro, SC 29488; (803) 549–2729.

West Columbia and Cayce (Lexington County)

Across the Congaree River from downtown Columbia are West Columbia and Cayce. Two of the parks, Guignard and Granby Gardens, have trails. They are maintained and supervised by the City of Cayce Dept. of Parks and Recreation.

Guignard Park

Facilities at Guignard Park include a picnic area, a children's playground, and an asphalt trail. The park was given to Cayce in 1961 by the heirs of John G. Guignard to be maintained as a public park, in a state of natural beauty preserving the wildflowers, trees, and shrubs, and to provide a "place of quiet and restfulness." For access cross the Congaree River on SC 215 from Columbia and take the first L on Deliesseline Road.

Guignard Park Trail

Length: 0.3 mi (0.5 km); easy; USGS Map: Southwest Columbia; trailhead: parking area.

Follow the paved trail under large loblolly pine, gum, oaks, beech, and maple. Landscaping consists of azaleas and ornamental shrubs. Near Axtell Street the trail loops back to the parking area.

Granby Gardens Park

The Granby Gardens Park facilities are a picnic shelter, a children's playground, and a nature trail. Access is at the jct of SC 2 and 12th Street. Turn N over the railroad, and go 0.2 mi to the Cayce Municipal Building driveway on the L. Park on the R.

Granby Gardens Nature Trail

Length: 0.8 mi (1.3 km); **easy**; USGS Map: Southwest Columbia; trailhead: parking area.

I followed the trail sign by a small stream on a wide, 20-station exercise trail, which meandered through the forest of large poplar, loblolly pine, and oaks. A sign described the route of the trails over a boardwalk and by the stream area where alder, bays, switchcane, and willow grew.

Information: Contact Director, Parks and Recreation, P.O. Box 2004, Cayce, SC 29171; (803) 796–9020.

Winnsboro (Fairfield County)

Winnsboro, chartered in 1785, is the county seat of Fairfield County and is named for Col. Richard Winn, a distinguished Revolutionary War officer and early town leader. Lord Cornwallis had his headquarters here from October 1780, to January 1781. One outstanding feature in this town of rare architectural style is the oldest running town clock in the nation—since 1833. Among its parks is Fortune Springs Park with facilities for swimming, tennis, a playground, and formal gardens.

Fortune Springs Park

Fortune Springs Trail

Length: 0.3 mi (0.5 km); **easy**; USGS Map: Winnsboro; trailhead: parking area.

From US 321 and SC 200 jct go one block W on SC 200 to Evans Street and turn L. Go 1 block on Evans Street and turn R on High Street for 2 blocks to Park Street.

We parked at the Fairfield County building and followed the trails, some of which were paved, around the beautiful reflection pool, lake, fountains, pavilion, and waterfalls. Large oaks, gum, willow, river birch, and pines partially shaded the many floral displays of azaleas and other flowering shubbery. We were there early one morning near the swimming pool and the lake when the Peking and mallard ducks had not been fed. They followed us around until we shared some of our whole-wheat bread.

Information: Contact Director, Winnsboro Parks and Recreation, Congress St., Winnsboro, SC 29180; (803) 635-4041.

CHAPTER V
Private and College Trails
Private Trails
Asbury Hills United Methodist Camp (Greenville County)

On a number of older maps, including some USGS maps, there is a little valley as beautiful as Eden called "The Youth Camp." That camp is no longer little or anonymous. It is a 1,800-acre historical preserve owned and maintained by the South Carolina Methodist Conference. A few years ago it changed its name from Methodist Youth Camp to Asbury Hills, a more appropriate title because Francis Asbury, "the prophet of the long road," visited the area on his route from western North Carolina to Charleston. "We found a new road, lately cut, which brought me in at the head of Little River, at the old fording place, and within hearing of the falls (Raven Cliff Falls) a few miles off of the head of Matthews Creek. . . ," wrote Asbury in his *Journal* in 1803.

Before 1958, the conference had no camp of its own, so it borrowed or rented camping facilities. The dream of a campground to fulfill the programs of the Board of Education came closer to reality in 1962 when the conference purchased 312 acres and subsequently added another 1,688 acres. Today the camp has lodges, cabins, a dining hall, a swimming pool, an infirmary, a library, and other facilities. "We are now conducting a fund-raising campaign to expand our services and facilities," said Wes Voigt, the jovial camp director who has been there since 1961. "I have been here so long some Methodists believe I don't work for a living." We talked about hiking. "Hikers are welcome. They don't have to be Methodist," he said, smiling. "All we need to know are their names and if they plan to camp."

Access: From the jct of SC 11 and US 276 go N on US 276 for 2 mi to the camp entrance on the L. After 0.7 mi reach the camp office building.

Blue Trail

Length: 0.8 mi (1.3 km); **easy**; USGS Map: Table Rock; trailhead: near base of dam.

From the dining hall I followed the road toward the dam and before the base of the dam turned L at the sign. The trail circled the lake by the canoe dock, crossed the Asbury Trail on a ridge, descended to a small cascade, and exited below the dam by a large hemlock. Vegetation along the trail was mountain laurel, false down foxglove, trailing arbutus, fetterbush, oaks, and pines.

Yellow Trail

Length: 1 mi (1.6 km); **easy**; USGS Map: Table Rock; trailhead: parking area at dining hall.

From the dining hall near the bridge, I ascended on a slope in an open forest with scattered mountain laurel on a yellow-blazed loop trail, passing patches of trailing arbutus. I descended to Matthews Creek at 0.4 mi and rock-hopped across. I ascended on steep slope in a mixture of rhododendron, fetterbush, ferns, and galax. I turned R on an old road at 0.5 mi, passed the Tree House Camp, a sheltered assembly platform, and rock-hopped Matthews Creek again. From here I returned to the dining hall at 1 mi.

Asbury Trail

Length: 5.4 mi rt (7.6 km); **moderate**; USGS Map: Table Rock; trailhead: east end of dam.

I began this unmarked trail, formerly called "The Loop," with Ray Matthews and Sammy Gooding. We walked to the east end of the dam and followed the old wagon road on which Francis Asbury rode his horse early in the nineteenth century. "It wouldn't have taken Asbury long to get to Charleston if he had a road like this all the way," Ray said, as we ascended an easy contour. After 1 mi we crossed a stream, turned R and had glimpses of Caesar's Head through the tops of the trees. Yellow root and crested dwarf iris bordered the road. At 1.7 mi we reached a campsite on the R and a jct with an old road on the L. (The road on the L follows Matthews Creek for 1.3 mi up to Raven Cliff Falls.) We continued ahead, rock-hopping across the cascading Matthews Creek. After passing a campsite on the L we ascended to a more recently used road. Here we turned R in our return to Asbury Hills. Numerous small streams trickled, bubbled, or splashed across the road each time we descended from the hillside. At one stream we saw bush honeysuckle (*Diervilla sessilifolia*), a yellow flowering shrub found only in high elevations of Greenville and Oconee counties in South Carolina.

Erosion caused by trespassing four-wheel-drive vehicles at 3.4 mi was so severe the creators of the ravines could no longer trespass. We continued to descend and reached US 276 at 4.3 mi. We entered a gate on the R and descended for 0.7 mi by the camp cabins to the jct with the camp entrance road. After turning R we hiked the paved road for another 0.4 mi to complete our loop of 5.4 mi.

Information: Contact Director, Asbury Hills United Methodist Camp, 150 Asbury Drive, Cleveland, SC 29635; (803) 836–3711.

Bethelwoods (York County)

Between York and Rock Hill, there is a little Eden with 150 acres of clean woodland and a lake with wood ducks. It is Bethelwoods, where "childhood is given back to children, family life is returned to the family, and the pleasurable art of conversation is rediscovered" in rustic cabins, at pioneer wagon camps, in fields and meadows, in a swimming pool, in canoes, and on trails. Bethelwoods is a Christian Education Center and Joint Camping Venture of Charleston-Atlantic and Providence presbyteries; it was formerly Piedmont Springs Bethel Presbytery, founded in 1936. It has programs for all ages and is open all year. Visitors are welcome and should request permission at the office to hike the trails. In addition to the trails described below, another is being developed around the perimeter of the camp.

Access: From the jct of SC 161 and SR 47 (6 mi E from downtown York and 9.5 mi W from I-77), turn on SR 47 and go 1.5 mi to SR 195. Turn L, and the camp entrance is on the L.

Bethelwoods Nature Trail and Wagon Camp Trail

Length: 1.6 mi rt ct (2.6 km); easy; USGS Map: Rock Hill; trailhead: office parking area.

To hike the nature trail, I walked from the office across the dam and entered a young forest of Virginia pine, red and white oaks, dogwood, sweet gum, and poplar. The trail was wide and clean. At 0.2 mi there was a tree house on the L. After entering a more mature forest, I curved L and reached the lake at 0.5 mi. Following the lakeshore I passed through wildflowers including milkweed, monkey flower, ironweed, lyre-leaf sage, everlasting, Solomon's seal, Maryland aster, and sericea.

Before beginning the next loop, I talked to Rebecca White, an administrative secretary who has been at the camp for more than 10 years. "I believe I love it here because of the program for all ages and the atmosphere," she said. From the office I followed the Wagon Camp Trail by the swimming pool to the Wagon Camp—a camp where campers sleep four to a wagon with built-in bunks and canvas covers—at 0.3 mi. I continued on a camp road to a field with scattered hickories and apple trees. At 0.5 mi I turned L on the wagon road by a large pen oak. At the wagon camp I turned R and backtracked to the office parking area at 0.8 mi.

Information: Contact Director, Bethelwoods, 922 West Mount Gallant Rd., York, SC 29745; (803) 366–3722.

The Bishop Gravatt Center (Aiken County)

The Bishop Gravatt Center is the camp and conference center for the Episcopal Diocese of Upper South Carolina. Since 1948 it has provided summer camping for children and youth. Located on 240 acres with two lakes, a complex of educational buildings, dining halls, and motel-type lodges, the center's recreational facilities are available year round for conferences and retreats.

Access: From the jct of I-20 and SR 49, go 0.8 mi NW on SR 49, and turn L on Kedron Church Road for 1.2 mi to Camp Gravatt Road, on the R.

Camp Gravatt Lake Trail

Length: 1.4 mi (2.2 km); easy; USGS Map: Ridge Spring; trailhead: parking area at dam.

Arriving at Camp Gravatt, I took the first road L, which curved around the lake to the dam, and parked. I met the congenial Rev. Clyde L. Ireland, the camp director, who gave me trail directions. He mentioned that I might see some wildlife—deer, wild turkey, fox, squirrel, and rabbit. I crossed the dam and entered the forest. An orange blaze was my guide through longleaf and shortleaf pine, white cedar, poplar, oaks, and gum. Wildflowers were orange milkwort, sensitive briar, aster, running pea, skullcap, butterfly weed, goat's rue, and trailing arbutus. After 0.3 mi I noticed a large patch of sundews on the trail. At 0.7 mi the orange-blazed trail took a sharp turn R off the road (a spur trail, the Hill Loop went L with a blue blaze). I crossed a feeder stream to the lake. A weather-worn sign said "Turner's Bridge," but the sign had outlasted the bridge. I came out of the woods to a vegetable garden and passed a dining hall and volleyball court. I turned R around a feeder stream to the lake; calicroot was flowering at 1.2 mi. After following the dirt road back to the dam I went to see the Reverend Ireland. He was in the kitchen. I asked about hikers who might wish to visit the camp in the future. "They would be welcome," he said, "but they might wish to check with us to see if we are open."

Information: The Bishop Gravatt Center, 1006 Camp Gravatt Road, Aiken, SC 29801; (803) 648–1817.

Camp Pee Dee (Marlboro County)

Camp Pee Dee is owned and operated by the New Harmony Presbytery. It serves 50 Presbyterian churches and is also available for rent to other church groups. For all others who wish to hike the Canoe Lake Nature Trail, permission is necessary from the camp superintendent.

Access: From SC 9 and SC 38 N jct in Bennettsville, go N on SC 38 for 8.9 mi to SR 165; turn L and go 1.4 mi to Aarons Temple Church and SR 257. Turn L on SR 257 and go 0.8 mi to the entrance of Camp Pee Dee on the R. It is 0.7 mi to the gate from here. From Wallace take SC 9 E 1.2 mi from US 1 jct to SR 165 at Wallace High School and go 8 mi to the camp entrance.

Canoe Lake Nature Trail

Length: 1.6 mi (2.6 km); **easy**; USGS Map: Wallace; trailhead: parking area by the lake.

From the camp entrance I went 0.4 mi L on a paved road to the gravel-road entrance to Canoe Lake. After parking, I hiked across the dam and turned L at 0.1 mi by the lake border, following a white-blazed trail. I passed through slash, loblolly, and longleaf pines, scrub oaks, sweet pepperbush, sweet bays, bracken, bee balm, henbit, rattlebox, woodland sage, and other wildflowers. At 0.7 mi I reached a former beaver colony with dozens of stumps left by beavers. It was a chilly winter day and quiet except for a few songbirds. All the beavers had gone. I thought about *Paddy*, an orphan beaver made famous by Canadian naturalist R. D. Lawrence.

I turned off an old fire road at 1 mi, crossed a small stream, and returned to the fire road at 1.1 mi. I left the fire road at 1.4 mi and completed the trail loop at 1.6 mi.

Information: Contact Camp Superintendent, Route 4, Box 232, Bennettsville, SC 29512; (803) 479–3051. Or contact, Executive Secretary, 108 North Cashua Dr. (P.O. Box 4025), Florence, SC 29502; (803) 662–8411.

Camp Thunderbird (York County)

Founded in 1936, Camp Thunderbird is one of the best summer camps in the state for boys and girls ages 7 to 16. It features a fleet of sailboats, motorboats, and canoes; an excellent comprehensive program in aquatic sports including whitewater; hiking, camping, and backpacking; golf; gymnastics; rappelling and rock climbing; tennis; equestrian sports; field sports, and nature study. Its objectives are to develop, through quality leadership, interpersonal relationships, spiritual growth, self reliance, and self confidence. The Environmental Education Center offers programs for school groups from September through May. The camp is owned and operated by the Young Men's Christian Association of Charlotte and Mecklenburg County (North Carolina). Visitors are welcome to hike the nature trail, but ask for permission at the camp office.

Access: On SC 49 0.3 mi W of the Buster Boyd Bridge at Lake Wylie, turn off SC 49 at the River Hill Plantation to the camp entrance on the L.

Camp Thunderbird Nature Trail

Length: 1.2 mi (1.9 km); easy; USGS Map: Lake Wylie; trailhead: at the rear of the Environmental Education Center.

Ask the office staff for a trail guide. This guide covers 12 stations and twice that many that explain piedmont trees, as well as explaining the rock formations, soil layers, forest succession, and ecology. It is a walking, living, outdoor classroom for any age.

Information: Contact Director, Camp Thunderbird, Route 7, Box 50, Clover, SC 29710; (803) 831–2121.

Francis Beidler Forest in Four Holes Swamp (Dorchester County)

The National Audubon Society, owner of the nation's oldest private sanctuary system, manages the 5,500-acre Francis Beidler Forest, one of its 80 wildlife preserves in the United States. It also owns the forest jointly with the Nature Conservancy. The forest is named in honor of the lumberman-conservationist who preserved the area from logging

in the late nineteenth century. His decision allows the public to see the largest remaining stands of bald cypress and tupelo gum in the world. In a cathedral setting these 1,000-year-old giants and other trees such as water ash, water elm, water hickory, and water locust tower over a classic blackwater swamp. It cost $2.8 million to purchase the land, and the society has also raised funds to build the longest boardwalk trail in the state, which is designed to accommodate the physically handicapped. A Visitor-Interpretive Center with all telephone and power lines underground welcomes the visitor from the individually designated parking spaces. No camping or pets are allowed. (A small fee is charged for a visit; the sanctuary is closed on Mondays.)

Access: The forest is 40 miles NW of Charleston off I-26. Take exit 187 to SC 27 and to US 78 following the signs. From I-95 jct with I-26 turn off I-26 at exit 177 to Harleyville, and follow the signs SE on US 178 to SR 28.

Four Holes Swamp Trail

Length: 1.6 mi (2.6 km); easy; USGS Map: Harleyville; trailhead: Visitor Center.

From the Visitor Center I followed the signs, and on the boardwalk I sensed that this hike would be different from any I had ever experienced. I felt suspended in a world changed only by the seasons—in the summer and fall the swamp has low water or spaces with none at all, and in the winter and spring the water level is full. This fluctuation allows observation of more than 120 species of birds and 50 species of mammals and reptiles.

Halfway along the boardwalk was a rain shelter and a spur section that led to Lake Goodson for a view of a more open area of water. Water rippled around the shadowy base of the cypress knees, making them look like brown stones in a lake. The coiled supplejack hung through the Spanish moss, ominous, endless. I could easily spend a day on this trail, resting and observing the tranquil splendor of an ecosystem that is fast becoming extinct. Mike Dawson, a sanctuary naturalist transplanted from New York, said that the "forest grows on you; each walk is a new classroom." Emerson would likely agree. In one of his lectures he stated: "I would study, I would know, I would admire forever."

I have hiked the winding boardwalk in all seasons. On one of my last trips, when the water was low I saw a large cottonmouth moccasin with his broad head resting on a small branch in the water, waiting for an unfortunate lizard or frog. Growing nearby were flowering dragon head and lavender *justicia*.

Information: Contact Sanctuary Director, Francis Beidler Forest, Route 1, Box 600, Harleyville, SC 29448; (803) 462–2150.

Harbison Recreation Center (Richland and Lexington Counties)

Harbison has the state's longest cement trail, a lighted trail that weaves among the pines and rings with the laughter of children every day. Harbison is a model development of beautiful residential areas, housing for senior citizens, shopping, offices, parks, greenways, schools, and recreation. The developers planned this city with a parklike atmosphere, housing to suit people of all ages, lakes for boating, and trails for bicycling, jogging, and hiking—a city with energy, vision, and a slogan of "we're building your tomorrow."

At the community center, designed for year-round fun and relaxation, is an Olympic indoor swimming pool, a gymnatorium, an auditorium, racquet/handball courts, exercise rooms, saunas, and facilities for art exhibits, recitals, and poetry readings. Although the development is private, Richard Friedberg, the development director, said that nominal fees are charged to nondevelopment visitors, but the trails are open to the public without charge.

Access: On US 176 NW of Columbia (4.3 mi from I-20 jct), turn at the entrance L (across from the Harbison State Forest). Follow Harbison Boulevard to Hillpine Road R, and turn L to the center. From I-26 (exit 101) take US 176 SE 1.7 mi to enter on the R.

Harbison Trails

Length: 7 mi rt ct (11.2 km); **easy;** USGS Map: Columbia N; trailhead: Community Recreation Center.

From the Community Recreation Center I followed the trail E on a main line of 8-foot-wide concrete (connector trails are 5 ft wide) to Creekside Place, curved R and later entered a tunnel under Piney Woods Road. Other tunnels followed at Hillpine and Harbison Boulevard. I followed a labyrinth of routes, all well marked, to Lakeside, circled the lake, and returned to the Community Center. The center's manager said that the trail system has more than 3,100 cubic yards of cement and that it is "part of a greenway system with approximately 9 additional miles planned." As the trails extend they will connect to the second lake, across I-26.

Wild vegetation on the trail includes pines, oaks, maple, hickory, sourwood, dogwood, ash, elm, and sumac. On one of my visits I saw ferns, false indigo, cattails, woodland sunflowers, and meadow pink near Lakeside. On a peninsula near a children's playground, Mark Austin and Jamie Scheuch were playing in the sand. We talked about the trails. They said what they liked best is that "the trails are lighted and we can walk after dark."

Support Facilities: (See Sesquicentennial State Park.)

Information: Contact Manager, Harbison Community Association, 106 Hillpine Rd., Columbia, SC 29212; (803) 781–2281.

Hilton Head Island (Beaufort County)

Hilton Head Island contains some of the world's finest resorts, some of which have parklike natural areas or preserves. A few have private trails that may be open to the public, depending upon the stages of development. In the mid-1950s the Byrnes Bridge connected the island to the mainland, resulting in a rapid growth of resort paradises with year-round facilities.

The Island has a history of at least 4,000 years, beginning with the American Indians who lived on the island. From 1526, when it was sighted by the Spanish, to the early

1700s, Spanish, French, and English pirates fought for its control. In 1663 English Capt. William Hilton, for whom the island is named, sailed the *Adventure* into Port Royal Sound and described the area as the "best and frutefullest ile ever was seen."

In the early eighteenth century, English settlers established plantations and used West African "Gullah" slaves to raise rice, indigo, and Sea Island cotton.

In 1941 Josephine Pinchney wrote *Hilton Head*, a historical novel based on the life and times of Henry Woodward (ca. 1646-1686), a surgeon befriended by the Indians in the Port Royal area. An early South Carolina hero, he has been called the "first English settler."

With the outbreak of the Civil War, approximately 25,000 Union troops and naval personnel occupied the island as a base for blockading Southern coastal cities, chiefly Charleston and Savannah. This occupation is covered in detail in Robert Carse's *Department of the South: Hilton Head Island in the Civil War*. After the war the island was left to the freed slaves, with the exception of a few large holdings of property retained by Northern investors as hunting areas. The former slaves developed their own culture—farming, fishing, education, religion, and dialect.

Nearly 6,000 Gullah dialect words have been identified among the Gullah of the island and other Sea Islands in South Carolina and Georgia. Some of them have been incorporated into standard English usage: *goober* for peanuts, *juke* as in jukebox, and *gumbo* for okra. Their rapid speech did not carry a drawl. A folk art group, Bessie Jones and the Sea Island Singers, has been touring America for a number of years to illustrate the island heritage. (Between Beaufort and Hunting Island on US 21 is Penn Center, a museum of the heritage of the black people of the sea islands.)

Access: Hilton Head Island is 40 mi NE from Savannah and 95 miles SW from Charleston. From the jct of SC 170 and US 278 follow US 278.

Support Facilities: Outdoor resorts on Hilton Head Island may be restricted to motor homes or full hook-up units. The nearest state-park campground is Hunting Island State Park (see Chapter III). A commercial campground is KOA-Point South, from exit 33 on I-95 and US 17, on US 17 behind Best Western Motel. Address: Route 1, Yemassee, SC 29945; (803) 726–5733/5728. Full svc, rec fac. including short hiking trails. Open all year.

Information: Contact Chamber of Commerce, P. O. Box 5647, Hilton Head Island, SC 29928; (803) 785–3673.

Hitchcock Woods (Aiken County)

A 1,420-acre preserve, Hitchcock Woods has an extraordinary network of dirt roads for hikers, joggers, or equestrians. It is one of the last virgin forests in the area. The tract was originally owned by William C. Whitney and Thomas Hitchcock who used it as a hunting preserve. After Whitney's death, Hitchcock purchased the estate and later he and his daughter, Helen Clark, gave it to the Hitchcock Foundation in 1939 to "never be sold to a private individual or firm."

Maintenance of the trails, bridges, and signs, and the management and protection of the natural resources in Hitchcock Woods are all directed by the trustees of the Hitchcock Foundation, a tax-exempt, nonprofit organization. The trustees request that users of the forest not litter, smoke, fish, hunt, build fires, or use motorized vehicles. (For more information, contact the Hitchcock Foundation, P. O. Box 1702, Aiken, SC 29802.)

Access: From downtown Aiken at the jct of Richland Avenue, US 78, SC 302, and Laurens Street, take Laurens S for 6 blocks to South Boundary Avenue and turn R. Park in the parking area at the gated road.

Hitchcock Woods Trails

Length: 20 mi (32 km); easy to moderate; USGS Map: Aiken; trailhead: end of South Boundary Street.

Each time I hike sections of this magnificent forest, I notice something new—a larger loblolly, or mulberry, or sweet gum or wildflower, or another cliff. Because the trails on the roads crisscross so frequently, and because spur trails require some backtracking, it was impossible to measure this network or describe how to hike it all. No camping is allowed, so I carried a day pack and carefully noted which direction I took at each intersection. In addition to all the roads, there are at least another 10 miles of dragline.

A linear gauge of distance from the trailhead to the memorial gate is 0.4 mi. Here is a sign that reads: "This entrance is created in memory of Francis R. Hitchcock by his friends, 1859-1926." From here it is 0.4 mi to the old Aiken Horse Show ring (a grassy field), but 0.6 mi if you ascend R on the road. From the ring it is another 1 mi to Barton's Lake, and another 1.3 mi to Dibble Road.

Information: Contact Greater Aiken Chamber of Commerce, 400 Laurens St. NW, Aiken, SC 29802; (803) 648-0485.

Lake Hartwell KOA (Anderson County)

Lake Hartwell KOA has 140 campsites and all the facilities familiar to campers who use their "year-round vacation wonderland" services. The trail described below is open to the public, but the KOA staff requests that anyone on the premises other than registered campers inform them.

Access: From I-85 and SC 187 (exit 14), go 1 mi SE on SR 187.

KOA Nature Trail

Length: 1.2 mi rt (1.9 km); **easy**; USGS Map: La France; trailhead: campsite 82.

From the office we walked to campsite 82 and followed a red-blazed trail through a pine forest with an understory of sassafras, strawberry bush, dogwood, gum, deerberry, and honeysuckle. We descended to a hardwood forest at 0.2 mi, crossed a ravine, and ascended to another stand of pine. At 0.3 mi we took the L fork and crossed a paved road, Wham

Circle, at 0.5 mi. We followed the trail to a narrow peninsula for excellent views of Lake Hartwell at 0.6 mi and then backtracked. (An alternate return is to hike the road R for a total of 1.5 mi.)

Information: Lake Hartwell KOA, Route 11, Box 551, Anderson, SC 29621; (803) 287–3161.

Magnolia Plantation and Gardens (Charleston County)

All the superlatives you have heard or read about this historic garden with the seven bridges are true. John Galsworthy, distinguished author and garden specialist, has said it is the "most beautiful in the world . . . beyond anything I have ever seen." "Acres upon acres of rapturous beauty," according to *Readers Digest*; and "Artists and poets have labored in vain to convey their impressions of the loveliness," *National Geographic* has written. Internationally known as America's oldest major garden (ca. 1685), this treasure house of beauty by the Ashley River is listed in the National Register of Historic Places. It is the 300-year-old ancestral home of the Drayton family, a family whose influence on colonial and early United States history is well documented.

The plantation was named "Magnolia" by Stephen Fox, the first owner, whose daughter Ann married Thomas Drayton, Jr., in the late seventeenth century. The gardens are now considered to be America's oldest man-made attraction. Originally a formal English garden designed by Thomas Drayton, Jr., it had expanded to ten acres by 1716. In 1825 John Grimke Drayton inherited the plantation and began to transform the gardens into a more informal and natural design. Since 1975 it has been owned by John Drayton Hastie (the ninth generation), who continues to develop and maintain its historic beauty as a nonprofit charitable foundation.

Open to the public since 1870, this garden of all seasons has more than 250 varieties of azaleas and 900 varieties of camellias. With these and all the outstanding displays of iris, tulips, jonquils, quince, hyacinths, and wisteria, it is obvious why some garden specialists say that springtime is its best season. Others say it is summer, with lilies, caladiums, canna, alliums, amaryllis, raphealepsis, oleander, pomegranate, hydrangeas, phlox, dahlias, roses, and mimosa. Summer blends into fall with roses, abelia, bougainvillea, hibiscus, cassia, lilies, and chrysanthemums. Horticulturists say there are several million plants here and that something is blooming every month.

The 500 acres contain more than the original garden area. There is a canoe and hiking trail through the water-fowl refuge; an eighteenth-century herb garden; the plantation house filled with educational displays of plantation life; a Biblical garden, which opened in February of 1983; a picnic area; a gift shop; a petting zoo; a seventeenth-century horticultural maze made of over 500 camellias; a topiary garden; the Audubon Swamp Garden; and the Carolina Woods Walk, which opened in 1988. The peak of azaleas is March 15 through April 30, and for camellias the peak is November 15 to March. There are no camping facilities. The gardens are open daily from 8:00 A.M. to dark, and there is an admissions charge. (Magnolia Gardens offers a special program called "Magnolia by Moonlight": groups can see sections of the gardens illuminated at night and can attend a wine and cheese party on the Plantation House porch. These and other activities, such as oyster roasts, fish frys, and receptions must have advance reservations.)

Access: On SC 61, Ashley River Road, go 6.5 mi NW from jct of SC 61 and SC 7 in Charleston.

Magnolia Gardens Trails

Length: 1.7 mi rt ct (2.7 km); **easy;** USGS Maps: Ladson, Johns Island; trailhead: parking area.

Although I had walked these combinations of courtly footpaths a number of times before, I set aside a day in June to walk and to measure them all and to hike the Wildlife Trail.

Walking among live oaks and peacocks, Eric Tang and I began the hike into the gardens in front of the main house

at the sign. We followed the 30 interpretive points. The first
stop was the Biblical garden of 50 species. At 0.4 mi we
reached the jct with the Wildlife Trail on the R. Then on
the L was the historic site where Adam Bennett, chief slave
to the Rev. John G. Drayton, was nearly hanged by General
Sherman's pillagers in their efforts to force Bennett to reveal
where the valuables of the plantation were buried. (It was
Bennett who later hiked the 250 miles to Flat Rock, N.C.,
to inform Drayton that though the house had been burned
to the ground, the "black roses," as Drayton affectionately
called his slaves, had not left and were continuing to take
care of the plantation and gardens.)

At 0.5 mi we came to the Drayton family underground
burial vault, which had been restored from the vandalism of
General Sherman's troops. We crossed two arched bridges
and reached the wildlife observation tower, dedicated to
George H. Burbage, at 0.7 mi. We returned to the main
garden area and crossed another arched bridge at signpost
#16. Another arched bridge followed, and a gazebo was on
the R at 1.1 mi. The fragrance of roses came at 1.3 mi,
shortly before we crossed another beautiful bridge. At the
nucleus of the gardens, there were large camellia japonicas
and decorative edges of azaleas at signpost #26. After a few
spur trails across the lawn, we reached signpost #30 at 1.7
mi.

Magnolia Wildlife Trail

Length: 3.4 mi (5.4 km); easy; USGS Maps: Ladson, Johns
Island; trailhead: parking area.

From the parking area we went back through the main
gardens to the Wildlife Trail entrance by the river. We followed the sign along the top of a dike and saw wax myrtle,
cedar, and small oaks on each side. A boreal breeze came
from across the marsh where we heard and saw egrets,
herons, ibis, rails, and marsh wrens—only a few of the 200
species of birds found in the preserve. Jets, like huge birds
from the marsh, lifted off from the International Airport

nearby. A number of turtles had come up on the open trail, dug holes, and were laying eggs. One turtle had finished and was covering her nest to let the sun provide incubation. At 1.2 mi we passed a lake drainpipe and the jct of a trail (0.4 mi) on the L leading to the observation tower. At 1.6 mi we turned R on a service road, and at 2 mi reached the Indian Mound, the largest prehistoric Indian burial mound on the East Coast. (Its artifacts are now in the Smithsonian Institution.) We entered a pine and oak forest and passed a nursery where attendants were preparing new plantings. At 2.4 mi we crossed the entrance paved road, entered another nursery, and turned sharply L at 2.6 mi. At 2.7 mi we passed the graves of Magnolia superintendent Adam Bennett, his wife Hannah, and their two sons, John and Ezekiel. (After Adam's death in 1910, his sons continued as superintendents until the 1940s.) We passed over a dike between lakes, reached a paved road at 3 mi, and turned R onto the road. We hiked back to the parking area at 3.4 mi. (A shorter route is to take the spur trail at 1.2 mi on the Wildlife Trail, go 0.4 mi to the observation tower, and return through the main gardens for a total of 2.3 mi.)

Support Facilities: One of the nearest campgrounds is Oak Plantation, a semiwooded campground on US 17, approximately 9 mi SW from the I-26 and US 17 jct. Full svc, rec fac. Open all year. Address: Route 2, Box 559, John's Island, SC 29455; (803) 766–5936.

Information: Contact Magnolia Plantation and Gardens, Route 4, Charleston, SC 29414; (803) 571–1266.

Middleton Place (Dorchester County)

We have J. J. Pringle Smith, a descendant of Henry Middleton, to thank for Middleton Place. A National Historic Landmark and America's oldest landscaped gardens, this majestic 110-acre rice plantation by the Ashley River was restored by Smith and his wife, Heningham, early in this century. Its original beauty and elegance, its "golden age," abruptly ended during the Civil War when maintenance vanished and General Sherman's troops burned the main plantation house in 1865. Only the south wing could be restored; it served as a family residence until it was opened to the public.

Its history begins with Henry Middleton in 1741. He designed the magnificent terraces, *allées,* and ornamental lakes to reflect the graceful designs of earlier French and English formal gardens.

From 1741 to 1865 the plantation was the family seat of four successive generations of Middletons—Henry, a president of the First Continental Congress; Arthur, a signer of the Declaration of Independence; the second Henry, governor of South Carolina and U.S. Minister to Russia; and Williams, a signer of the Ordinance of Secession in 1860.

The gardens and stableyards are open every day all year from 9:00 A.M. to 5:00 P.M.; the Middleton Place house is open from 10:00 A.M. to 4:30 P.M., but closed on Monday mornings. Admission is charged, and group rates are available by reservation. There is a picnic area, but camping on the property is not permitted. The Pavilion Restaurant is open daily 9:00 A.M. to 5:00 P.M. and serves light lunch, snacks, and beverages. Exclusive luncheons, parties, and banquets can be arranged by reservation. Among the annual events held here are May Faire in early May, the Spoleto Festival Finale (which has been known to swell attendance on the terraces to 6,000) in early June, the Scottish Games in mid-September, and the Plantation Days in mid-November.

Access: From downtown Charleston go 14 mi NW on SC 61 to entrance on R, or from jct of SC 61 and SC 165 at Cooks Cross Roads (S of Summerville) go 4.3 mi on SC 61 to entrance on L.

Middleton Place Trails

Length: 1.8 mi (2.9 km); **easy;** USGS Map: Stallsville; trailhead: parking area.

From the parking area my wife and I followed the signs to the R of a reflection pool and along a border of ornamental shrubs to the ruins of the 1741 house and to the restored 1755 south wing. From here we walked to the spring house and then to the edge of the main parterres where the original camellias given to the Middletons by André Michaux were planted. They were the first camellias planted in an American garden. The view of the terraces and the butterfly lakes is impressive from here. After we passed Arthur Middleton's tomb, we walked through a camellia *allée* and more formal gardens, passed huge crepe myrtles, and reached Cypress Lake. To our L was a path into the forest. Curving R, around a pool with azaleas, kalmia, palmetto, Spanish moss, and lilies, we admired the "wood nymph," a graceful marble statue that was buried for security during the Civil War.

Although we had heard of the 1,000-year-old Middleton Oak, it was not until we saw it that we understood its regal significance. We were told by a garden attendant that it was used "as an Indian 'Trail Tree,' a type of landmark or distance marker on the way to 'Whitepoint' or the Charleston peninsula."

From the sundial gardens we walked along the flooded rice fields to the butterfly lakes and the edge of the Ashley River. After turning R, through the azalea hillside, we crossed a bridge over an old rice millpond to visit the stableyards, a living outdoor museum with an active display of heritage crafts. At 1.8 mi we returned to the parking area.

Information: Middleton Place, Ashley River Road, Charleston, SC 29414; (803) 556–6020.

Paper Companies Recreation Areas

Two of the three major paper industries have trails open to the public: International Paper Company and West Virginia Pulp and Paper Company (WESTVACO).

International Paper Company (Horry County)

International Paper Company has been operating in South Carolina since construction of its Georgetown paper mill in 1936. It manages timberlands in North Carolina, South

Carolina, and Georgia for timber production, while maintaining prime wildlife habitat and environmental quality. In Bainbridge, Georgia, it operates a wildlife and forest research center. In South Carolina the Indian Camp Forest Trail is being "refurbished," according to a report from Emily Williamson, public relations coordinator.

Indian Camp Forest Trail

Length: 0.3 mi (0.6 km); **easy**; USGS Map: Conway; trailhead: behind the maintenance building.

From the jct of US 501 and SC 544 near Conway, go S on SC 544, passing the University of South Carolina Coastal Carolina Campus for 1.5 mi to company's sign on R. Park near the maintenance building.

This short nature trail is a botanical garden, an open aviary, and an example of what private timber industries can offer the public. Although owned by the International Paper Company, the trail is a cooperative project between the company and the Horry-Georgetown Technical Education Center. Open from sunrise to sunset, without charge, it has 66 interpretive trail markers with information about Southern forests.

After beginning the trail near a stand of slash pine, we descended from a dry hillside forest to a hardwood mesic area. We crossed Quail Creek and circled back to follow its banks before ascending to the end of the loop. Among the oaks along the trail were swamp chestnut, laurel, water, white, red, blackjack, and post. Other trees were hickory, ash, mulberry, willow, and loblolly pine. Flowering shrubs and wildflowers included trillium, dogwood, meadow beauty, orchids, blazingstar, sweet pepperbush, and beautyberry. More than 25 species of birds live in the area. As all four of America's poisonous snakes have been seen in the area, it is wise to stay on the trail.

Information: Contact International Paper Co., Route 6, Box 123, Conway, SC 29526; (803) 347-3791, or International Paper Co., P.O. Box 518, Georgetown, SC 29440; (803) 546–2573.

Westvaco (Colleton County)
Westvaco Corporation has timber management in South Carolina, Virginia, West Virginia, Tennessee, and Kentucky. For more than 85 years, the company has made its lands available for hunting, fishing, nature study, and other recreational and educational activites. The company has designated appropriate sites on its lands for biological study and protection of wildlife. One of its protected public areas is the Edisto Nature Trail at Jacksonboro. According to Casey Canonge, Jr., public affairs forester in the Timberlands Division in Summerville, the company has "several areas with unique features such as Wassamassaw Swamp and Edisto Spruce Pine natural areas, but access is for educational and research purposes."

Edisto Nature Trail
Length: 1 mi (1.6 km); **easy;** USGS Map: Jacksonboro; trailhead: parking area.

On US 17N in Jacksonboro at the trail parking area, we examined the trail design for information and then hiked counterclockwise by 51 numbered interpretive markers. Some of the vascular plants were wax myrtle, black cherry, black and sweet gums, Devil's walking stick, Alabama supplejack, hackberry, switchcane, catalpa, yaupon, water hickory, sugarberry, and oaks. At 0.4 mi we crossed two boardwalks over marsh near an old phosphate mine. At 0.5 mi we passed an old barge canal that once went to the Edisto River and, at 0.6 mi, an old railroad tram used at the former phosphate factory. After hiking through areas that once were rice fields, we returned to the parking area.

Information: Westvaco Timberland Division, Southern Woodlands, P.O. Box 1950, Summerville, SC 29484; (803) 871–5000.

Champion International Corporation

A third paper company, the Champion International Corporation, has nearly 200,000 acres in South Carolina Wildlife Management lands "available for all reasonable public use." (See Wildlife Management Areas.) With nine regions in the nation, the company owns and manages forests throughout the South, the Lake States, the Rocky Mountains, and on the West Coast, as well as in Canada and Brazil. Its primary management objective on this and all tracts of fee lands is commercial timber production, but the corporation is also involved in numerous university research programs.

Although camping is not allowed, hikers will find many old logging roads suitable for nature study. On one occasion in the central part of the state, I found on one nature study hike an extremely fragrant white wild azalea, a species that Doug Rayne, botanist of the South Carolina Heritage Program, thinks is *Rhododendron viscosum*. Growing near it by a stream was a climbing hydrangea, *Decumaria barbara*, an aerial rooted vine that is also extremely fragrant.

Information: Contact Manager of Forest Lands, Champion International Corporation, 37 Villa Rd., Suite 402, Greenville, SC 29615; (803) 271–8404.

Peachtree Rock Preserve (Lexington County)

Organized in 1951, the Nature Conservancy is an international nonprofit organization committed to protecting natural diversity. It maintains a system of more than 900 natural sanctuaries in the United States and has more than 500,000 members. Among those natural sanctuaries is the Peachtree Rock Preserve, a 306-acre natural area purchased by the South Carolina Nature Conservancy in 1980.

A concentration of more than 350 species of plants and more than 50 species of birds makes the preserve an extraordinary classroom for nature study, and it is only 16 miles from Columbia, the state capital. Other distinctive features in the preserve are the sandhills and sandstone outcrops.

The preserve contains typical pine-scrub oak sandhills, with stands of mature longleaf pine. There are also hardwood coves with meandering streams. With these abound smaller plant communities, such as 10 acres of evergreen shrub bogs and 15 acres of seepage slopes. In addition, the rock formations have numerous cryptogamic flora. Of the nine species of reptiles, only the Carolina pigmy rattlesnake is poisonous. During one of my early summer visits, I saw a flicker, downy woodpecker, Carolina wren, Carolina chickadee, vireo, towhee, and of course a noisy mockingbird—all in one location.

Access: From Columbia take SC 302/215 SW past the Metropolitan Airport to jct with SC 6 in Edmund. Follow SC 302 and 6 to a fork. Take SC 6 0.7 mi to second paved road on L, Bethel Church Road. After 0.2 mi turn R at sign on dirt road and go 0.1 mi to parking area on L. (If from I-20, take SC 6, exit 55, for 9.3 mi to Bethel Church Road.)

Peachtree Rock Trail

Length: 3.6 mi ct (5.8 km); **moderate**; USGS Map: Pelion E; trailhead: parking area.

I followed the trail sign through young loblolly pines, turkey oak, bracken, and sparkleberry bushes until the trail divided at 0.1 mi. To the L was a 15-foot delicate waterfall. To the R was Peachtree Rock, a large sandstone rock balancing like a top, with mountain laurel scattered among the trees. The rock has marine fossils and intertidal deposits, evidence of its origin nearly 50 million years ago. Hard oxidized red sandstone, mottled red-yellow clay with a mixture of quartz pebbles, shell hash, kaolin sands and silica gave a history of its creation. Indicative of an ancient maritime environment are the tubelike burrows of an aquatic animal called *Calianassa major*.

I chose to first follow the trails to the R of Peachtree Rock. On these I crossed small streams flowing (sometime underground) to Hunt Creek. Titi, switchcane, and sensitive ferns were prominent. On a more open area I saw sticky foxglove, a number of *vaccinium*, St. John's wort, and sandwort. Although the *Manual of the Vascular Flora of the Carolinas* does not list it in Lexington County, I am almost sure I saw *Silene caroliniana* along the trail. A spur trail led to an area of galax and woody goldenrod.

After 1 mi I hiked R at the fork of two old roads near a sawdust pile. At 1.6 mi I backtracked and turned R, up an incline to see an enormous white sand dune at 1.8 mi. Among the sparse vegetation were lichens such as cushion moss and spikemoss. Bits of red ferruginous rocks appeared more red than ususal from the heavy dew. At 2 mi I faced a large colorful rock formation. Tan pebbles, pin-purple kaolin, shining mica, and quartz grains shadowed, reflected, merged to remind me of a Boccioni painting, and an observation of Alexander Pope in his *Essay on Man*: "All Nature is but art."

I ascended through a ground cover of evergreen sand myrtle, titi, and sweet pepperbush. A large cirque was to my L. At 2.4 mi I reached an old road, turned L, and passed the cemetery of the Bethel Methodist Church on the R. From here I descended to remnants of an old whiskey still and reached the waterfalls at 3.1 mi. After examining a number of spur trails, I returned to the parking area for a total of 3.6 mi. (This route can also be reversed to follow the conservancy's trail guide.)

Information: Contact The South Carolina Nature Conservancy, P.O. Box 5475, Columbia, SC 29250; (803) 254–9049.

Riverbanks Zoological Park and Gardens (Lexington County)

Riverbanks Zoo opened in April 1974 and has since received international recognition and awards for its excellence in design, animal collections, and conservation programs. Some of its outstanding features and accomplishments include the largest group of black howler monkeys in the world; the first successful hatching of the milky eagle owl in the Western Hemisphere; being the first zoo in the world to breed the South American Toco toucan; being instrumental in developing the computerized International Species Inventory System (ISIS); having one of the nation's finest aviaries and the largest environmental-type displays of polar bears and sea lions in North America. On exhibit are more than 185 individual mammals representing 52 species and more than 500 birds, representing 140 species.

The zoo's education department offers a wide variety of programs for school groups, families, scout groups, and adults. (There is a fee for all programs.) These include a Zoo Nature Trail walk and a special overnight Zoo Camp for students in grades 4 through 12. The camp involves a study of what is behind the scenes in zoo maintenance, animal hospitals, a commisary, and several animal holding areas. There is a minimum group size of 20 and a maximum of 30; the fee is $30 for each individual. Educational Department programs, some of which require a deposit, must be reserved in advance by calling (803) 256-4773.

Information: Contact Riverbanks Zoological Park, (P.O. Box 1060) 500 Wildlife Parkway, Columbia, SC 29202; (803) 256-4773.

Stumphouse Tunnel Park (Oconee County)

During the 1830s commercial interests between the Midwest and the seaport at Charleston led to plans for a connecting railroad. South Carolina's John C. Calhoun was on the original surveying team, and it was his support that kept the idea alive after the first abandonment of plans. Two years after his death, the state legislature chartered the Blue Ridge Railroad Company and endorsed bonds for more than $1,250,000 for stockholders to raise contractual funds of $17,000,400. Doubt about the wisdom of a tunnel through Stumphouse Mounatain led to a delay in plans until the company had assurance from H. B. Latrobe, an engineer specialist of the Baltimore and Ohio Railroad, that it was the best route. Construction began in January 1855.

The tracks would start in Belton, pass through Anderson, Pendleton, and Walhalla. From there they would gradually ascend around the southeast slopes of Turnip Top **Mountain** and tunnel through Saddle Mountain, Middle Tunnel Ridge, and Stumphouse Mountain. Three other states, Georgia, North Carolina, and Tennessee, would have companies build the railroad to its western terminus in Knoxville. A total of 13 tunnels were planned for a combined 13,820 feet, and the largest—5,863 feet—would be through Stumphouse Mountain.

The contractor for the Stumphouse tunnel was George Collyer, whose company began work in May 1856. To speed up the project, contractors had teams of workers at both ends of the tunnel. The laborers were mainly immigrants who worked 12 hours a day, six days a week, with only simple tools: sledgehammers, chisels, hand drills and black powder for blasting. At the peak of construction, a community of about 1,500 men, women, and children lived in a village called Tunnel Hill. But after three years and 4,363 feet into the tunnel, the contractor ran out of money, and the state refused to grant additional funds because of its pending secession from the United States. Tunnel Hill no longer had a purpose, and it died with the dream of the Blue Ridge Railroad.

Ownership of the area over the years has been a mixture of government and private ownership. Today the park is owned by the Pendleton District Historical and Recreational Commission, a government agency, but the Blue Ridge Railroad Historical Trail is on private property. It is open (free) during daylight hours for picnicking, visiting the Isaqueena Falls and the tunnel, and hiking. There is a small campground with sanitation facilities, and a nominal fee is required for overnight camping. Oliver Ridley, park ranger, showed us a stone culvert where a stream flows from the former railroad bed. "The state used all the tunnel rocks for gravel on the highways in the 1920s," Ridley said.

Access: From SC 28 turn on SR 226 (0.3 mi SE of Pickens Ranger District hq and 6 mi NW of Walhalla), and go 0.4 mi to parking area.

Isaqueena Falls Trail

Length: 0.2 mi rt (0.3 km); **moderate**; USGS Map: Walhalla; trailhead: top of falls area.

From the picnic area near the top of the falls, we followed the footbridge across the stream and descended on switchbacks on an exceptionally steep trail to the base of the 220-foot falls. We returned by the same route. The legend about the falls concerns a Cherokee maiden, Cateechee, who was called Isaqueena (also spelled Issaqueena) in Choctaw. Prior to the outbreak of the Cherokee War, Cateechee (meaning "Deer Head") had fallen in love with an English trader, Allan Francis. She overheard plans that the Cherokees were going to attack and massacre the inhabitants at Ninety Six. During the night she rode the distance to warn them. The village was saved, and Isaqueena married Francis. Later she was captured by the Cherokees, and in her escape she jumped off the top of the falls, landed on a ledge, and hid from her pursuers, who thought she was dead. Francis rescued her (probably having seen it happen), they canoed down Cane Creek, and lived happily ever after. (See Ninety-Six National Historic Site in Chapter II. For information on the Cateechee auto-trail, contact the DAR at 2003 Laurel Dr., Anderson, SC 29621.)

Blue Ridge Railroad Historical Trail

Length: 7.1 mi (11.4 km); **moderate** to **strenuous**; USGS Map: Walhalla; trailhead: Stumphouse Mountain tunnel.

We took our heavy-duty flashlights and walked 1,640 ft to the dead-end of the 25-foot-high and 17-foot-wide tunnel. We climbed up to the top tier of blue granite and cut out the lights to stand motionless and quiet. The temperature was 50 degrees, and the humidity was 90 percent. A stone and brick wall installed by Clemson University in the tunnel made light from the entrance appear as a pin point. Our reactions: "I could touch the dark, it was like velvet" . . . "I felt a vibration as if from the traffic overhead" . . . "I heard my heart" . . . "I heard a faint cathedral choir."

That was how Kevin Clarey, Taylor Watts, Les Parks, Dick Hunt, and I began our hike on the Blue Ridge Railroad Historical Trail. After 0.3 mi we walked back into daylight and followed the park road for 0.3 mi to cross a bridge over Cane Creek near the top of Isaqueena Falls. We took a sharp L up a steep path through rhododendron until we reached the old railroad bed.

(The trail was devised and developed by Boy Scout Troop 219 and sponsored by the Baraccas Men's Class, Seneca Baptist Church in Seneca in 1976. Boy Scouts who hike the trail are eligible for the Blue Ridge Railroad Trail patch and medal. The trail is listed in the National Register of Historic Railroad Trails.)

We turned R and followed a red-arrow marker through a border of hardwoods, elderberry, grape, blackberry, and raspberry vines. We bypasssed a caved-in cut at 0.8 mi. At 1.1 mi it was 90 yards L off the trail to a small opening of the 385-foot Middle Tunnel, which long ago filled with water. The trail skirted R on a slope with pine and oaks and honeysuckle, where timber cutting has opened new roads. We reached the N end of the tunnel at 1.4 mi. Ahead we crossed a deep ravine on what is a good example of the contractor's plans to fill all ravines and hollows with earth and rock; an arched rock culvert is used for drainage without wooden trestles.

At 1.8 mi we entered a deep cut across the ridge and crossed a ravine. Logging roads altered the old railroad bed where we crossed small streams for a short distance. At 2.7 mi we reached the S end of the 616-foot Saddle Tunnel, of which only 200 ft were ever completed. It too is filled with water and fallen earth at the entrance. Les, a Boy Scout, was ahead of us, and we heard him scream, "It's a nickie! It's a nickie!" By the time we reached him, the rattlesnake had vanished.

We climbed steeply, following the logo signs, to a ridge with wildflowers and turned L at 2.8 mi. We detoured around a large hornet nest and descended on a fresh dirt slide road made by a timber harvest of oaks, pines, and poplars. We reached the N end of Saddle Tunnel at 3.2 mi. Timber equipment had made the railroad bed wider as we passed through a deep cut at 3.4 mi. At 3.8 mi we turned off the lumber road and followed the logo signs onto the railroad bed for a section of undulating treadway. Cuts and ravines had not been completed at 3.8 mi, 4 mi, and 4.1 mi.

We reached graveled SR 174 at 4.2 mi, turned R, and followed SR 174 for 0.1 mi before turning R into a pine forest and the "white cliffs" exposed by the excavations. At 4.6 mi we went straight ahead at the fork and crossed a small stream at 4.7 mi. Back on the railroad bed, we crossed a timbered area where fallen pines covered the trail markers. After 0.1 mi we descended steeply again into a ravine, where mountain laurel, trailing arbutus, and gold star were prominent under the locust and poplar.

We climbed back to the railroad bed and noticed some mysterious rock shaped like a tombstone at 5 mi. Soon we ascended over the edge of a deep cut and descended steeply to reach a ravine at 5.2 mi. Twice we ascended steeply to the top of deep cuts, and we reached the top of the second at 5.5 mi. We descended and then ascended to an exceptionally deep cut where the trail was dangerously close to a precipice at 5.6 mi. At 5.8 mi we took a sharp L onto the railroad cut. After five more dips the trail leveled out, and we passed a private home on the L at 6.7 mi.

At 6.9 mi we came out in a clearing where large oaks were near the R border. (The No Trespassing signs here do not apply to hikers.) At 7.1 mi we arrived at a dirt road near SR 181.

To reach this point, E terminus, from downtown Walhalla take SR 148, N Church Street, at jct with SC 28 for 1 mi to SC 174. Turn L on SC 174, and go 1.7 mi to SR 181. Turn L on SR 181 for 0.1 mi to R turn on dirt road. (For the complete Blue Ridge Railroad Trail, go to West Union on SC 28, and turn on SR 324, Torrington Street, at the S&W Grocery and Exxon Station. Cross the Southern

RR toward the sawmill, and begin the foot trail on the L in the forest. It goes NW on the old railroad bed to Cane Creek, turns R and comes back to Torrington Street to cross the bridge and return along the edge of a field to Brown's Lake at the dam. From here it follows the exit road to SC 183, N. Catherine Street, and turns R. From SC 183 it turns L on SR 397 toward the Walhalla High School where it takes a sharp R in the forest. After a L it crosses SR 397 again, passes the Walhalla Middle School, and follows the old railroad bed to a road. Here it turns R to SR 58, takes a L on SR 58 and goes to the jct of SR 181. At SR 181 it turns L, passes the grocery store and Exxon station on the R, crosses SR 174 and goes 0.1 mi to a dirt road on the R, referred to above at 7.1 mi. Total distance is approximately 5 mi.) (A shortcut on the trail from here is to take SR 174 N for 2.3 mi to the trail jct on the L.)

Information: Contact Executive Director, Blue Ridge Council, Boy Scouts of America, P.O. Box 6628, Station B, Greenville, SC 29606; (803) 233–8363; or contact Pendleton District Historical and Recreational Commission, 125 East Queen St., P.O. Box 565, Pendleton, SC 29670; (803) 646–3782.

Truluck Vineyards (Florence County)

There is a touch of France in the Old South, a touch made possible by the ingenuity, foresight, and determination of Dr. James P. Truluck, Jr., of Lake City. His touch began as a dream in 1959 when he was on a tour of duty with the U.S. Air Force in France. "He was a country boy hankering for culture, and he visited French vineyards in his off hours, developing a taste for wine," Thomas C. Cothran reported in the *Kalamazoo Gazette*. Truluck recognized the similarities of the soil and the climate in France to his native low country in the Palmetto State.

As a result he created his own hybrid vineyard by grafting some of the best French grapevines on tougher native American stock, and by 1976 his winery was completed. Six varietals, four blends, and seven specialties are now produced.

Winery tours and wine tasting are Tuesday through Saturday, 10:30 A.M. to 5:30 P.M.

Access: In Lake City at the jct of US 52 and SR 10 (near David's Restaurant), take SR 10, which becomes SR 85, and go 3.2 mi E to entrance on R.

Truluck Vineyards Trail

Length: 1.2 mi (1.9 km); **easy**; USGS Map: Hyman; trailhead: vineyards office.

After entering the gate we drove through the vineyard toward the winery and office. At a corner there was a sign, "Ne piquez pas les grappes." Since it was June, two months before harvest time, the sign didn't apply to my hiking team. At the winery we were welcomed first by a strutting peacock, then staff personnel Dorothy "Dot" Hanna and Karen Warner. We talked about the trail and vineyard. Dot, who has worked here since 1972, said that her "favorite wine is 'Carlos,' sweet and grapey, a native muscadine. But I enjoy meeting the visitors more than tasting wine." They showed us where we could walk or drive around the lake. When we crossed the lake dam, the ducks, geese, and swans gave us another welcome. Then we turned L, walked between rows of grapevines to a small forest of sweet gum, pine, and oaks. After passing a residence we curved L, reentered the vineyard, followed the road, and completed a loop to the office. "You will have to come back the last weekend of July," Dot said. "That is when we have a French festival, a 'Day in France.'"

"Merci beaucoup, nous allons essayer," I said. *"Au revoir."*

Information: Contact Truluck Vineyards, P.O. Drawer 1265, Lake City, SC 29560; (803) 389–3400.

World of Energy (Oconee County)

Keowee-Toxaway Nature Trail

Length: 0.3 mi (0.5 km); **easy**; USGS Map: Old Pickins; trailhead: parking area.

For access to the trail from Pickens take SC 183 W, and from Walhalla take SC 183 N 10.5 mi to Lake Keowee. Follow signs to World of Energy. From Seneca take SC 130 N to SC 183 for 8 mi, and continue on SC 183-130 to the visitor center entrance on the R.

This trail is at the Duke Power Company's Keowee-Toxaway Complex, where the Oconee Nuclear Station began operation in 1973; the visitor center, the World of Energy, opened in 1969, and it offers an outstanding tour of seven exhibit areas explaining three energy sources: water, coal, and nuclear fission.

From the parking and picnic area, we descended on steps from the large entrance sign into the forest. Some plants were labeled; my team of hikers saw oaks, dogwood, hickory, holly, sourwood, ferns, bloodroot, wild hydrangea, squirrel cup, Hercules club, Oconee bells, Solomon's seal, sericea, wild azalea, five fingers, and Bowman's root. There were scenic views of Lake Keowee from the footbridges. The World of Energy is open Monday through Saturday, 9:00 A.M. to 5:00 P.M.; Sunday, 12:00 to 5:00 P.M.; closed on major holidays.

Information: Contact World of Energy, P.O. Box 1687, Clemson, SC 29633; (803) 882–5620.

COLLEGE TRAILS
Clemson University (Oconee, Pickens, and Anderson Counties)

Lake Issaqueena Recreation Area

Indian Creek Forest Trail and Lawrence Trail
Length: 3.1 mi rt ct (5 km); easy; USGS Map: Clemson; trailhead: parking area.

From the jct of US 76 and SC 122 in Clemson, I drove N on SC 133 for 3.8 mi to a Shell service station on the L (Lawrence Chapel was ahead on the L). I turned L, then R, into the 17,000-acre Clemson Experimental Forest. After 0.5 mi on a graveled road, I reached the Indian Creek Forest Trail parking and picnic area on the L.

I had a drink from the nearby springhouse and crossed Indian Creek into a hardwood forest, passed another spring by picnic tables, and followed a well-graded and clean trail. Mountain laurel and white pine were below the trail slope, Indian pipe and black cohosh were on the trail borders. At 0.4 mi I crossed a footbridge at a cove. A cemented stone resting bench was on the L. Twisted stalk and crested dwarf iris bloomed here. At 0.5 mi was a fork. To my L began the Lawrence Trail, and the Indian Creek Forest Trail continued on my R. I turned R, crossed a stone bridge at 0.6 mi, and passed through a small meadow to ascend on the ridge slope. At 0.9 mi I returned to the parking area.

I went back on the Indian Creek Forest Trail to the Lawrence Trail and followed upstream, crossed the stream in a cove with a mixed forest, and descended slightly to a L curve at 0.3 mi. Following the N side of the ridge, I saw signs of timber harvesting and an old logging road at 0.8 mi. Descending through a pine forest, I reached an old roadbed at 1.1 mi at a trail jct with the Issaqueena Trail. (Straight ahead it is 2 mi one-way on the Issaqueena Trail to the dam.) I turned R 100 yards to Indian Creek and Willow Springs picnic area. I drank from the clean cement spring and walked up the road for 0.6 mi to the point of origin at Indian Creek parking area for a round-trip total of 2.2 mi. (From Willow Springs picnic area, it is 0.5 mi to the Lakeside area and another 0.5 mi to the Wildcat Creek recreation area. After another 2 mi on the graveled road there is a jct with SC 37-27; 0.5 mi farther is the falls area at the dam.)

Issaqueena Trail

Length: 4 mi rt (6.4 km); **easy;** USGS Map: Clemson; trailhead: Issaqueena Lake dam.

From the Indian Creek area I returned to the forest entrance and turned R toward the Issaqueena Lookout Tower on the R. After enjoying a panoramic view from the tower, I continued on the paved road for 0.4 mi to a graveled road on the R. From here to the dam it was 1.5 mi. I followed the well-designed trail up the E side of Lake Issaqueena through dense rhododendron and mountain laurel. At 0.4 mi I crossed a small stream, curved around from the cove, and saw a huge tulip poplar at 0.5 mi on the R, measuring 14 ft in cir. The views of the lake from the trail were impressive. Maiden hair fern, crane-fly orchids, and crested dwarf iris grew in the damp coves. At 0.8 mi I crossed another small stream. By the edge of the lake a family of beaver had chiseled out a section of saplings to reroof their lodge. I turned R, toward the Indian Creek cove at 1.6 mi. To my L were water lilies, and in the path were ladies tresses. Christmas ferns and wood betony grew on both sides of the trail. Wild azaleas and filberts were scattered in the open forest, and rose pink and bear's foot were prominent. At 1.9 mi I entered a stand of white pine and poplar to reach the jct with the Lawrence Trail at 2 mi. I backtracked.

On the way back the angle of the late afternoon sun made the lake look as if it were glazed with shimmering silver and pink flakes. It was an Emerson sunset, "the world through a prism."

Outdoor Research Laboratory

Beaver Dam Trail and Firetower Trail

Length: 1.8 mi rt ct (3.9 km); easy; USGS Map: Clemson; trailhead: Outdoor Lab parking area.

From US 76 Dick Hunt and I turned on SR 56 SW of Pendleton and drove 2.4 mi to the Clemson University Outdoor Lab. We met the lab director, Charlie White, who told us there are three campgrounds: Camp Sertoma, Jaycees Camp Hope, and Camp Logan. They all have dormitories or cottages, cafeteria, and recreational areas. "The facilities are open for rent to groups for overnight or day use," White said. Physical fitness and nature study are part of the lab's program.

From the parking area at the lab office, Kresge Hall, we entered a pine forest on a winding, graded white-blazed trail. Common on the trail were dogwood, reindeer moss, hawthorn, and jessamine. At 0.3 mi we crossed a footbridge and at 0.4 mi reached a beaver dam. Growing in the area were switchcane, elderberry, papaw, Devil's walking stick, ferns, alder, cattails, joe-pye weed, trillium, cohosh, and wild azaleas. At 0.6 mi we crossed a footbridge over a small stream and crossed another stream at 0.7 mi. Ascending we passed sassafras and goldenrod. At 0.8 mi we reached the paved entrance road, turned L, walked on the paved road for 0.25 mi, and turned R onto the trail (not the old road). From here we ascended to the Clemson Lookout Tower at 1.1 mi. We could not climb the tower, but we tried our agility at rope swinging from a large red oak. We descended on a yellow-blazed trail, crossed a service road at 1.4 mi, entered Camp Logan at 1.5 mi, and returned to the parking area. The paved trails, which accommodate the handicapped, are between the camps and the lakeside.

Treaty Oak Area

Treaty Oak Trail

Length: **0.4 mi** (0.6 km); **easy**; USGS Map: Clemson; trailhead: parking area.

From US 76 in Clemson, take SR 22 (0.5 mi W of the CN & W railroad track), go 1 mi to jct with SR 149 (SR 37 in Oconee County) and go 0.7 mi to the parking area on the R, near the "Hopewell" sign. Although the original tree is dead and its location under Lake Hartwell, the DAR marker indicates that on Nov. 28, 1785, the U.S. Government signed its first treaty with the Cherokee Indian Nation there (a treaty that was subsequently broken). Jess Grove of the College of Forest and Recreation Resources told me that the "signing was supposedly under a red oak." (If you visit from the Outdoor Lab on SR 65, go 0.6 mi to SR 122 on L. Follow SR 122 into Pickens County where it becomes SR 155 and go 2 mi to SR 149, CN & W railroad crossing.

Turn L and the Treaty Oak parking area is on the R after 0.2 mi.)

Horticultural Gardens

Horticultural Gardens Trails

Length: 1.5 mi rt ct (2.6 km); **easy**; USGS Map: Clemson; trailhead: parking area.

On US 76 in Clemson, slightly W of the National Guard Armory, turn S at the gardens sign on Perimeter Road.

We entered the garden at the parking area near the bright red caboose on the Southern Railroad. The list of what was in the gardens made us realize we would need at least half a day to see everything. (A full day would be better for a student of botany or horticulture.) We began on the trail to the R toward the picnic area, and read the labels along the way. We examined the new arboretum and continued on counterclockwise to the Garden of Meditation at 0.2 mi. We went upstream to the Spring House, Tea House, and Wildflower Collection. Backtracking, we chose to ascend on the Nature Trail through a hardwood forest. At 0.4 mi was a soil profile. Bird-watching stations followed. A sign read: "The forest is the poor man's overcoat." At 0.6 mi we reached the Woody Ornamental Research Area and turned L to the Mini-Garden and Dwarf Vegetable Display. We lingered on the Braille Trail, amazed at the time and effort that must have gone into it. More than 80 Braille signs explained the cabin, grist mill, spring house, and plant life. At 0.9 mi we backtracked to the Hortitherapy Garden, circled the lake, and followed through the azalea and camellia trails to another arboretum at 1.3 mi. Ahead of us were floral displays for thousands of flowers. Continuing ahead we crossed a service road and entered the Rhododendron Trail. At 1.6 mi we returned to the parking area. The largest horticultural gardens in the South, the arboretums have at least 18 of the state's largest trees.

Information: Contact College of Forest and Recreational Resources, Clemson University, Clemson, SC 29631; (803) 656–3215.

Coker College (Darlington County)

Kalmia Gardens Trail

Length: 1 mi (1.6 km); **easy**; USGS Map: Hartsville S; trailhead: parking area.

From the jct of SC 151 and US 15 (5th Street) in downtown Hartsville, go W on SC 151 (Carolina Street) for 2.5 mi to the entrance of the 30-acre Kalmia Gardens of Coker College on the R. The historic site was the home of Capt. Thomas E. Hart, who settled in the area in 1817. A justice of the peace, educator, merchant, farmer, and postmaster, he died in 1842. Hartsville is named in his honor. The house and gardens are now owned and maintained by Coker College (1908), a small, private, coed, liberal arts, four-year institution. "We are planning to identify and label all the plants along the trail," said George P. Sawyer, professor of biology and director of the gardens. "We also plan an exercise and jogging trail," he said.

I followed the trail signs from the front of the house through thousands of azaleas and camellias under a magnificent canopy of mixed forest. At the first major fork I took the R which led through a labyrinth of spur trails to the swamp at 0.4 mi. From this area I returned on a different trail to an observation deck. Banks of mountain laurel and galax were on the L. Cypress and gum were prominent on the R. After resting on one of the seats by a small pool in the center of the loop, observing the birds, and enjoying the tranquil scenery, I ascended to the lawn on the NE side of the house. The gardens are open to the public daily during daylight hours without charge.

Information: Contact Director, Kalmia Gardens of Coker College, Coker College, Hartsville, SC 29550; (803) 332–1381.

APPENDIX

National and Regional Organizations and Clubs

American Camping
   Association, Inc.
Bradford Woods
Martinsville, IN 46151
(317) 342–8456

American Hiking Society
1015 Thirty-First St., NW
Washington, DC 20007
(703) 385–3252

American Trails Inc.
1400 Sixteenth St., NW
#300
Washington, DC 20036

Appalachian Trail
   Conference, Inc.
P.O. Box 807
Harpers Ferry, WV 25425
(304) 535–6331

Center for Environmental
   Education, Inc.
1725 Desales St., NW
Suite 500
Washington, DC 20036
(202) 429–5609

Clean Water Action
   Project
317 Pennsylvania Ave., SE
Washington, DC 20003
(202) 547–1196

Defenders of Wildlife
1244 Nineteenth St., NW
Washington, DC 20036
(202) 659–9510

Friends of the Earth
530 Seventh St., SE
Washington, DC 20003
(202) 543–4312

National Audubon Society
950 Third Ave.
New York, NY 10022
(212) 832–3200

National Campers and
   Hikers Association
7172 Transit Rd.
Buffalo, NY 14221
(716) 634–5433

National Geographic
   Society
17th and M Sts., NW
Washington, DC 20036
(202) 857-7000

National Parks and

Conservation Association
1015 Thirty-First St., NW
Washington, DC 20007
(202) 944–8530

National Wildlife
Federation
1400 Sixteenth St., NW
Washington, DC 20036
(202) 797–6800

Rails-to-Trails Conservancy
1400 Sixteenth St., NW
Suite 300
Washington, DC 20036
(202) 797–5400

The Nature Conservancy
1815 North Lynn St.
Arlington, VA 22209
(703) 841–5300

The Sierra Club
730 Polk St.
San Francisco, CA 94109
(415) 776–2211

The Wilderness Society
1400 I St. NW, 10th Fl.
Washington, DC 20005
(202) 842–3400

State and Nearby Area Citizens' Groups

Audubon Society of
Greenville
4001 Pelham Road
Greer, SC 29651
(803) 268–4034

Bartram Trail Society
(Georgia)
Highway 106, Box 803
Scaly Mountain, NC 28755

Bartram Trail Society
(North Carolina)
Route 3, Box 406
Sylva, NC 28723
(704) 293–9661

Boy Scouts of America
1825 Gadsden St.
(P.O. Box 144)
Columbia, SC 29202
(803) 765–9070

Foothills Trail Conference,
Inc.
P.O. Box 3041
Greenville, SC 29602
(803) 232–2681

Georgia Appalachian Trail
Club
P.O. Box 654
Atlanta, GA 30301
(404) 636–8164

Girl Scouts of America
2712 Middleburg Dr.
Columbia, SC 29204
(803) 252–8962

Nantahala Appalachian
Trail Club
15 White Oak St., Apt-3
Franklin, NC 28734
(704) 524–8759

Nature Conservancy
of South Carolina

2320 Devine St.
Columbia, SC 29205
(803) 254—9049

Sierra Club Chapter
  (South Carolina)
2530 Devine St.
Room 300-B
Columbia, SC 29205
(803) 256–8487
  (Contact the
  Chapter for addresses
  and telephone numbers
  of the Clemson
  Group;
  Henry's Knob Group
  John Bachman Group;
  Nancy Cathcart Group;
  Robert Lunz Group;
  and the William Bartram
  Group.)

South Carolina Association
  of Conservation
P.O. Box 463
Newberry, SC 29108
(803) 276–1526

South Carolina Forestry
  Association
4811 Broad River Rd.
Columbia, SC 29221
(803) 798–4170

South Carolina Wildlife
  Federation
Box 61159
Columbia, SC 29260
(803) 782–8626

Wildlife Society

of South Carolina
  Chapter
P.O. Box 779
Walterboro, SC 29488
(803) 549–2507

United States Government Departments

Department of Agriculture
Forest Service
P.O. Box 96090
Washington, DC 20013
(202) 447–3957
  and 447–3760
  for information

Department of Agriculture
Regional Forester,
  Southern
Suite 600
1720 Peachtree Road, NW
Atlanta, GA 30367
(404) 347–4177

Department of Commerce
  National Marine Fisheries
  Service
1335 East-West Highway
Silver Spring, MD 20910
(301) 427–2239

Department of the Interior
National Park Service
Interior Bldg.
(P.O. Box 37127)
Washington, DC 20013
(202) 343–6843

Department of the Interior
National Park Regional
  Director
75 Spring St., SW
Atlanta, GA 30303
(404) 221–5185

Department of the Interior
Fish and Wildlife
  Service Area Manager
75 Spring St.
Room 1200, SW
Atlanta, GA 30303
(404) 331–3588

United States Congressional Committees

Committee on Agriculture,
  Nutrition and Forestry
  (Senate)
Room 328-A Russell Bldg.
Washington, DC 20510
(202) 224–2035

Committee on Energy and
  Natural Resources
  (Senate)
SD-364, Dirksen Bldg.
Washington, DC 20510
(202) 224–4971

Committee on Environment
  and Public Works
  (Senate)
SD-458, Dirksen Bldg.
Washington, DC 20510

(202) 224–6176

Committee on Agriculture
(House)
Room 1301
Longworth House Office
  Bldg.
Washington, DC 20515
(202) 225–2171

Committee on Interior
  and Insular Affairs
  (House)
Room 1324
Longworth House Office
  Bldg.
Washington, DC 20515
(202) 225–2761

State Government Agencies

Department of Agriculture
Wade Hampton
  Office Bldg.
Box 11280
Columbia, SC 29211
(803) 734–2210

Department of Health
  and Environmental
  Control
Marion Sims Bldg.
2600 Bull St.
Columbia, SC 29201
(803) 734–4880

Department of Parks
  Recreation and Tourism

Suite 113
Edgar Brown Bldg.
1205 Pendleton St.
Columbia, SC 29201
(803) 734–0157

Forestry Commission
Box 21707
Columbia, SC 29221
(803) 737–8800

Geological Survey
Budget and Control Board
Harbison Forest Road
Columbia, SC 29210
(803) 737–9440

South Carolina Coastal
   Council
4280 Executive Place North
Suite 300
Charleston, SC 29405
(803) 744–5838

State Land Resources
   Conservation Commission
2221 Devine St.
Suite 222
Columbia, SC 29205
(803) 734–9100

Water Resources
   Commission
1201 Main St., Suite 1100
Columbia, SC 29201
(803) 737–0800

Wildlife and Marine
   Resources Department
Div. of Information
   and Public Affairs

Dennis Bldg.
(P.O. Box 167)
Columbia, SC 29202
(803) 734–3888

State and Adjoining National Forests

Supervisor's Office
   (Marion and Sumter NFs)
Strom Thurmond Federal
   Bldg.
1835 Assembly St.
(P.O. Box 2227)
Columbia, SC 29202
(803) 765–5222

Francis Marion National
   Forest
Wambaw District
South Pinckney St.
(P.O. Box 788)
McClellanville, SC 29458
(803) 887–3257

Witherbee District
HC 69, Box 1532
Moncks Corner, SC 29461
(803) 336–3248

Sumter National Forest
Andrew Pickens District
Star Route
Walhalla, SC 29691
(803) 638–9568

Edgefield District
321 Bacon St.
(P.O. Box 30)

Edgefield, SC 29824
(803) 637–5396

Enoree District
Route 1, Box 179
Whitmire, SC 29178
(803) 276–4810

Long Cane District
Room 201, Federal Bldg.
(P.O. Box 3168)
Greenwood, SC 29646
(803) 229–2406

Tyger District
Duncan By-Pass
Highway 176 (Drawer 10)
Union, SC 29379
(803) 427–9858

Chattahoochee National
  Forest
Tallulah Ranger District
P.O. Box 438
Clayton, GA 30525
(404) 782–3320

Nantahala National Forest
Highlands Ranger District
Route 2, Box 385
Highlands, NC 28741
(704) 526–3765

River Recreation Teams

The following nearby
whitewater outfitters
are among 40 in
the Eastern Professional
River Outfitters
Association.
For a complete
directory of the
Association, contact
any of these.

Wildwater Ltd.
Box 100-E
Long Creek, SC 29658
(803) 647–9587

Nantahala Outdoor
  Center, Inc.
US 19W Box 41
Bryson City, NC 28713
(704) 488–2175/6900

Rolling Thunder River Co.
P.O. Box 88
Almond, NC 28702
(704) 488–2030

Southeastern Expeditions,
  Inc.
1955 Cliff Walley Way
NE, Suite 220
Atlanta, GA 30329
(404) 329–0433

Cherokee Adventures, Inc.
P.O. Box E-836
Erwin, TN 37650
(615) 743–8666/7733

Ocoee Outdoors, Inc.
P.O. Box 72
Ocoee, TN 37361
(615) 338-2438

Sunburst Adventures
P.O. Box 329E

Benton, TN 37307
(615) 338–8388

Trail Supplies

The following list of
stores has a
partial or complete range
of supplies
for outdoor recreation.
Department stores
also may have supplies
in their sports
departments. (Because
stores may change
addresses or names,
please consult a current
telephone directory
for information.)

Grady Sport Shop
3440 Clemson Blvd.
Anderson, SC 29621

Grego & Company
287 King Street
Charleston, SC 29401

Outdoor Outfitters
1662 Savannah Highway
Charleston, SC 29407

R & M Sporting Goods
112 Citadel Mall
Charleston, SC 29407

Trail Center, Inc.
5728 Dorchester Rd.
Charleston, SC 29405

Clemson University

Bookstore
Clemson University
Clemson, SC 29631

Judge Kellers Store
119 College Avenue
Clemson, SC 29631

Athletic Attic
Columbia Mall
7201 Two Notch Rd.
Columbia, SC 29204

Backcountry Sports
1230 St. Andrews Rd.
Columbia, SC 29210

Backpacker
940 Harden Street
Columbia, SC 29205

Dunhams Omni Sports
5510 Two Notch Rd.
Columbia, SC 29223

Moe Levy
1300 Assembly Street and
1103 Lady Street
Columbia, SC 29201

USC Campus Bookstore
Russell House
University of South
Carolina
Columbia, SC 29208

Francis Marion College
P.O. Box 7500
Florence, SC 29501

Arnex Inc., The Woods
52 Airview Drive
Greenville, SC 29607

Athletic Attic
Greenville Mall
1025 Woodruff Rd.
Greenville, SC 29607

Bob Jones University
Campus Stores
Greenville, SC 29614

Hammett Learning World
1175 Woods Crossing
Greenville, SC 29607

Sam Wyche Sports World
1224 Poinsett Hwy.
Greenville, SC 29609

Athletic Attic
Crosscreek Mall
Bypass, NW
Greenwood, SC 29646

Ship-Oar-Shore
35 Lagoon Rd.
and Port Royal Plaza
and Coligny Plaza
and Shelter Cove Mall
Hilton Head Island, SC
29928

Outfitters Outlet Co.
Route 3
Lake City, SC 29560

Carolina Outdoors
851 Houston Northcutt
Blvd.
Patriots Plaza
Mt. Pleasant, SC 29464

Low Country Outfitter
10177 N. Kings Hwy.

Myrtle Beach, SC 29577

Newberry College Store
Kaufman Hall
Newberry, SC 29108

R & M Sporting Goods
B-16 Northwoods Mall
North Charleston, SC
29418

Marine Corps Exchange
Marine Corps Depot
Parris Island, SC 29905

Buddin, Inc.
2129 Cherry Rd.
Rock Hill, SC 29730

Harris Sporting Goods
123 Bypass
Seneca, SC 29678

Jantzen Southern
Dock #2, Mountain
View Dr.
Seneca, SC 29678

C & H Sales, Inc.
Asheville Highway
Spartanburg, SC 29303

T.C. Sports
West Gate Mall
Spartanburg, SC 29303

Simpson Plaza Hardware
Palmetto Plaza Shopping
Center
Sumter, SC 29150

Sunrift Adventure
426 Poinsett Highway
Travelers Rest, SC 29690

River Runners, Inc.
410 Meeting St.
West Columbia, SC 29169

Jantzen Southern
403 Holland St.
Westminster, SC 29693

General Index

Trail Index

Trails labeled with a (B) are bicycle trails, (E) equestrian trails, (P) for the physically handicapped, (R) river trails, and (V) vehicular trails. All other trails are (H) for hiking, walking, or jogging. Some trails are multiple use. Examples are all (B) (E) and (P) trails are (H) trails also. The highway bicycle trails would be an exception.

324

About the Author

Allen de Hart has been hiking, designing, and constructing and writing about trails since he was a teenager. In his home state of Virginia, news reporters call him the hiker's guru. He has hiked more than 8,500 different trails and over 17,000 miles in 46 states and 18 foreign countries. He completed the Appalachian Trail in 1978, the Buckeye Trail in 1981, and the Florida Trail in 1988. A graduate of the Adjutant General's Corps of the U.S. Army and with graduate degrees in history from the University of Virginia, he is currently a professor of history in the Social and Behavioral Science Department at Louisburg College in North Carolina, where he is also director of public affairs. He is founder of two botanical gardens. Books he has authored include *Hiking and Backpacking, North Carolina Hiking Trails, Hiking the Old Dominion, Hiking and Backpacking Basics, Hiking the Mountain State: The Trails of West Virginia,* and *Monongahela National Forest Hiking Guide* (with Bruce Sundquist). He has also written numerous articles on specific trails and prepared special features on the Appalachian Trail hut system, hiking and rafting in the Grand Canyon, canoeing in the Okefenokee Swamp, and climbing the peaks of Colorado and California.